Respectable

Respectable

The Experience of Class

LYNSEY HANLEY

ALLEN LANE
an imprint of
PENGUIN BOOKS

ALLEN LANE

UK | USA | Canada | Ireland | Australia
India | New Zealand | South Africa

Allen Lane is part of the Penguin Random House group of companies
whose addresses can be found at global.penguinrandomhouse.com.

First published 2016
001

Lyrics from 'Kinky Afro' by Paul Anthony Ryder, Gary Kenneth Whelan, Mark Philip Day,
Paul Richard Davis and Shaun William Ryder are reproduced by kind permission of Warner/Chappell
Music Publishing Ltd (PRS) and London Music (GB 1) (PRS); copyright © 1990 by William George
Entertainment Ltd. Universal Music Publishing Ltd. All Rights Reserved. International copyright
secured. Used by permission of Music Sales Ltd.

Set in 12/14.75 pt Bembo Book MT Std
Typeset by Jouve (UK), Milton Keynes
Printed in Great Britain by Clays Ltd, St Ives plc

A CIP catalogue record for this book is available from the British Library

ISBN: 978-1-846-14206-2

For my parents

Contents

Introduction

I can't remember the day I started calling dinner 'lunch' and tea 'dinner', but I know that it happened, because that's what I call them now. That must mean I'm middle class, where once I was working class; though, no matter how posh I get, I can't bring myself to call (what I now call) dinner 'supper'. Supper for me means (with apologies to the writer Stuart Maconie) having a Kit-Kat in your dressing gown in front of something racy on Channel 4.

Social mobility has its limits: limits which, perhaps, you have to set yourself in order to stay at least halfway related to the person you started out as. It is often talked of as a ladder, which you can climb from bottom to top. The walls are less talked about. This book is about how people try to get over them, whether they manage to or not. I grew up on a West Midlands council estate as part of an extended family which would once have been described as 'respectable working class'. I went to school in the eighties and early nineties on the same estate, in an educational environment which didn't expect or prepare young people to stay on beyond sixteen, and progressed from there to a sixth-form college in a middle-class area full of straight-A students. I went on to the University of London, and from *there*, eventually, I got to *here*: writing books about the anxiety induced by being socially mobile. The questions for me have always been: how did that happen? Why does it induce such anxiety? Why is it such a big deal to change social class?

I felt a need to try to write about this subject for a number of reasons. First, as you may already have worked out, because the subject of class obsesses me, as it does a lot of people who started life in one class and have ended up in another. Changing class is like emigrating from one side of the world to the other, where you have to rescind your old passport, learn a new language and make gargantuan efforts if you are not to lose touch completely with the people and habits of your old life, even if they are among the relationships and things that are dearest to your heart. The effect of this is psychologically disruptive, sometimes extremely so; yet it's rarely discussed alongside the received wisdom about social mobility, which is that it is unequivocally a Good Thing for individuals and for society as a whole.

Second, and related to the first point, was my desire to explore more fully the idea of the 'wall in the head'. When, in 1989, the Berlin Wall came down, this phrase (*der Mauer im Kopf* in German) was used to describe the lingering psychological effects on former East Germans of having been shut in by concrete for nearly thirty years. It seemed to sum up the gap between the life I'd been primed to expect – through innumerable cultural and educational signals – and the life I've ended up having. I borrowed the phrase 'wall in the head' as the title for a chapter in my first book, which was about housing, as it seemed to fit exactly what I'd experienced as a child and adolescent living on a council estate – or, rather, what I realized *after leaving* that it was what I'd experienced. The estate stayed with me long after I moved elsewhere, partly in the form of a strange kind of vertigo when presented with opportunities and experiences I'd grown up assuming were far beyond my reach. I also felt its presence as early as my first term at university, when I got it into my head that everyone in the student union bar wanted to hear a version of my life story which crossed the 'books on prescription' section of the library with Monty Python's Four Yorkshiremen sketch. The wall in my head manifested itself in a desperate sense that I had to change my destiny at the same time as believing I had no right to do so. Any elements of struggle in the journey from one class to another felt as though they came from forces present inside me, rather than forces from outside. Social factors affecting my experience of life – the area I lived in, the schools I went to, my family's income and status – filtered inwards and expressed themselves psychologically. This is because, as I hope to show in this book, the higher your social status, the more self-confidence tends to be ingrained in you. The further up the social ladder you are, the more external influences are set up to favour you and your kind, to the extent that privilege becomes invisible and so weightless that – literally – you don't know how lucky you are. At the other end of the social scale, there is an acute sense of how little social trust or esteem is placed in you as an individual, a feeling that is absorbed and then expressed in low self-confidence.

I was nowhere near the bottom of that scale. As I'll go on to explain, I had 'respectability' on my side, which increased my chances of acceptance on the journey from working class to middle class. But there was a place I wanted to get to – more accurately, there was a feeling I wanted to attain, a feeling of freedom – and the obstacles to reaching it were almost always, I believed, generated from within. For instance, once I left my secondary school, where few people managed to achieve good passes in their GCSEs, and went to a college where it was usual to get As and Bs, I kept fluffing my exams and missing deadlines for coursework. Not because I was daft, and only partly because I was ill-primed for post-compulsory learning. It was because I assumed that anyone marking my work would see it for what it was: a half-baked, cringeworthy, autodidact's attempt to pass as someone who'd always known this stuff. It was only out of sheer pig-headedness that I didn't drop out. After graduating with a lower-second-class degree, I failed the probation periods of my first two jobs after university, unaware that one of the primary skills needed to succeed in professional life is the ability to wing it with style.

Third, I wanted to think and talk about how social class is reinforced and regenerated over time, through language and culture. At what point does talking about a 'wall in the head', where people set their own limits and restrict their own potential in accordance with their delimited social status, become a self-fulfilling prophecy? Class encourages people to become stuck in ruts that don't look like ruts: you can be yourself, but only as far as your way of 'being yourself' stays within well-defined social parameters. It is hard to be accepted by the group without staying within those limits. Within the working class, an individual's desire to present a respectable self-image can be altered – some would say damaged – by the lack of autonomy and control that is forced upon people from the outside by government policy, employers' practices and the insidious influence of class distinction itself, increasingly expressed through the cultural choices we make.

What I aim to explore in this book is the relationship between those choices: those that are offered and those that we make from the ones we have access to. That, essentially, is what inequality means in terms of how we experience it. Less money means fewer options – but not always, and not automatically, worse ones. Less power in crucial areas, such as work, education and housing, means fewer options as well, though in this case it also tends to restrict the ability to accrue more power. The combined forces of outright snobbery and tacit distinction are, I will argue, the most psychologically damaging aspect of class, because they contribute to this undermining of self-belief. Our culture contains many silent symbols more powerful than money. It contains keys that can't be bought, which gain access to rooms whose existence you can barely imagine, unless you get to enter them.

Social and cultural capital works on a compound-interest

model: the more you have, the more you get. The more knowledge and influence you accrue, the more you get to know other people with knowledge and influence, and the more knowledge and influence you acquire to share among people who have it already. Mainstream media, including social media, function both as an expression and as a propagator of this model. Micro-blogs and social networks give an impressive illusion of levelling the landscape of communication, a permanent vox pop session in which everyone gets to have a go – or, conversely, in which everyone is condemned to be the author of their own timeline. What social media actually do is emphasize and intensify the existing imbalances of power, in terms of who gets to have a voice and who can be persuaded to listen to it. This is because well-educated and well-connected people know how to use their voice – their language, their tone, their aggregated knowledge – to their advantage. Social networks serve this advantage to an exaggerated degree, allowing such well-connectedness to be flaunted to others and made use of professionally as well as socially. The tone of conversation is set early on, attracting those comfortable with that tone and repelling those who aren't.

For individuals to thrive at the bottom of a pronounced and visible class hierarchy, and to overcome the pressure – exerted from all sides – to stay where they are and yet also strive to escape, suggests a confounding order of things: an apparent rebellion, but a kind of orderliness as well. A class system needs both socially mobile people and socially immobile people in order to prove its worth. The upwardly mobile are held up as proof that the class structure isn't half as rigid as it looks, while those who don't move out of the working class – because, of course, it's fine to be socially immobile as long as you're middle class – are held to be somehow parasitic for their refusal to 'do the right thing' and create a morally acceptable level of surplus value. This isn't a new phenomenon. The cultural critic Richard

Hoggart, who died in 2014, aged ninety-five, spent his working life insisting on the central importance of social class in British society. Hoggart noted consistently that its ability to shape and distort experience had not diminished in the lifetime of the post-war welfare state, but kept finding new ways to distinguish as the living standards of the population improved as a whole. Hoggart lived long enough to document apparently huge changes in society, all the while noting that many of those changes were on the surface only. They must have been. The first time I read his book *The Uses of Literacy*, published in 1957, I felt he could have been writing about my own childhood, which took place sixty years after his. When he writes about the 'fine topcoat' of empty salmon and fruit tins on the Hunslet middens at Sunday teatime in the nineteen thirties, I'm instantly transported back to my parents' kitchen in Birmingham in the late eighties, sticking on Radio 1 to hear the Top 40 countdown, getting out the can opener, mashing the salmon with vinegar and plopping Dream Topping on the peaches. I felt kinship with Hoggart's essential loneliness as every exam he passed took him further away – in travel and in daily experience – from his working-class neighbourhood and closer to a place that was more comfortable in every way except for the emotions that accompanied him on his journey.

'Each decade we shiftily declare we have buried class,' wrote Hoggart in 1989; yet 'each decade the coffin stays empty'.[1] Had the social changes he documented been deeper and more effective at erasing class distinctions, I wouldn't have spent the last fifteen years or so repeatedly looking to his work for its continued relevance to my life. I am, in his words, one of 'the uprooted and the anxious': at once socially mobile and psychologically stuck, or at least divided, somewhere between our place of origin and the place we must inhabit in order to 'get on'. His work is the guiding spirit of this book and forms its intellectual backbone.

PART ONE

There

1.   You're Not Supposed To

The desire for self-improvement, in certain circumstances, can turn you into a lunatic. In 1993, when I was seventeen, I was doing five A-levels and four jobs, scuttling between them by bus on the south-eastern periphery of Birmingham. My main job was working in an east Birmingham branch of Greggs, the baker's shop; the second was selling Avon cosmetics; the third, a paper round; and the fourth, making cakes and chocolates and selling them door to door. The last one involved buying large amounts of baking ingredients from an Aldi supermarket five miles from the estate where I lived with my parents. The box I carried back from the bus stop was so heavy that every few steps I had to shunt it back into my arms using my knee. With every shunt I muttered, self-pityingly, 'these things are sent to try us': completely inaccurate because everything I was doing, I had chosen to do. The box had no handles. It contained a bag of plain flour and a bag of self-raising, a bag of sugar, a bag of currants, a large tub of margarine, several bars of cooking chocolate, some glacé cherries and a dozen boxed eggs. I'd taken the bus to Aldi because it was so much cheaper than the Food Giant nearby. I spent about £8 on my ingredients, and expected to make about £60 from the results. The plan was to make cakes and chocolates and sell them to people living on our road. I would make the boxes myself by covering cereal boxes with snazzy paper, and I'd fill them with homemade fudge and truffles. I would write the menu, photocopy it at college and distribute it by hand while doing one of my other jobs, which was delivering one of the local freesheets once a week.

You could say I needed the money, but I didn't need it in the sense that, without it, I would have gone hungry. My family didn't need it — not in the way that, a generation or so earlier, they would have needed a seventeen-year-old's wages in order to maintain household solvency. I don't think I needed the money at all: what I needed was the feeling that my life was going places, namely, somewhere other than the place in which it was currently stuck. It wasn't money that was going to get me out of that place, a large estate built to house 60,000 people from inner Birmingham on its farthest outskirts — not money on the scale I was earning, anyway. As much as the five A-levels, it was the desperation. I didn't really need to do four jobs — poorly paid though all of them were — but I still did them.

I tried explaining this strategy to my friend Richard, whose mother did everything for him. I told him that working in a bakery had its obvious compensations. We were the first to smell the pasties as they fattened and browned in industrial chrome ovens, the slim doors of which opened like letterboxes for our paddles to reach in and turn the trays halfway through baking time. We didn't bake our own loaves, or fold our own pastries: that was done in a factory near the centre of Birmingham that must have smelled like heaven with gravy on top in the middle of the night, when the night shift churned out thousands of steak bakes for delivery to the shops at dawn. We didn't fill the doughnuts with jam; neither did we roast the chicken that went in the baguettes, or crumb the ham, or chop the onions for the vat of tomato soup which, in the immortal words of Alan Partridge, was perennially 'hotter than the sun, Lynn!'

All this preparation was done somewhere else, in places we'd never visited. (At least I've seen the Heinz factory in Wigan — the largest food production site in Europe, where the soup would have been made — when travelling up the M6. God alone knows where the chicken came from.) Our job was to take half-baked goods and finish them off in such a way as to maximize their tastiness. We gave doughnuts and yum-yums another coat of sugar before bagging them up in fours, and made egg wash from powdered egg and water for the 'bake-off': a pastry brush dipped in this primrose emulsion covered two or three frozen pasties, which entered the oven sallow and odourless and came out bronzed and ambrosial, transfigured by heat. I remember wrestling massive trays of pasties on and off the floor of the oven with scorched mitts, then the struggle to prise them off the baking parchment where they were glued down by dried egg wash. Over the course of the working day, the floor would accumulate crumbs of bread, pastry, meat fat and butter, over which my plimsolls first slid and then stuck, getting gunkier and less comfortable every time I walked from the oven to the till and back. By five o'clock my shoes had an auxiliary sole made of ham scraps, which I'd slough off with the scraping tool (like an indoor hoe, it was used for unsticking food detritus from the floor prior to sweeping and mopping) before putting the shoes in a bread bag next to my uniform, a sort of cream housecoat with a matching cream apron and peaked hairnet.

I also told Richard that I had no argument with being on my feet all day, and that the customers were invariably incredibly friendly. They were conspiratorial about their finances and wincingly frank about their toilet trouble. We had counterfeit note detectors next to the till, although they were never needed because you could tell from a mile off when someone was trying it on with a fake £20. It wasn't that people didn't generally pay with £20 notes – they were quite common, especially on Saturdays and among older women with better-paid husbands who expected an inch of gammon in their sandwiches. It was that people in possession of fake notes couldn't fake ignorance of the fact. When passing one over the counter they would scrunch up the note in an attempt to disguise it, which meant that you couldn't help but take more notice of it than of one that was uncrumpled. They would search for a detail – a speckled egg on an Easter Nest cake, or a fly on the sticky strip behind you – and fix their eyes on it while you attempted to force this dodgy-looking note under the ultraviolet beam of the detector. You knew you would have to say, 'Erm, I'm sorry, we can't take this note.' They knew they would have to say, 'Why, it's fine, I got it in my change the last shop I was in.' It seemed obvious to me that no one would try to buy food with pretend money just because they fancied it, because they thought it would be fun. They may not literally have starved that night, but a chance to make things more bearable that day would have been lost. Pasties, pastries and pies, to George Orwell, were nothing more than 'cheap luxuries which mitigate the surface of life'; to the cultural critic Richard Hoggart, a desire for 'something tasty' bore proof of the working-class gift – the necessity – for finding pleasure where you can get it. (Have you ever seen anyone walking away from an ice cream van with a freshly piped cornet, or leaving a bakery with a cake – any cake – without a smile on their face?) A rough/respectable view of human nourishment.

I suppose I should start where I always start in my own mind, where every day I ask myself a version of the same question: how did I get from *there* to *here*? Is *there* working at Greggs and humping boxes from a bus stop? Is *here* writing a book about that experience? And why does it matter so much that I spend so much time asking myself the same question, or questions, over and over again? You don't want to hear all that David Copperfield kind of crap, as Holden Caulfield pointed out in *Catcher in the Rye*. Well, let me tell you, I'm pretty sick of it myself, but it's probably fair to say that I'm a screw-up. I am a British person for whom the facts of social class matter. They matter to me, in all probability, because I'm from somewhere, class-wise, that doesn't quite fit. I grew up *respectable* : neither rough nor posh, neither rich nor especially poor. Far from middle class, but not quite classically working class, either. Clerk class; foreman class; skilled tradesman class. A space filled with uncertainty and anxiety about the ease of falling and the unlikelihood of climbing. A set of containing walls which, like all other self-perceptions, dissolve the moment you check to see if they wobble. It is because of respectability that I don't want my son's hair to grow too long or be cut too short. Because of it, I go in second class even when first class is cheaper, then I spend the journey griping about how it's not as nice as first class, and how in Poland they give you free tea and biscuits whatever class you're in. It's about being *sensible*, and not being caught out. You can't let yourself go . . . except when you do, and the plug of repression pops out with the force of a champagne cork.

The confusion is endless and self-defeating, and comes from having grown up 'respectable' in an area perceived, from outside and to an extent from within, as 'rough'. We were an estate of ex-Brummies, quarantined from the city and the suburbs proper by geography, appearance and perception, transported from the city to the green belt in a series of clearances at the end of the sixties. The estate was one of the largest sanctioned by Richard Crossman, Labour's utilitarian minister of housing, and was treated from its birth by the local press as a social experiment doomed to fail by dint of its population. Most of my peers regarded themselves as 'respectable', too, whether or not they seemed that way to others. Everyone was careful not to classify themselves as 'rough'. Rather, it was about 'giving a shit' or 'not giving a shit': what you would do or what you wouldn't do in order to maintain dignity and self-respect in the face of another individual or an institution. ('Ooh, that Darren,' you might say, in a tone expressing admiration as

much as disdain, 'he doesn't give a shit.') For us children, that
institution was school: a secondary modern in all but name,
an estate school which deformed and stymied our hopes as
readily as the rest of our environment. It seemed to provide
concrete evidence of the overarching structure of things: the
knowledge that some things were out of reach for no other
reason than that we were growing up in the wrong place to
get hold of them. (Whether 'respectable' or 'rough', we were
united in regarding our estate as somewhere to get out of, but
for one additional confusion: I didn't realize we lived on an
estate, or that it meant anything in particular to do so. I just
thought we lived in a place where all the houses happened to
look the same.)

When we were growing up, in the eighties and early nineties,
it was very hard to imagine a time when Britain might not be
ruled by the Conservatives, and therefore it was just as hard to
imagine a time when you could go about your life without the
sensation of being followed, not quite high enough above your
head, by a lowering, ever-pissing black cloud. By the time I
started working at Greggs in June 1992, I'd lived much of my
life in the knowledge of this black cloud. There seemed to be no
way out except for the ways you found yourself. A decade or so
earlier, Norman Tebbit had stated that because his dad had had 'got
on his bike and looked for work' in the Depression, so should
everyone then being slowly starved, of food or opportunity, out
of their home towns. Back in 1961, the year my father had started
work, three-quarters of employed people in England and Wales
were manual or low-grade clerical workers, of whom 69 per
cent were male.[1] When I left university, thirty-six years later,
the proportion of manual and routine workers in the employed
population had fallen to just under half.

From the sixties, when docks and mines began to close and
Harold Wilson's Labour government anticipated the coming

death of heavy industry by heralding 'the white heat of the technological revolution', Britain began to move from a 'production' model of what it meant to be working class – the class that makes things – to a 'consumption' model – the class that buys things. In theory, this ought to have made the experience of being working class a lot more like the experience of being middle class, in the sense that anyone who had enough money could express their worldview partly through what they bought, and was freed from some of the more stifling aspects of social interdependence by home and car ownership. This argument appeared to be borne out by the findings of the sociologist John Goldthorpe and his colleagues in their 1969 study of 'the affluent worker' – men employed in the light-industrial occupation of car production, mostly living in the south-east of England, whose lifestyles were comparable to those of the better-paid lower-middle class. They simultaneously identified themselves as members of the working class and presented a strongly individualized account of their lives, aims and political outlook. It seemed at that time that you could stay in your class, enjoying the comfort of like minds, while no longer having to believe in the necessity of collective struggle.

Yet anyone who didn't have a job – which at times in the eighties and nineties meant 3 or 4 million people – was excluded from this process. Instead their position, their status in society, was diminished in three ways. First, through the dismantling of trades union power, which had helped to integrate the jobless into the wider working population by establishing and then protecting rights and benefits when they were out of work. Second, through negative propaganda, in tacit collusion between government and newspaper owners, which sought to isolate the badly off and the bolshy from an upwardly mobile, consumerist working class. Third, through populist policy-making: the Right to Buy, which divided local authority tenants into the 'aspirational' and the 'non-aspirational' depending on whether or not they bought their council house, being a prime example.

The idea that working-class respectability no longer exists appeals to people who believe that the social and political changes of the last thirty-five years have sorted the wheat from the chaff. From this viewpoint, anyone who proved they could string a sentence together and brush their own hair has – rightfully, it's believed – gained admittance to the swollen middle class, leaving behind a disreputable and undeserving lumpenproletariat to wallow in their own shite. Diametrically opposed to this viewpoint, coming from the left, is the idea that working-class respectability died with the unions and with heavy industry, leaving a demoralized and demonized group no longer able to hold its head high and represent itself on its own terms. (Not only that, but seeking to be respectable in the first place was a manifestation of false consciousness rather than a universal desire for dignity.)

Both, in their different ways, are wrong. Respectability is still there as a signal component of what it means to be working class, either through its affirmation or its repudiation. You either define yourself by your respectability – whether that's purely in your own eyes or in the eyes of an alternately vigilant and ignorant wider society – or you define yourself against it. In many ways, indeed, respectability is a defining factor of working-class experience in the whole. It expresses the need to defend yourself and those you love against threats, whether real or perceived, to your existence.

Respectability is not necessarily, and not in itself, as precarious as it seems to the people who strive for it. Rather, its importance tends to fade in conditions of greater security. Such security may come from having more money, higher occupational standing and greater facility with the consumer products which doubly serve as social signifiers. Language, too. In order to be self-deprecating in conversation, a middle-class person might make a big deal of what a slob he or she is (or what a slob they would be if they didn't have a dishwasher, in some instances a human one). This is a mystery to many working-class people, for whom the maintenance of self-respect in private and public is a fundamental priority.

What has changed since the seventies is the meaning attached to working-class respectability. In the eighties it came to be regarded as shorthand for the emergent and politically favoured affluent wing of the working class, many members of which bit the Tories' hands off when offered council houses at knock-down prices. A split that was already present was deliberately driven open, and to a great extent it worked. Organized labour no longer had a chance against The Man once you had to pick sides: unambitious council tenant or aspirational owner-occupier, sponging welfare dependant or dynamic entrepreneur. Respectability was recast, through policy and media, not just as a way for individuals and communities to hold depredation at bay, but as a crusade against evil. But the thing is, there's nothing inherently good or bad about being respectable. Respectability is a property of your specific circumstances: circumstances which permit you, or at least make it easier, to maintain the appearance and feeling of self-respect. The more desperate your circumstances, the less likely you are to be seen as respectable by other people, but it doesn't necessarily affect your own perception of how respectable you are. You might simply choose to define it in different ways. To say proudly, 'We ain't ever gonna be respectable' (as Mel & Kim, the cockney pop duo to whom I owe this book's title, sang in 1987) is a way of preserving dignity against those who insist on respectability as a precondition for acceptance.

In his book *The Uses of Literacy* Richard Hoggart combined a testimony of his parents' and grandparents' lives immured in poverty in post-Victorian Leeds with a reckoning of the likely effects – for good and ill – of greater affluence on working-class daily life. The working-class world of 'resistance and adaptation' to an unforgiving urban environment was, he feared, soon to give way to a faux-classless landscape, in which all were encouraged to regard themselves as no better or worse than the next man, yet without the economic or social means to make that perception a reality. He told of 'persuaders' whose job it was to tell you that the class war was over, *daddio*, and all that was left to do was to consume cultural goods where once you would have helped to create them.[2]

In the book's opening lines, Hoggart notes that it was widely believed that a 'bloodless revolution' had taken place in Britain following the end of the Second World War. The founding of the welfare state and the slow re-emergence of a consumer economy after fifteen years of wartime austerity led many to believe that class divisions were diminishing. In some ways they were right: the war essentially put an end to domestic service, while the coming of the NHS in 1948 created a far healthier generation (the healthiest to date, perhaps). Yet the revolution, it turned out, was bloodless because it never actually happened. The coffin of class remained open, whether deliberately or by default, through the mechanisms of a class-bound education system, class-segregated housing, a media and cultural landscape that has persistently reinforced class prejudice, and a bizarre historic tendency among British voters to elect governments which act against their own interests. Seventy years after the Butler Act created the tripartite system of grammar, technical and secondary schools, and fifty years after most of them were replaced with comprehensives, our social class still largely determines the type and quality of education we receive.

The effects of class are the hardest of all social evils to slay because they are the most given to mutation. Like the 'invisible hand' of capitalism itself, they shift shape in order to go unnoticed.

What we are left to grapple with are the signs of class, the consequences of it and the injuries it inflicts on civil society. These 'hidden injuries of class', to use the sociologist Richard Sennett's phrase, abound because of the intimate connection between how we feel about ourselves in relation to others, the relationship between what we start out wanting for ourselves and our loved ones and what we're able to achieve, and our relationship to a social and economic structure that we did nothing to bring about. We articulate this latter relationship, mostly though not always unconsciously, in what we do and the way we behave. We carry and clothe ourselves according to our class; we're educated broadly according to our class; we eat and drink increasingly according to our class; and we make use of the physical and cultural resources around us according to our class. We use them, whether consciously or otherwise, as signs that show to ourselves and others where we belong.

Not only does the coffin of class remain empty, but we carry that knowledge within us and wear it like a giant yoke. The facts of class manifest themselves in many small tragedies, ignorance being only the most common of them. The richness of life is vast, and we all have some measure of it, which is why stultified dreams are the cause of so much bitterness. It's one thing to have a vague idea that a better life than the one we have is possible, quite another to equip ourselves with the knowledge to fulfil it. The geographer Danny Dorling, author of an 'atlas' of social identity in Britain, states:

> Most people think they are average when asked. In most things, most are not. Most say they are normal, but our atlas shows that what is normal changes rapidly as you travel across the social topography of human identity in Britain – from the fertile crescent of advantage, where to succeed is to do nothing out of the ordinary, to the peaks of despair, where to just get by is extraordinary.[3]

No one ever used the term 'working class' when we were growing up. Instead it was 'people like us', or 'the likes of us', or 'people round 'ere', by which I took to mean a discrete group bound by occupation and geography who could expect certain things out of life but not others. When reference to respectability was made, it was often through the use of the malapropism 'respectful'. When I left home in 1994 to go to university, my respectable post office account was filled with the respectable proceeds of four jobs and a local authority maintenance grant. I was said to be one of a dying breed, since all those who hadn't done the same and fled their hometowns, in a spirit of mania and desperation as much as aspiration, had come to be characterized as losers. Only losers took the bus. Only losers rented their houses off the council. Only losers didn't spend their lives trying to ape the middle class. Yet my obsession with self-improvement had been bound up not with the desire to become middle class, but with the desire to avoid being exploited. How you'd get into your head so young that your destiny, should you not work desperately to avoid it, lay in exploitation, is an interesting question.

At that age exploitation may have meant being forced to listen to New Kids on the Block and have the girls in my tutor group experiment on my hair – 'Cause the thing is, Lyns, you don't help yourself do ya?' – but there was also an inkling that it could get a lot worse. There was an understanding, for example, that men were a certain way and that, because they were all alike, the only safe bet was to avoid them as far as possible except when you needed one to make you look normal. 'Men are all the same,' I was always being told. 'The thing about men is they're like this.' I was convinced that all men were not the same, that human individuality was not unique to women. My obedience and future-fixation, mistaken by teachers for qualities that others would benefit from emulating, stemmed in part from being an only child, a girl who hadn't been handed a succession of siblings to help raise, and who was more attuned to the way adults communicated than the way children did. In fact, I was fixated on becoming an adult because I had no idea how to be a child.

At that age, in response to the brutalizing potential of secondary school, I retreated into an internal world in which kindness dominated. I would try to think of kindness wherever it appeared, and it would always seem to be somewhere else: somewhere quite far away. This meant that my mind was always somewhere else, somewhere quite far away, too. Boys, as long as they weren't social outcasts, had footballs to play with, and girls had each other. Girls talked about the things and people of their immediate surroundings, but I needed to get away. I had no idea how to articulate this, and consented to be tolerated as a mildly stinking presence on the edge of the group, with nothing to say: if you clung to the edge you'd at least look as if you were trying. By the time we were fifteen, some of the girls at the centre of that group would move on to discussing when would be a good time to get engaged, whether before leaving school or waiting till just after. They would be aware that once they had said yes to marriage they might never be able to say no to anything again.

There were other things I needed to get away from. Casual violence – symbolic, domestic and public – was endemic in the place and times in which I grew up. Casual racism was part of the fabric of daily conversation. Casual cynicism pervaded: a consequence of casual exploitation and casual displacement, which fed into people's souls and manifested in their treating everything like one great frigging joke, because that's how they felt they'd been treated their entire lives. To be casual about horrific things was a cover for fear. I was much too respectable to be casual in that way, and instead took everything incredibly

seriously – which of course I was told not to do, because everything was a frigging joke and there was no point pretending
otherwise.

You may wonder what led to this collective conviction that
there was no point. It might be argued that another primary
aspect of working-class experience, a feeling which most defines
a certain way of being in the world, is loss. Loss is everywhere:
the loss of optimism as experience victory-laps hope; the loss of
loved ones too soon to war, to workplace accidents or to
ill-health; the loss of a sense of home, going back generations as
families move repeatedly in search of relief from poverty; the
loss of close ties as families are broken up in a similar way by
moves down south, to America, Canada, Australia; and the loss
of a sense of place as families attempt to remain rooted in a
changing environment, such as when a local works that once
employed just about everyone in the area closes down. Every
generation is faced with a choice – whether or not to compen-
sate for the losses they know their parents and grandparents
endured by staying close and not threatening the sense of life
as they know it. Others see this profound loss as a family legacy whose continued transmission they must break for the sake
of their own children. To do the latter may require leaving –
physically and socially, if not emotionally – the environment in
which your character was formed. In so doing, you risk creating
another disjuncture, another source of loss, in the history of
your family. The place you came from, so this new story goes,
wasn't good enough for you. You had to find somewhere else
that was better in order to make the loss disappear; yet it can
physically disappear only if you never go back. Meanwhile, the
sense of it still lingers. The difficulty comes when you have a
thought that goes along the lines of 'I believe life can be better
than this'; a thought which is then interpreted by other people as
'You believe you're better than me.'

In the mid-seventies, a sociologist called Paul Willis investigated the ways in which a group of schoolboys in the industrial Midlands town of Wolverhampton subverted all attempts by teachers to get them to face up to the reality of a world outside the one they knew. Willis concluded in his book – pithily entitled *Learning to Labour: How Working Class Kids Get Working Class Jobs* – that boys and girls respond in much the same ways to the imposition of values and practices which not only seem ridiculous to them, but seem dedicated to diverting them away from ways of life they know to be 'real', settled and achievable. 'The lads', as Willis called them, worked hard to gain victories on their own terms: they were obsessed with 'having a laff', which meant getting one over on the teacher, developing a parallel language of in-jokes and shared mumbles, and doing just enough work to avoid serious opprobrium while giving no indication of their actual capabilities.[4]

I know these lads. You know, the funny thing is I never sat in the front row at school. I was always at the back: in the same row as the lads, but never with them. I thought they were throwing their lives away. They knew they were throwing their lives away, and yet they refused to acknowledge that that was what they were doing. The cost of one of them saying, '*Come on lads*, we can have a laff outside of school, we're here to learn so we don't have to do jobs we hate later on,' would have been too much for any one of them to stand. In any case, Willis argued, working-class males are trusted so little within the wider social structure (beginning at school and extending into the workplace), that even if 'the lads' had changed their minds and decided to work hard, there was no guarantee that it would have got them better jobs. Willis wasn't exactly saying that resistance, in the form of mild yet persistent insubordination, was futile; more that it was the boys' own practices – their habits of playing up, of sticking together, of 'having a laff' – as much as the unfairness of 'the system', which led them to become trapped in low-paid and unfulfilling jobs. He concluded: 'there is an element of self-damnation in the taking on of subordinate roles in Western capitalism . . . however, this damnation is experienced, paradoxically, as true learning, affirmation, appropriation, and as a form of resistance'.[5] Solidarity made sense to the lads because they understood that they were all headed for the same destiny and would need mates when they got there. In this way a survival strategy becomes a self-fulfilling prophecy.

Thirty years later, the social anthropologist Simon Charlesworth was to regard this particular form of stubbornness as something that is carried through into adult life, once the 'working-class kid' realizes he has cornered himself into a 'working-class job', or a working-class life on the dole, for real. Among men in his home town of Rotherham, Charlesworth observed 'a general obstinacy towards the world, an identity that in other social universes would be seen as rude and impolite'.[6] The uses of obstinacy are manifold: the 'good worker' can refuse obstinately to be ground down by the bastards and instead find his own way through it. The 'bad worker' can be a ringleader of the exploited or just someone who gets on everyone's wick. Again, the cost of this is departure from the group, or refusing membership of it in the first place.

This can be seen in two ways. As Hoggart observed of the fifties factory floor, the worst way for a worker to be seen in the eyes of his comrades is as someone who's 'keen': an individual's keenness at work can show up his workmates and force them either to work harder – for no extra reward – or to edge him out of association with them. (The next thing you know he's a foreman, in the pockets of the bosses, and therefore showing that he was never 'one of us' in the first place.) An alternative model of fifties rebellion is Alan Sillitoe's Arthur Seaton, from *Saturday Night and Sunday Morning*, who doesn't disdain keenness in order to stick with the group, but because he thinks the whole lot – work, solidarity, society – is a mug's game.

Not a lot had changed by the time I came of age. Keenness is the curse of the respectable, and I was as keen as mustard. In addition to the job at Greggs, I got the job with Avon. This second job I could fit around the first, and the A-levels, by delivering the catalogues to every house and flat on our road in the evenings. A week later, again after college and tea, I'd collect the catalogues and any orders that had been placed and go home to fill in the order form, which in its turn would be collected by the local supervisor. A week after that, a big box would arrive containing shampoos, lipsticks, shower mittens and earrings, destined for the grown-up party bags that I'd take round to their purchasers' houses. Getting the money was harder than getting the orders, I remember – in all probability because ordering from catalogues never does feel like proper shopping. I have never been good at doorstepping, and sometimes it felt like extortion to ask someone – a young woman whose flat smelled of hassle, who ordered some eye shadow just to feel normal for a bit – for the £2 or £3 they owed. Then again, I was seventeen and neither sensitive nor experienced enough to realize I could just let them off paying. With keenness and respectability came an inflexible sense of rectitude: discretion was not my middle name.

At my school there were teachers who loved the very bones of us, who would always have chosen to teach us over any well-primed middle-class kids. There were also teachers who couldn't understand why we didn't love them, considering everything they tried to do for us. Lastly there were teachers who loathed us because we disgusted them. But even the teachers who loved us didn't see great futures for us – not incredible, un-thought-of futures, at least. I always believed I had a future:

I could envision one, right from the beginning – but that vision didn't come from school. I always imagined Chelmsley Wood, where we were from and where we were schooled, was a place I would one day leave. *Any day now.*

There's a song by the band Broadcast, whose singer Trish Keenan came from the same place as me, the first lines of which invite the eponymous Michael on a trip back to Chelmsley Wood. The first time I heard it I fell off my chair. I knew Broadcast were from Birmingham, but had always imagined that they were from somewhere where people did interesting things, such as Moseley. (Come on, we're talking about Birmingham here. Of course you've never heard of Moseley. It's a part of Birmingham where I've heard interesting things take place.) The music of Broadcast had a spooky, edge-of-frightening quality to it, right from the start. Their early song 'The Book Lovers' strongly transmitted a sense that going to the library could be dangerous. 'Michael A Grammar', their song mentioning Chelmsley Wood, is jauntier, but not without edges. I got no clues from a decade's worth of casual listening that they were from anywhere else but somewhere quite bohemian and therefore quite posh: perhaps the name 'Chelmsley Wood' just scanned better. But that didn't sound right, either. In order to write a song about it you have to know it's there, and not many people do know it's there, unless it's the place they actually come from.

Then one day I went to see Broadcast play live, at the Barbican Centre in London. They had performed shyly, glacially even, for half an hour when Keenan asked, into the half-lit mass of faces:

'Is anyone here from Chelmsley Wood?'

'I AM! I AM!'

That was me in the gods, too far away for her to hear. She went on to complain that even her old school had a bleak name:

'It was called Archbishop Grimshaw. The name says it all.' That the audience reacted with polite bemusement is exactly what you'd expect. But someone had said the words 'Chelmsley Wood' on stage at the Barbican: it was like receiving confirmation of your existence. Trish Keenan and I exchanged emails, a few years before her death from pneumonia in 2011, on the vexed subject of Where We Were From. What has always stayed in my mind is her telling me that she had never quite managed to convince her partner what it meant to Come From Chelmsley Wood: 'I try to explain to my boyfriend [about it] but unless you've lived a council estate life you don't know how deep it goes and what it does to people.'

'You don't know how deep it goes and what it does to people.' It sounds like a description of abuse, doesn't it? At the very least, it suggests that something has been withheld, something essential to wellbeing, from one segment of humanity by another. She was right. 'Now live in it,' writes Paul Farley in his poem 'Brutalist', an anti-fantasy about tower blocks and the people who make others live in them. If I had lived 'a council estate life' all my life, and not just for the first half of it, I would be fifty years older. In my easy life I am not ageing; I skip along with no weight or aches. When I was growing up, the thing I aspired to most desperately was autonomy, the ability to move around weightlessly knowing I was trusted – and that I trusted myself – to do just that. The interesting thing about entering the middle class is that everything you have known is turned on its head. You go from being invisible to society, and yet at the same time the object of constant scrutiny and mistrust, to being at once anonymous and in possession of a voice. You are trusted to get on with things, and encouraged to go on endlessly about the way in which you do them.

Today I'm doing my work in the same library I grew up

visiting. I am struck by how many of the people in on a quiet
Wednesday are here because they have been sent here, by the
Job Centre or the careers service, to be told how to look for
work. A small queue of men forms for this purpose – and
they are all men, the women here having been encouraged by
their doctor or support worker to take part in community
activities, today's being a Christmas card-making session. The
healthiest-looking people are those who work here, or for
the auxiliary services that take up daily or weekly residence.
The people who don't work here often look tired and grey,
either swollen or emaciated, and wear worn-down shoes. The
other libraries that I use – city centrepieces, university reading
rooms and branch libraries in pleasant suburbs – house their
share of misfits, but are generally visited from day to day by
people who simply enjoy going to the library, who enjoy taking
their children there and who see a trip to the library as part of a
full life. No one has forced them to be there on pain of losing the
money on which they have to subsist; no one has badgered them
into going because it would do them good to get out of the
house while they wait six months to receive Cognitive Behaviour Therapy. The library here, because nothing can any longer
exist for its own sake, also serves as a citizens' advice bureau, job
centre and public health information centre. For better or worse,
books to read for pleasure are no longer the main event. Any
pleasure to be gained has to be measured in terms of economic
and mental health outcomes.

It doesn't necessarily matter to everyone that this is the case.
The older men who sit together, researching the crossword
answers and arguing about history, ignore the way their library
is being forced to change and carry on doing what they've
always done. They manage to congregate – to read and discuss,
in a library of all places! – without being asked if they need a job
or a health check or benefits advice. If people didn't continue to

use libraries like this, we'd be told that libraries have outgrown their usefulness.

While working in the library I go downstairs to Greggs to get a cup of tea. (In recent years the library has been moved from its original purpose-built home into the shopping precinct.) In the time it takes to reach the bottom of the staircase I overhear a total of two sentences: one, by a woman speaking into a phone, is 'FUCK OFF about your Rizlas, I don't wanna hear it,' and the other, from a young man to a young woman, is, 'I can't hear a FUCKing thing you're saying with you walking ahead of me.' My bones turn to glass again and I remember that often things do seem terrible just because of where you are. I'm thrown back into a world of ignorance and everyday violence – and if that sounds extreme, you needed to hear the way in which those 'fucks' were said: the desperation and life-fatigue of the first and the casual aggression of the second. I remember that, although I had quite a life here before I was eighteen, it wasn't one to feel unduly nostalgic about. People so often suppress anger about their circumstances – because of the constant need to feel as though they are decent and reasonable, whether or not their version of decent and reasonable looks anything like yours – that it forces itself out like steam at jarring points in the day. A violent hiss over something trivial.

The American psychotherapist and social activist Michael Lerner, having practised in a working-class district of Oakland, California, in the seventies and eighties, developed a compelling theory. To Lerner, 'surplus powerlessness' explained why relatively few working-class adults challenged unfair working practices, low status and inadequate pay, whether unofficially or as members of a union. 'Powerlessness corrupts,' he wrote, because it crushes out of all proportion our sense of what is worthwhile and possible: 'We look at our world and our own behaviour and we tell ourselves that, although we really aren't living the lives we want to live, there is nothing we can do about it.'[7] Yet those who lack power in the public sphere are often very powerful in the domestic one, which is both an affirmation of individual resilience and a sign of how people who are thwarted in one area of life don't necessarily lose their power in another. People create spheres of influence wherever they can: they make rules even where there appears to be no order and no reason.

British society is not so much a pyramid as a diamond, with the lives of those at the top and the bottom resembling each other's in ways not obvious to the wide band in the middle. At the top and at the bottom, it's all about who you know, and about those around you seeking to maintain networks and familiarity, whether or not that helps you as an individual. At the bottom, as at the top, everyone knows each other: not in the comforting, borrowing-a-cup-of-sugar way that those in the habit of sanctify-ing working-class life seek to encourage, but in the war-by-text-message, baseball-bat-through-your-window-for-slagging-off-your-brother's-girlfriend-on-Facebook kind of way. People who feel themselves stuck here complain that everyone knows everyone else, and that this intrusiveness prevents them from getting on with their lives. I sometimes overhear such conversa-tions on the bus and wonder how knowing so many people can be so bad for you. It's a trap, or a series of traps, just as public school and Oxford are, designed by your peers to keep you in line. The contrast, of course, between the traps at the top and those at the bottom is that the former set you up for a smooth path through life and the latter for an extraordinarily difficult one. But there is a concentration of power at both ends of the diamond: the only difference is the milieu in which that power can be used. In the middle, power is diffused by dint of sheer numbers, and yet it is in the middle that power is aggregated and gets used most effectively. Because of its size it is the middle class, and not the '1 per cent', which sets the rules. This much larger group has the combined wealth, the qualifications, the social and cultural capital and, perhaps above all, the electoral influence to dictate much of our government policy, from tax to education.

I'm trying here to make an argument not in favour of people's autonomy, but in recognition of the fact that it already exists. I want it to be acknowledged that 'helplessness' or 'dependency' – as it's defined by politicians seeking to blame individuals for structural failings – is an adoptive or adaptive stance rather than an innate fact of character. You can express your power, maintain the illusion of autonomy, preserve your dignity, whatever you need to do, by refusing to comply with what is asked of you by society. To feel as though you lack power is to believe that none of your actions has any consequence: which means, perversely, that you give yourself the licence to do what you like on the assumption that it won't matter. That's kind of what it means to be 'rough': to draw what strength you can from your place on the margins, to let it all go to pieces and not really 'give a shit'. To be 'respectable' is to define yourself against that feeling: it is to believe, and to enact, the idea that you do have power as an individual, as a household or as a community in spite of your relative powerlessness in society. We are free in ways we often cannot comprehend, and bound in ways that are far beyond our strength as individuals to control. Self-possession – the ability to decide for yourself which of society's strictures matter and which ones don't – is compromised by the need to look and feel dignified in a society which seeks in innumerable ways, big and small, to make you look and feel *un*-dignified. Because of this, the efforts we sometimes see people make to preserve their dignity and self-respect actually work against them. When I lived in inner London I would often see teenage boys ride bikes in circles on the streets around our block of flats, some wearing curlers in their hair and some sucking dummies. They would wear their

jeans in a way that made them walk as if they'd just soiled themselves. It was upsetting to see them: to be dignified, to go for
dignity, in this way, on these streets, when on any other street
they would just get laughed at or run away from. I think back to
'the lads' of Paul Willis's book, and the boys with whom I sat
in the back row at school, who sought each other's respect
through endless, circular attempts to show each other how little
they cared about the outside world. Though they'd rather have
died than admit it, they cared about each other instead. It was
just that the psychological need to preserve self-respect in that
context absorbed all their energy, leaving none to see what
their efforts looked like to everyone else. The boys I used to
see in London were trying to avoid looking soft and being
humiliated in the situation in which they found themselves. To
engage in such avoidance, to enter a situation in which nothing
else mattered except the approval of peers, not only put them in
danger of direct violence, but also of the indirect, symbolic violence of being disdained by wider society. One of the effects of
their efforts was to enable other, less trapped, people to say, 'these
people – they're not like us'. Not that it mattered to them, when
to 'fit in' better on their particular street felt comfortable, partici-
patory and assertive. What might begin as a mutual ignorance
and suspicion becomes ingrained: groups of humans living in the
same city become alien to each other.

One evening when I was home from London, while the
adverts were on, my dad said to me: 'Have you ever been
down at the shops and just looked around and thought, all these
wasted lives?' I didn't want to say that I had, because to do so –
especially once you've left – is to suggest that you're somewhat
detached from it. Surely, to think of people walking around a
barren precinct their whole lives, waiting in the bitter cold with
Farmfoods bags for buses that never come, suggests something
depressive in you, rather than in the scene itself. *Now live in it.*

Places such as Chelmsley Wood, and the lives lived in them, don't enter the wider consciousness except through portmanteau terms such as *council estate* and *deprivation*, or, to the well intentioned, *community* and *regeneration*. These days I live in a nice suburb, which never gets described by other people as a 'community': it is a distinctive neighbourhood, with specific characteristics and residents who are assumed to have autonomous lives.

I have a map in my mind of where I grew up, on this largest of estates. How can that be so, when it feels as though I never knew anyone here, as though I passed through it like a ghost? I must have walked along every walkway at some point without being able to tell you why. There were always errands to run, I guess, and walls to jump. Shortcuts to discover. Trying to find the way out took eighteen years, during which I went to playschool, in the square church hall, then primary and secondary schools, in square brown buildings, and caught a million buses through the estate. I wore out my shoes delivering the newspapers and the Avon catalogues, and running up and down the Greggs shop floor between the bread slicer and the trays of doughnuts for sugaring and bagging. Yes, I had quite a life here before I left. I had a childhood here; the lion's share of my education took place here. I'd always thought my life started only when I left, but perhaps that's because it's what I told myself would happen: I'll get out of here and then I'll really start living.

But isn't part of living savouring that freshly sugared doughnut? I can taste the jam in it now, and can tell you it tastes just as good in east Birmingham as it would anywhere else. Part of living is finding a quicker way home through the oddly cherished walkways. We knew we were living at New Year's Eve parties, at the social club near my parents' house, when the floor was packed and, for once, nobody cared about your haircut or what your dancing was like. That one night a year, for several years, came quite close to redeeming all the others. The DJ would build up the set, easing in with hits from the current Top 40, merging into lesser-known Motown and Northern Soul tracks for the connoisseurs. A brief break for the buffet and he'd ramp it straight back up: 'Jimmy Mack' by Martha Reeves, The Velvelettes' 'Needle in a Haystack', a tasteful lovers' rock slowie, before ending with the party full Monty: 'Tainted Love', 'We Are Family' and 'Oops Upside Your Head'. For no reason I can fathom, we 'danced' this sitting down in a conga line. It was the one night of the year I didn't want to be anywhere else. It took a long time to understand why.

There was a richness of its own there, back on the plains of council estate life, but not one that could stand up, could bear comparison, to the diversity I found beyond its confines. That's a painful, probably erroneous, truth I keep coming back to: an unreliable memory, which nevertheless feels solid and right to me. There's a difference between what we are all looking for and what some of us are given, and it has to be measured and confronted if we're to get anywhere at all. It was a long time before I returned to my parents' home with a sense of having understood something about the place and times in which I grew up that I hadn't got the hang of before. It was a contained childhood in a contained place: not contained in the sense that you couldn't move, but in the way that the estate, in its own infancy and adolescence, was growing up apart from the city that brought it into being. We were out on a limb here, and that altered the perceptions of adults who were used to being at the centre of things, or at least better contained within the body of the city. The estate was erected so as to have invisible walls around it, to which we reacted as if they were real.

2.   This Is My Truth

We ate a lot of mince in Chelmsley Wood. We were shorter and shyer than the teams of schoolkids from the other half of the borough we'd occasionally beat at skittleball. When our primary school teachers saved up yogurt pots to bring in for seed-planting, I remember that the labels were always from Sainsbury's, not Somerfield or Kwik Save. Because of this their lives seemed redolent of another, impossibly profligate world: you got the impression they didn't shop at the indoor market. They all had cars because they all lived far from us: another way in which they were different. To be honest, they probably ate mince in the suburbs too, but in exotic dishes such as lasagne.

At primary school, a group of us who showed some promise in maths were driven by our teacher to a school on the other side of Solihull, a borough better known for being posh than for having council estates. The children we were seated with spoke like adults to us, and like adults to adults.

A rangy boy pushed his glasses up his nose, which sat between glowing, success-flushed cheeks. 'Well, I think we should break off into pairs and work out one quarter of the sum each. What do you think?'

I remember us sitting there, the short, mince-fed kids, so shocked by his front that we couldn't even find the voices to tell him to get lost. Even then, I would have described him as different from us, but wouldn't have known why. Now, of course, I know that what made him seem so different was that he was middle class.

Let's imagine that I'm telling all this – what I'm about to

say – to a friend. Say it's Richard, who used to visit me in the
Solihull branch of Greggs when I did extra shifts at half-term.
Say he had an interest in finding out more about my life: why
this shy-to-the-point-of-catatonic girl he first met in the summer of 1992 managed in spite of her near silence to flaunt a
massive chip on her shoulder.

The time and place we met were not auspicious. To arrive at
a suburban sixth-form college, having been educated entirely on
a council estate a few miles away, and realize that I had spent the
previous sixteen years in a parallel universe, wasn't going to
help, chip-wise. (My husband has never forgotten the first time
he saw a garlic crusher, when, having left Birkenhead, he arrived
at university in London. It seemed so ridiculous to him – so
superfluous – that he burst out laughing.) The fact that, in places
like Solihull proper, thirteen years of Conservative rule had
further enriched people who were already doing very nicely
while dessicating the social fabric of places like Chelmsley Wood
didn't help matters. *Help yourself to a pasty while the manager's not
looking, Rich, there's a good 'un. I'll tell you all about it.*

It was the second week in September, and two school-leavers
emerged from the park gate to begin afresh in another set of
rooms full of tables and chairs. Outside, everything was green
and dewy-smelling: a thin jam of crushed chestnut husks, slippery underfoot, formed a path from the bus stop to the college
threshold. There was the damp and the discomfort of wet coats.
New Doc Martens trod rainy mush into the foyer, where a flap
of little pages pinned to the walls directed each new student
towards the expectant chambers that led off it. They were sixteen years old and bursting to tell the world of their arrival.
Their new rucksacks contained Kit-Kats, the foil wrappers
waiting to be sliced down with a careful thumbnail under the
desk; books to read with new words in them. Tapes rattled
around at the bottom, next to used-up batteries, to be wound

around with an index finger while waiting to register for the secular trinity of English, history and politics. You could hear a babbling brook of jacket press-studs being popped and the easy, measured sound of people with at least two words for every feeling. Copies of *Ulysses* were flipped open next to a cup of instant coffee – the very measure of adulthood when, six months earlier, the only thing you could get out of a school vending machine was a can of Sunkist – next to someone now free to sit on tables, rather than chairs, without the threat of detention. Heaven for anyone whose waking and sleeping life until that day had consisted of one sustained, unbroken, cheerful pine for freedom.

I was pretty much the same then as I am now. It's just that all that was really me – all that was most me – was hidden under a bushel of anxiety. My mind had been an eager little constellation until then. It didn't know about the universe. That was me, there, preparing for it all with a series of ring-binders neatly felt-tipped with my full name – graffiti of a sort – and just behind, the one who would see life in me, taller by a head and shoulders, with a CD Walkman on and a copy of *Private Eye* rolled under his arm.

It was not a good day to be wearing what I was wearing on my first day at college. Doc Martens and hiking socks cut it well with sheer leggings back then, but warm feet were no consolation for cold, wet everything else. I caught the bus and shook silently in my seat all the way there. I realize now that this was caused by the longing for a warm, still hand on my shoulder that would stop me from thinking and permit me to sleep. I needed to know it was going to be all right. There was an underlying conviction that everything would be all right, but no evidence yet to uphold it.

One of the lists attached to the wall of the college foyer told me to turn right and then left for history. This wasn't what I'd originally signed up for. Because I'd gone to a school where people didn't do A-levels – if they were doing all right, they signed up for the gas board or the Rover works – there was no guidance, none at least to suggest which of the blasted things were most likely to get me into university. *University*. The word evoked something as distant as Mars. It was a destination so elevated, so suggestive of human effort and dedicated self-direction that one could perhaps reach it and die happy. University, in my mind, was the laboratory of human curiosity where ignorance was banished and thoughtfulness encouraged. If I could just get there, I believed, my life would be transformed utterly. In my final month at school and in the absence of advice I wrote on the application form my intention to study A-levels in English language, art and social biology, which was the closest to sociology the sixth-form college offered. In hindsight, those choices would have got me somewhere, just not where I wanted to go; what mattered for the course of my future life was that the form and my predicted GCSE grades were enough to get me through the door.

Social biology went out of the window as soon as it became clear that it was something closer to hard science than applied daydreaming. Art was my favourite subject but so is everybody's. That left English language, which I'd understood to be close to linguistics – a way to grasp and master the language as it's used in society. Once I'd replaced the first two choices with history (my best subject after English) and politics (the nearest thing to sociology), English language stuck out somewhat. Apparently, English literature, politics and history was what you did, so that's what I did. The lack of intellectual rigour that went into these decisions terrifies me now. I made them on my own, unguided except for instinct. Which way would my life have gone had I not found the room for history, had I not walked into it, signed my name on the sheet and recognized the tall teenager to my left, who looked as though he spent every minute of his day thinking?

I watched Richard as he introduced himself to Dr Burgess, the head of department, and signed the take-up form in mannered italics using a fibre-tip pen taken from his top pocket. Imagine introducing yourself to an adult! Sheesh, he must really take himself seriously, I thought.

'Are you down for politics as well as history?' he asked me, clicking the cap back on to his fibre-tip pen. 'Because if you do them with English you can go for one of the low-ranking Cambridge colleges – Robinson, Churchill.'

'Mmm. Oh yeah? Ooh no. I mean yes.' The challenge he had set me was to answer clearly, without looking away. I looked away. I remembered him from the summer open day, when we were piled into a small carpet-squared room for a general knowledge quiz. He couldn't find a seat initially. When he found one, he pulled the chair at right angles to the table, all the better to spring into action with his fibre-tip pen and mannered italics as soon as each question was asked. It must be great to be that smart, I thought.

On our last day at secondary school, Mr B, my humanities teacher, had called me in to his office and issued a friendly warning: 'You're going to be there with kids from Solihull who've all been at school together and have got ten As each. They've had each other to compete with since they were four. You haven't been competing with anybody. They've got there because they've done well, as you have, but it's not going to be what you've been used to. It's going to be hard. I'm just telling you so you'll be prepared.'

He wasn't telling me this because I was certifiably 'bright'; no one would have been more aware than him that I'd sweated my guts out to get As and Bs when other kids, in other schools, would have bagged them with their eyes shut. It was more to do with him having recognized what Richard Hoggart called 'white-collar leanings' in our family, which had unwittingly set me apart at school and, it turned out, would set me apart again – for the opposite reasons – at college. There had been other kids from our school who'd gone to sixth form and experienced something like culture shock, arriving utterly unprepared for the difficulty of A-levels and coming away empty-handed, their sense of inadequacy trebled.

As Mr B was talking, the rosy-cheeked expert from the primary school maths workshop surfaced in my mind. *Bloody hell, they're all going to be like him, aren't they?* I had a rough idea of what Mr B meant, but no real sense of what it would feel like to arrive at a place that you imagined would be a level plain – where all A-grades meant the same thing – only to find that your estimation of your own skills put you somewhere in a ditch.

'I'm from Chelmsley Wood,' I told Richard, in the way Basil Fawlty would say 'He's from Barcelona.' I felt this would explain everything. I wanted to tell him that this meant growing up in a place where men had been kicked to death on the street and where there are people who joke about running over black people at pedestrian crossings. (As time has worn on, this has become my standard self-description: 'I'm from Chelmsley Wood,' as if it explains anything.) It turned out that Richard was from everywhere: Essex, Suffolk, Cheshire, Solihull. His father's own desire to climb socially had made his son rootless. Perhaps due to his family's habit of moving and getting-used-to, moving and getting-used-to, Richard seemed worldly as well as smart. He also seemed empathetic. He saw in me, the squashed and hopeful sixteen-year-old sitting next to him in class, a lost person who wanted to learn how to find things out.

Mr B had been right about sixth form, though as it turned out Richard was as unsettled as me, albeit for quite different reasons. He had spent some of his secondary schooling in the private sector where, he told me some years later, 'If the teachers thought you hadn't tried your best they'd tear up your work and make you do it again. I was always being told, "This isn't your best, you can do better than this."' Later on Richard found himself at one of those Solihull comprehensive schools where, Mr B had assumed, a culture of excellence was well established. 'When I went there I couldn't believe I wasn't being told to try harder,' he said. 'The teachers didn't think they needed to: it was a comprehensive so they didn't want to hold anyone back, but they were damned if they were going to encourage anyone to do better.'

Why would you be told in one institution that you can do better and not in another? For the powerful, excellence in education and culture is both a demand and a right. For the powerless, excellence has to be self-generated, because it isn't otherwise expected. In the mid-twentieth century, both Hoggart and the Welsh literary theorist Raymond Williams put out powerful arguments for the creation of a common culture that did not aim, consciously or otherwise, to keep the classes at cross purposes. Williams and Hoggart were two 'uprooted' and 'anxious' boys – to use Hoggart's words – from South Wales and northern England respectively, who won scholarships to grammar school from working-class backgrounds and who, in their own elegant ways, stormed academia. Because they were interlopers, they were able to forge a new intellectual discipline, that of looking closely at the information we consume and create, and articulating what it reveals about relationships in society. Both Williams and Hoggart were among the first critics to treat working-class culture as a subject worthy of discussion in its own right, and to set out ways in which the streams of high and low or popular culture could rightfully be united. They did this by asserting the inherent universality, and therefore the very ordinariness, of human cultures. Through decades of contributions to public life in Britain, Williams and Hoggart between them conveyed an important message with consistency and power. We must speak clearly to each other, they said, or we will remain divided. But, despite their efforts, divided we remain.

To realize – even to accept – that there are other strands of cultural life than the ones you're used to takes more than simple exposure. These things are all around you, all the time. It's more that you start sniffing at something, like the Bisto Kids at a fleeting whiff of roast beef, and you follow your nose. As you do so, a door opens into a room filled with stimuli you never knew existed: not only new things to see, but new ways of seeing. The room seems to become bigger and fuller the more time you spend in it, making the one to which you'd previously been confined feel at once claustrophobic and sparsely furnished. You start to look again, with fresh eyes, at aspects of the culture that you're used to – in my case, popular culture, which took in pop music and the magazines featuring it, the output of the main television channels, mainstream American films, tabloid newspapers. In so doing, you become attuned to the broader idea of what all but the finest examples of them are suggesting collectively about the level of your comprehension and by extension your intelligence. Over a period of time a single, strong message begins to emerge: that, as someone from a working-class family, in a working-class environment, and experiencing a level of education tailored to and directed at a perceived idea of working-class children's abilities, you are expected to reach a certain level of understanding and no higher. Sure, you'll be able to intuit things with that 'natural' antenna for cant which street-level authenticity affords; but without exposure to a wider picture you'll struggle to gain a broad and nuanced understanding of the society in which we live. Still, no matter: for the likes of you, entertainment is meant to be about forgetting, not remembering; for escape, not for transcendence.

This realization can make things psychologically tricky for anyone in the process of navigating the space between what they once knew and what they're about to find out. Did you hear that door slam shut just then? Which side – *whose* side – were you on when it did? Hoggart refers in a 1966 essay, 'Growing Up', to having suffered a 'nervous breakdown' during the arduous process of educating himself out of his original class.[1] Having grown up in poverty, he was used to fearing the unknown, and commented on the way his grandmother methodically smoothed the hem of her pinny as she mentally costed the household budget down to the half-penny. He no more wanted to forget her distress than to remain locked inside it: a classic double-bind. Even in working-class families where the threat of absolute penury disappeared with the coming of the welfare state, the behaviour associated with it can persist. Everything and everyone is a refuge; to feel comfortable is to stay close, never to leave the nest. This state of being may remain comforting for some, but can become stifling for others, particularly when they begin to notice that there is a larger world outside.

On that first day of college, I made a decision – only half aware that I was doing it – to take up the opportunity that was being presented to me. It was an opportunity to turn decisively away from what I'd learned about the world to that point, and turn towards another way of looking at things. I didn't realize at the time that this change of direction wasn't just a choice: in fact, it would be absolutely necessary in order both to survive this form of education and to thrive in the professional class. 'Survival' is not too strong a word to use. I had to avoid falling into the void between two worlds, the working-class world and the middle-class world. I had to choose between rooms. The years that followed would be a slow process of guidance on the part of friends and teachers, and mimesis on mine, after which I snatched the baton and ran for my life. But that first day at college was the point at which everything began to change, because it was the day on which my veil of ignorance – my belief that meritocracy was a reality – started to lift.

What lies in the second room has the potential to unlock every subsequent door with which you're confronted in life, at the same time as closing off – in a crucial, saddening way – the door back to the first. The more time you spend in this second room, the way you use words – the order you put them in, the number of clauses and qualifiers you include in a sentence, even the sounds of the words themselves – begins to change. It's not simply a matter of becoming more verbose. It involves learning another language entirely, one which places at its centre the act of thinking, and thinking about doing things in the future as opposed to doing them right now.

Back in the fifties, the socio-linguist Basil Bernstein argued that working-class and middle-class people communicate on such entirely different terms that the former are automatically disadvantaged by an education system which values abstract learning over the affirmation of shared experience. Bernstein asserted that the way middle-class people use language is not superior to the way working-class people use it. It's simply that the former is more powerful and effective in the society we have, and for this reason schools and teachers often unwittingly reinforce the idea that one way of using language has to be got rid of in order to learn the other. Telling someone they could become a lawyer is only going to make sense if their entire experience has been geared towards such a thing seeming possible. The difficulties I had in adapting from a working-class school to the middle-class world of sixth-form college had everything to do with language and its intimate relationship with class.

Analysing the way members of the working class and the middle class use language in everyday situations, Bernstein realized that working-class speech focuses on describing acts as they are taking place, or, if they took place in the past, *as if* they are taking place in the present. In one example, a working-class person recalls having been unable to buy a ticket from the driver on the bus the previous morning: 'He says, "I can't sell you a ticket, you'll have to get one out of the machine," but I go, "The machine's not working." I'm going up the bloody wall by now so I'm just getting off and he says, "Oh all right then, I'll let you off this time."' On the other hand, middle-class speech gravitates towards classifying and contextualizing events, making them stand as concepts almost regardless of whether or not they actually happened. A middle-class person describing the same exchange would aim to give an impression of place, control and perception: 'I tried to buy a ticket on the bus this morning but the driver insisted I get off and buy one from the machine. When I told him the machine wasn't working, he let me stay on just as I was about to get off in a huff.' The working-class and middle-class methods – to put crude brackets around each – of relating the same story diverge from the outset. The former aims to include you, the listener, in the flow of the telling; the latter aims to assert the speaker's authority and accuracy.

What gives middle-class speech its power, I'd argue, is not its 'formality' – as Bernstein describes this 'elaborated' code in opposition to the 'informal' or 'restricted' code of working-class speech – but its ability to translate material security into security of the self.[2] It confirms the grasp the person has both on their own life as an individual and on their effectiveness, their agency, in the world. Working-class children are often described as 'passive learners', who appear not to know how or are reluctant to take part in their own learning. But in order to be regarded as an 'active learner' you would have an idea of how taking part – how giving a shit – might benefit you a long way into the future.

The middle-class approach to life, expressed through the middle-class approach to language, is founded on a bedrock of security: an understanding that the future will be as good as, if not better than, the present. By comparison the working-class approach to life and therefore to language embodies generations of uncertainty. For how long can we keep the family together? Will our child survive? Will I still have a job tomorrow or next week? Can we make plans that will work out?

The very idea of 'compensatory' education to improve the systemic position of 'deprived children', suggested Bernstein, is based on a notion that the informal language code is inherently deficient, rather than a rational, if embedded, response to circumstances. It's only deficient in the sense that formal education is based on the formal code, and can therefore be made use of by jettisoning the informal code. Once applied, and without this understanding, Bernstein writes, 'these labels do their own sad work'. This is as true now as when he wrote it in 1970.

The use of informal code in working-class speech persists even when material circumstances improve. Why? Because working-class families and communities generally *do* stay together, and because for that very reason collective memories are long. We learn to speak using the language of the people around us, using the same accent, the same turns of phrase and the same points of reference, in order to get along in that society. To learn the new language, perhaps even to be aware that another one exists, you have to leave that family and community – literally, psychologically or both.

This has extraordinary implications in terms of the hidden ways in which class can have a decisive influence on aspects of people's lives. Going to a working-class school in a working-class area, with all your working-class mates, gives you little incentive to learn the language of your middle-class teachers. Instrumental appeals to 'get on in life' may work, but only if those appeals are consistent and come from more than one set of people: not just your teachers, but your parents, peers and neighbours.

Another quality that Bernstein identified in working-class speech is its fragmentary nature. By sticking with the description of individual events rather than unifying them into a larger narrative, you accept the contingency of things: after all, your circumstances might have changed by tomorrow, and in any case what you've said is likely to have significance only in the specific context in which you said it. Middle-class speech, by comparison, smacks of grandeur, because it seeks to place feelings and events in a universal context, with the inference that the individual speaker and his perceptions matter in the greater scheme of things. A bit of polish, like a 'phone voice', can be learned easily through simple imitation. Mastering a code without first being given the equipment to unlock it is another matter. Given that formal schooling is about learning universal principles, a working-class child who enters school using a form of speech geared towards communicating, in Bernstein's words, 'particularistic' rather than 'universalistic' meanings is immediately at a disadvantage. Informal speech makes sense only in terms of the direct relationships it describes, whereas formal speech works towards defining and then communicating overall ideas and concepts.

Bernstein's work may be relatively old, but more recent research suggests that it has remained relevant, perhaps depressingly so. Paul Kerswill, a socio-linguist working at Lancaster University, found in the mid-2000s that the use of speech by working-class and middle-class adolescents in Reading and Milton Keynes was polarized by class, in spite of Milton Keynes's nominal status as a 'classless' new town. The tropes of working-class speech persist, he argues, as an act of political resistance against the ways of ' "posh" people': remembering to say 'I ain't done it yet', rather than 'I haven't done it yet', is how you stick it to The Man. (While you might also expect middle-class teen-agers to shave off some of the vocal vestiges of their privilege, Kerswill reports that, in Milton Keynes and Reading at least, their recorded use of working-class motifs such as the double negative – 'I didn't do nothing' – 'was so rare as to be negligible'.)[3]

Here, again, is where divided loyalties come in. Why should you ditch the language you learned among the people you love, and which enables you to communicate with them? A 'phone voice' is just that: a voice used for, and only on, specific occasions. Putting on a posh voice when you think it would be useful doesn't change you at your core, whereas learning the formal code of middle-class speech brings about permanent change, not only because it *works* – it gets things done, it makes people regard you differently no matter how you regard yourself – but because it causes you to think differently. One significant way it does this is by elevating the status of ideas at the expense of relation-ships, taking your feet off the ground and putting your head in the clouds. There is nothing wrong with talking about ideas, but how you do it – and whether it's 'all right' to do it at all – is treated very differently according to the social group in which you find yourself.

The Swiss linguist and thinker Ferdinand de Saussure describes language as a form of treasure which is shared with others when we speak. Treasure is also something that can be hoarded. If you keep all the good words – the rich, descriptive, wild, long words – to yourself then you retain their high value. Share them with the masses and you end up, suggest both Saus-sure and the French sociologist Pierre Bourdieu, with the linguistic means to create a society of equals, which is exactly what the hoarders of cultural capital don't want.[4] Communica-tion is the battlefield on which the slights and injuries of class are played out, which is why we go to such great lengths to avoid communicating with people from other classes. If you want to make someone wish the ground would swallow them whole, you correct their malapropism; and if you want to remind someone of the dire cost of getting above their station, you ask them: have you swallowed a fucking dictionary?

Once I began to absorb the rules of middle-class speech, and as I spent more time away from home, the way I used words began to change. I came from a family that was interested in words, and in 'safe' circumstances – such as at home or when talking to my teachers – I already used a relatively wide vocabulary. But, looking back, I made a psychologically significant compromise in order to learn the new language that was necessary to move from one stream of education – the working-class stream, which makes fewer conceptual or linguistic demands on its participants – into another. I kept my fairly strong Birmingham accent, which gets stronger if I become relaxed or animated. I can wow you with abstract concepts till the cows come home, but I'll still pronounce cows 'kews' and home 'howme'. Yet I was locked out of my own life until I learned how to speak, not 'proper', but in a way that gave voice to ideas. It was as though someone had dangled a key and shown me how best to use it.

Those who identify themselves as being working class may point out, perhaps with satisfaction, that a middle-class person can't flit between an informal and a formal way of communicating as easily as this, and therefore is just as limited in his or her ability to move comfortably between social groups. If you are someone equally comfortable in both codes, you have the ability to negotiate a safe register to speak according to the situation you find yourself in. In other words, you can bend the ear of those in authority and therefore get things done. This is what enables middle-class people to dismiss so easily what working-class people have to offer. Which is not to say the middle classes don't nick, or borrow freely from them: coolness, 'authenticity', an apparent ability to dress up prejudice as 'common sense'. That's the most ridiculous thing about such condescension, born of ignorance: that because working-class people are supposed to 'tell it like it is', we're meant to take the 'it' as self-evident truth, rather than what 'it' often is – a cocktail of self-righteousness and cant. Richard Hoggart regarded this indulgence as an 'excuse for gross insensitivity; that insensitivity feeds on its own pride, the "hubris" of the "ordinary chap" '.[5]

Of all the stultifying effects of class, the tendency of each class to make a virtue out of its own habits is the strongest. Habits form culture, and culture is the total expression of a group of people in their specific environment. In this way, a culture represents the accumulation of habits which differ between groups according to their environment: it goes on, it lives, and it changes as it does so. My childhood habits were different as a result of having grown up in my parents' house and not that of my grandparents. HP Sauce, not Daddie's. The *Mirror*, not the *Sun*. BBC, not ITV (apart from *Corrie* and *Auf Wiedersehen, Pet*). Butter, not marge. Mortgage, not rent. Boiled eggs, not brawn. Duvets, not blankets. *Woman's Own*, not the *Weekly News*. My nan gardened for the veg and my mum for the flowers, but both shared an attachment to leaf tea and Fairy Liquid.

Together these influences help to shape our idea of what culture is, and can and should be, and tend to determine what role and what attitudes we have towards shaping it. The word I fall upon here is 'collusion' – but that sounds quite a lot meaner than it should; and 'swapping' sounds too equal, since I hope to illustrate over the course of this book the vast inequalities evident in how culture gets produced, promoted and disseminated. A more generous definition of the interaction between people and

culture in society comes from Raymond Williams, in his land-
mark book *The Long Revolution*: 'A series of unique individuals,
in real relationships, learning and contributing to a changing
pattern.'[6] It doesn't matter that all habits are the specific products of necessity, and that working-class habits have arisen out
of dispossession, from generations' worth of narrowed offerings. *This* is what we do. People like us don't do *that*. We take
this knowledge right inside us, in the form of internal, and
eternal, vigilance. The French philosopher Michel Foucault
puts it a different way: 'There is no need for arms, physical violence, material constraints. Just a gaze. An inspecting gaze, a
gaze which each individual under its weight will end by interior-
ising to the point that he is his own overseer.'[7] That gaze may
begin as someone else's, Foucault warns; but in the end we won't
need someone else's strictures to restrict ourselves, for we'll have
become our own policeman.

To be dispossessed, and to adopt in response to this dispossession a position of wilful ignorance, is one way of meeting life as
you find it, of creating the terms for a liveable life using what is
in front of you and denying the existence of the rest, because
it's too late to find a way into it. It's easier to switch off than to
remain switched on, not least when to remain engaged and
open to hope keeps you exposed to the grinding realities of your
situation. It may also expose something you hadn't noticed, or
had cause to register, before: the levelling agenda of your peers.
Think you're better than us, do you?

The problem is, the more you shrink your own world, the
more likely you are to be frightened by the unexpected, and the
unexpected can't be avoided in life. We may find hope of a sort
in the fact that people with limited choices still make choices:
even to abdicate responsibility for making informed decisions is a
choice in itself. It's a way of coping. Both Foucault and Bourdieu
wrote extensively about the nature of power as it's experienced by

individuals: how it can sometimes be easier to turn on ourselves and those around us than on vague, even unidentifiable, oppressors. Bourdieu, the master anatomist of social difference, also makes the connection between the words 'habit' and 'habitat' with his use of the term 'habitus' as a way to explore how hierarchies in society come to be mirrored not only domestically, but psychologically, even bodily. Habitus is how you – your mind, your body, your imagination – express your relationship to the environment that shapes you. Bourdieu describes the phenomenon of 'habitus divided against itself': a painful state of divided loyalty that occurs when you try, or are forced through social mobility, to alter your class-bound habits. It echoes the biblical phrase 'a house divided against itself cannot stand'. I know exactly what this feels like: it's the wall in the head by another name. What that phrase means to me is the feeling of division, of torn allegiance, that we might experience between the 'home' we know and the possibility of a different kind of 'home'.

'I was driven by my childhood to get on,' Richard Hoggart told the *Guardian* in a 2004 interview,

> but not in the sense of becoming a millionaire or anything like that. The ambition was to do something useful and interesting and somehow involving my writing. And I did have an impulse to criticise because there was a lot to criticise. I was brought up in a world where just about everyone assumed they would stay there all their lives and I resented that deeply. There are two types of life; the first is the escalator life, where you move inexorably upwards, the other type is the carousel where you go round and round. One of my arguments is that there are enough people making it their business to ensure that people stay on the carousel.[8]

One sort of home can be found on the carousel, a life both bound and freed by knowing what is about to come next. Schooling has given you literacy but not the ability to decipher the hidden codes of a social structure in which you haven't made the rules; yet that degree of literacy gives you another power, the power to turn your nose up at something offered to you even if it would be in your interests to take it. You have the power to cut off your nose to spite your face, and abundant temptations to wield it. The risk of joining the escalator, which has the effect of making life's possibilities seem limitless, is that you never quite get comfortable, feeling at home both everywhere and nowhere. You can travel the world yet refuse to be parted from your accent or your football shirt, whichever matters most to the preservation of your identity.

The escalator, which I jumped on and clung to as much out of desperation as enthusiasm, never stops. But stepping on it gives you the least visible and most powerful of advantages, that of cultural capital. It teaches you the right names to drop, the right holiday places to mention, the right way to use cutlery, the right way to go about getting what you want. Such information is absorbed slowly, over time: you may not even notice what's happening, only that the slow accumulation of knowledge appears to smooth your path through life and give you greater power. When politicians talk about the 'sharp elbows' used by the middle classes to avoid the possibility of their children attending working-class schools, what they mean is that members of the middle class tend to have the cultural capital to get their own way. They – we – know how to negotiate and feel they have the right to do so; they know how to argue without looking boorish, and they know who they need to get on their side. They are not scared of authority because possessing the habits of the middle class confers authority upon them.

Yet Bourdieu rightly sees hope of a sort in the carousel life. In his books *Distinction*, about the relationship between cultural 'taste' and power, and *The Weight of the World*, which explores the way in which working-class people carry the heaviest burdens of society without being accorded any of the respect, he sees potential in the fact that people with limited choices still make choices about the kind of life they want to live. I saw early on what carrying the weight of the world does to people, and decided I wasn't having any of it. This is another way of saying I never wanted the responsibility of living as others have to. A combination of luck, circumstances and desperation enabled me to pull off this sneaky trick.

How do we survive in the midst of all this? The difficulty of defining yourself, your family and your community as 'us', meaning you don't trust or share the same values as 'them', is that it immediately sets limits. You decide that some things are for the likes of you in the same way that you feel that someone has already made this decision for you. You retain a keen awareness of your own intelligence but are troubled by the idea that, if you were so clever, surely you would have found the way to an easier life, on 'their' side. But would you even want to? Hoggart wrote of this dilemma in *The Uses of Literacy*:

> 'They' are 'the people at the top', 'the higher-ups', the people who give you your dole, call you up, tell you to go to war, fine you, made you split the family in the thirties to avoid a reduction in the Means Test allowance, 'get yer in the end', 'aren't really to be trusted', 'talk posh', 'are all twisters really', 'never tell yer owt' (e.g. about a relative in hospital), 'clap yer in clink', 'are all in a click [clique] together', 'treat y'like muck'.[9]

Or, in the words of Susan, a woman interviewed in the early nineties by the sociologist Beverley Skeggs: 'You know they're weighing you up . . . no matter what you do they've got your number. To them you're never fit, never up to their standards.'[10] That same tension remains present in my mind in the recurring thought that I'm not living the life I should be living. A common tendency among the socially mobile is to feel always that they are living the life of Riley, but on borrowed time: that at any moment someone is going to tap them on the shoulder and tell them it's time to go back. I have this feeling all the time, and the greatest fear that accompanies it is not of losing the substantial privileges that come with being middle class, but of knowing that, if I had to go back, I'd fit in even less now than I did back then.

There was one phrase I used to hear all the time at the large, tatty, hugely undersubscribed schools I attended in Chelmsley Wood between 1980 and 1992: 'The problem is, they just don't want to learn.' Some teachers – those who were newly qualified or particularly ground down – would say it directly to us. Parents would say it to each other, because it was always someone else's child who 'didn't want to learn', and I would say it to myself. The reason I did relatively well at school, I was told and told myself, was because *I wanted to learn*, while the others *didn't want to learn*. I would get all my GCSEs because I was the sort of child who would anyway: one who didn't need to be pushed because I pushed myself. 'A pleasure to teach', they would write in reports, which sounded suspiciously like 'makes my job easier'. And the others? Well, if they *didn't want to learn*, you *couldn't make them*.

Being told I was 'the sort of child' who would do well, regardless of circumstances, led me to do well. It wasn't *expected* of me: it was *assumed*. 'Expectations' are standard for middle-class children, who, despite varying levels of motivation, tend to knuckle down and deliver good results because it is expected of them. 'Assumptions' suggest that any success achieved by a child who *isn't* middle class must have an innate rather than environmental basis. The fact that I 'succeeded', in the sense that I passed a lot of exams, gained a university degree and now work in a profession, is unusual in the social context of where I grew up and how

I was educated, but less so in the context of my immediate family. Being an only child also helped in this respect: a quirk of fate that gave me more material resources, more adult attention and therefore greater early articulacy, and my own bedroom. Not only that, but becoming ill with an allergic reaction at the age of five meant I twice spent half a term out of school, effectively being home educated by my mum and grandad. Much of my knowledge and particular perception of the world was incubated in those unusual circumstances. Without doubt, spending months at home staring out of the window or building Lego cities with my mum turned me into a rampant daydreamer and someone who struggled to make friends up until adolescence. I sometimes wonder if my body, in collusion with my mind, became ill so that I wouldn't have to go to school, an environment for which I was psychologically too 'soft', neither able to dish it out nor take it. Even at that age, I was rubbish at being working class.

We were weird, anyway; there were other factors at play. We were technically part of the lower-middle class – my dad was a utilities clerk – though it didn't feel that way. (You tend to think of lower-middle-class people having cars and living on private estates, though statistically there were many more 'people like us' living in areas like ours before government policy sought to make council estates places where only the very poor lived.) He earned less than the dads who worked on the track at Land Rover or Longbridge up the road, with no possibility of night shifts or paid overtime. But he wore a tie, that's the point. His boss had a daughter who'd gone to university, as had my mother's cousin. I knew that universities existed: I grew up believing they were places where you could learn everything there was to know and that no one would tell you to stop or would slag you off for it. They sounded like paradise on earth.

Coming from this background made me, in Bourdieu's

words, a member of 'the least disadvantaged of the most disadvantaged' stratum. In spite of this, because I completed my years of compulsory education in an exclusively working-class environment and grew up on a council estate, I find it difficult to think of myself as coming from anything other than a working-class background. This was reflected in other strong ways, for instance in our closeness to members of our extended family – my nan and grandad lived a few doors from us, and my great-aunt and great-grandmother a couple of hundred yards away – and in the fact that my parents regarded themselves firmly, and correctly, as 'decent' but definitely not posh. We belonged to 'us', not 'them': a knowledge which translated into having a real enthusiasm for those aspects of life which we regarded as being open to us, but a tenser relationship – somewhere between suspicion and yearning – with those things about which we weren't so sure. This included higher education: we were, relatively speaking, so near to it and yet so far from it.

I suppose I'm arguing that to move from the working class to the middle class has always been a lonely journey: arguing, even, for the idea that it can't be achieved without the possession of a chip of ice in your heart. Since the end of the Second World War, Britain's welfare capitalism has allowed most members of the working class to experience a large degree of upward economic mobility, but not the same degree of social mobility. It is still something that's achieved only by scattered individuals with the aid of their families, teachers, mentors and role models.

So, social mobility is a potentially lonely experience, no matter where you start from. But the further down the social and economic scale you are, the higher the risks of getting things wrong and falling into that even lonelier chasm where you start to leave one class yet can't quite make it into another. For their 1962 book *Education and the Working Class* the sociologists Brian Jackson and Dennis Marsden, uprooted grammar-school graduates like Hoggart and Williams, interviewed parents in the Yorkshire town of Huddersfield about their perceptions of the school system, which assigned the majority of their children to secondary moderns. The mother of a boy attending the town's grammar school told Jackson and Marsden that her son didn't play with the other children on their newly built estate because she felt that the standards upheld by their parents left much to be desired – so much so that she felt her own household stood alone in maintaining the visible self-respect required to 'get on'. Perhaps unsurprisingly, her son had been the only boy in his immediate neighbourhood to have passed the 11-plus, thereby playing his own part in fulfilling his family's wish to stand apart from their neighbours, while embarking on a journey towards the middle class for which his mother appears to have primed him. From his mother's fastidious respectability you can imagine a boy whose side parting is so neat that it might have been set with a slide rule and compass.[11]

Other parents with similar hopes, but without either the systemic knowledge to take advantage of the new tripartite system or the desire to differentiate themselves from their neighbours, were found by Jackson and Marsden to be mystified and hurt by their children's lack of educational progress. Their study, like Hoggart's *The Uses of Literacy*, mapped a complex landscape of intra-class mistrust that is utterly recognizable to me, exposing both a communication gulf between middle-class teachers and working-class parents and the scandal of children's educational trajectories falling short for no other reason than an ingrained lack of confidence. Their study shed light on the psychological effects of class, effects which were preventing millions of working-class children and adults from taking advantage of the ways in which society's structure seemed to be shifting in their favour in the decades after the war. Fifteen years into the tripartite experiment, they revealed how grammar schools were not so much liberating 'bright' working-class kids from substandard schooling as pre-selecting those already well placed to gain from them. Those few who made it to grammar schools from rougher backgrounds, they showed, often found the dissonance between school and home life intolerable.

In the years since leaving school I've met and become friends with countless people for whom school was an extension of a loving home environment – an environment shared by a large number, perhaps a majority, of children at those schools – and who formed large, tight-knit friendship groups that have lasted into adulthood. I wonder if we were atomized at my school because the school became an extension of our atomized families, detached from the city, consumed by troubles and worry, ingrained with insecurity. Whether we were aware of it or not, we came to school full of anxieties that we didn't know what to do about, because we had already learned from our class-infused landscape that this was what our lives were going to be like and we were just meant to get on with it. As I suggested earlier, the intention was – it must have been – to remind us that we were unlikely to become the sorts of adults who could expect to have much control over our lives. Once at school, we were silently encouraged to embody this expectation. Many of us would have subsequently been exposed to the idea that things could be different – but we didn't know that at the time.

Of course, it suited me very well to know that *I wanted to learn* and *the others didn't*, a belief which served only to make me feel more certain that I could shape my own destiny. Everything I did, whether I intended it to be or not, was in opposition to what everyone else did, and this knowledge became a reward in itself. I could say, *I'm different, me*, and that was not only all right but better than being like everyone else. If you could learn in a school like ours, which had 600 unfilled places – effectively a school abandoned by the community as much as by the local authority and by central government – then you could convince yourself that hard work and merit alone would lead you to prevail. No one would step in to disabuse you of that notion, in spite of its wrongness, because to do so would expose the injustice of the whole system.

But what happens to girls who instead refuse to be good, out of solidarity or from being on better, more open terms with their anger? Does it necessarily follow that they come to be exploited, first by parents, then by boys, by men, by bosses, and then by children? I was prepared to do whatever it took to avoid being exploited, something which I took to be inevitable without years of studying, years of wearing a yoke I designed myself. It would mean turning my nose up at rebellion and self-gratification, and willingly overlooking the symbolic violence of being treated as a special case to the detriment of others. I had this strong conviction that if I could be 'good' for that long, it would mean that one day I'd get to throw off my self-made yoke and be free on my own terms.

In her 1982 book *The Tidy House* the historian Carolyn Steedman, who worked as a primary school teacher in London in the seventies, recorded her working-class pupils' unfolding responses to the environment in which they were being raised. Listening closely to what they said and paying detailed attention to what they wrote, she began to understand that their experiences were forming their language and the use they could make of it in the world in which they lived. There was a sort of resignation, as well as rapture, in their accounts of the world, which they could have learned only from being surrounded by people used to deferring or denying what they wished for in life. They were, in effect, learning to fail – or at least learning how to be disappointed, dispossessed, depressed and permanently accustomed to not getting what they needed from the people and institutions they relied upon. Given the choices that had so far been presented to them, learning to be just like their parents made perfect sense.[12]

I equated getting an education with becoming equal to others who didn't face a similar fate. So all this learning, this endless refusal to fit in and accept an 'easy life', all this was, after all, done for instrumental reasons. It was about nothing more than wanting, needing, to get to a different place. It had nothing to do with wanting to be posher and everything to do with not wanting to suffer; though let's not overlook the fact that I snobbishly equated being posher with being more civilized. I was obedient to the very idea of obedience, so I just smiled all the time and thought it best of all things to be cheerful and stoical, doing everything I could to realize a dream and to prevent it from being deferred or closed down. Indeed, I smilingly and mercilessly refused to entertain its deferral.

My enduring image of the university as nirvana was confirmed at the age of ten when, through the efforts of our creative and inspired headmaster, our primary school took part in a borough-wide performance and singing competition held at the arts centre of Warwick University. Warwick, I know now, is a very posh university, one of the high-ranking 'plate glass' institutions, like Lancaster and York, established in the sixties to absorb the growing numbers of eighteen-year-olds passing A-levels and expecting to stay on in education. On the day of the competition we were first taken to a room on the campus – concrete and brick, set in green belt, not unlike the estate where we lived – with a window looking out on to a thoroughfare full of students on their way to class. And now I can see her walking past, directly in front of me: an undergraduate wearing an ankle-length tie-dye skirt that swished along over plain black pumps. It was 1986, I think. She was – you could see – a self-possessed, independent young adult, lost in thought while absent-mindedly draining a carton of Ribena through a straw. It

seemed barely possible that you might be able to walk alone,
undisturbed in your thoughts, drinking Ribena you bought
with your own money at a time of your choosing. I realize now
that it wasn't a done deal to have that much freedom: most of us
at her age are already half-expecting to be channelled into a
certain kind of life, one in which an act as trivial as being able to
buy a carton of pop when you fancy it feels like a victory over
dark forces. That was what university represented. I wanted to
be someone who went to university, because it meant being able
to access a kind of adulthood which – I believed, somehow even
then – it otherwise wouldn't be possible to attain. There's a parallel me somewhere, one who froze at the door of the sixth-form
college, wondering if I shouldn't have just given in and taken
the BTec; or one who didn't even get as far as the door. If I had
frozen and refused to go in, refused to talk to anyone and refused
to sign the form and refused to take a leap of faith and refused to
take myself seriously, I would never have left the first room. I
would still be living a life that had its ups and downs, its rich
enjoyments and its sources of despair. But had I not somehow
got beyond that door, much of what I know to be part of me
would still be hidden from view. *The question is, Rich, how do you
get there?*

3. Respectable in the Eighties

I have this early memory of sitting at home, around about 1984, comparing the different ways in which my parents' *Daily Mirror* and my grandparents' copy of the *Sun* reported the same events. I vaguely recall making a mental note never to take the latter when I grew up. I took against the *Sun* pretty quickly. Although I was only eight, it was clear to me that these papers represented two opposing sides, two potential forms of our experience – working-class experience – and each had a take on how we should look at events going on around us. Not that that's quite how I would have thought of it at the time, of course. The *Mirror* could be coarse enough, but at least the glamour models were relegated to a more modest page five and wore bras: these were the little things that mattered. It possessed or rather retained a sense that although there was some level on which working-class people were unshockable, because they'd seen more than anyone deserved to, it didn't mean they didn't have morals. 'It's just like a comic, really, isn't it?' my nan would say as she flicked through the *Sun* on the kitchen counter-top, but it was 'their' paper and they had chosen it.

Another memory is of drinking oxtail Cup-a-Soup and reading *Titbits*, with *Gardening Time* on the TV, at my great-grandmother's flat, a few hundred yards along a branching set of tarmacked paths from where I lived with my parents. I remember my mum (pronounced 'mom' in Brummie) getting the warm white bread from the bakers' hatch at the back of Kwik Save, and the orange breadcrumbs on the ham. Why did we buy our bread unsliced, I wonder, when you could get someone else to slice it for you? I think my mum liked real things: pre-sliced bread wasn't so much common as just ersatz. It's the warmest memories that last longest, and you realize you have no idea why you find yourself thirty years later no longer eating fresh, fluffy bread made by someone else, or machine-powdered soup, but instead making your own bread and your own soup. Something made you stop doing one thing and start doing another; or, as in the case of the unsliced bread, made you carry on doing something even when you no longer had to. Texture versus pap.

I see in the landscape that surrounds me as I write today – reddening leaves, a beck gathering force as it reaches the lake, a plain telegraph pole carrying four lines of communication – all the things I am convinced were once denied to me, and continue to be denied to others, by our circumstances. The landscape which helped to shape my early experiences had to an extent been subject to a flattening of such diversity; and when you come from a flat or flattened landscape every bump you come across seems magical. Both my mother and father had spent their early years, the immediate postwar years, living in multiple-family accommodation in the inner districts of Birmingham as their parents waited to be assigned new council housing on the outskirts of the city. My dad moved as a child with his family from Balsall Heath to a new estate in Long-bridge, to the south-west of Birmingham, while my mum and her parents moved first to a flat in Nechells, just outside the city centre, then to a second flat further east in Kitts Green. Eventually, in 1969, my maternal grandparents were given the keys to a brand-new two-bedroomed house in Chelmsley Wood, the large new estate which was being built another few miles to the east. They got their first garden in the last of a series of moves in concentric rings, growing ever wider, in search of greater comfort. I grew up 'on Chemsley [*sic*]', as it's for ever known by locals, around the corner from one set of grandparents. My great-aunt and great-grandmother also lived a short walk away, in a flat they'd moved to in 1970 from the house they'd shared in the Rhondda pit village of Maerdy. Our experience showed that you could recreate something like a traditional, organic, extended family structure in planned surroundings that were apparently geared towards nuclear families.

The estate, comprising nearly 20,000 houses and flats, was – is – self-contained. We were about fifteen minutes' walk from a shopping centre large enough to contain branches of Woolworths, Mothercare, Fine Fare, Currys, Argos and Wilkinson's. You could walk to primary school without having to cross a road; great trains of children would follow each other at half-past eight every morning to the single-storey building. Its windows were so huge that on thundery days every room would go pitch black and you felt you were sitting in the storm cloud until the fluorescent strip lights juddered on. As early as the age of four or five, when I could first read, word got round the houses near us that I loved pop music, especially The Police and Duran Duran. It may have had something to do with our neighbours knowing I was often unwell and had to stay in a lot, but much older girls would bring round their finished-with copies of *Jackie* and I'd put up the posters of Madness and Adam Ant next to my alphabet frieze. I remember reading the testimony of an agoraphobic teenager who'd found the courage to leave her house for the first time in a year after getting a nice letter back from Sting. (Now, obviously, I doubt I'd have been able to read the word 'agoraphobia', but the idea that a girl might freeze, terrified, every time she opened the front door had a curious resonance for me.)

I'd never been inside a church until I joined the Brownies, but I knew long before that what it meant to have something to worship. When Sting went on the Saturday morning TV show *Tiswas* I hung on his every word, which, as far as I remember, comprised a dour treatise on the Troubles in Northern Ireland.

Thirty-odd years later I can relive each second of going into Woolworth's with money I'd received for my fifth birthday: walking in, barely registering the pick-and-mix aisle, being lifted towards the counter by my dad, handing over £1.55 for a copy of The Police's new single 'Spirits in the Material World', the assistant going off to match the record with the sleeve and coming back with them, putting both in a white paper bag. I wasn't interested in much else apart from pop music and pop stars, not truly, from that point until my late teens. I think it's unlikely you could become so obsessed with an alternative world at such a young age unless there was something to run away from: spectres of the past, portents of the future. Things you could no more be consciously aware of at that age than physics or *realpolitik*.

The Irish hunger striker Bobby Sands's name, along with the term 'H-blocks', seemed to come up every night on the news, and a large memorial – 'BOBBY SANDS RIP' – was painted on a railway bridge about a mile from our house after his death. Many families on the estate came from first- and second-generation Irish Catholic stock, with relatives both in Ireland and inner-city Birmingham, from where our parents and grandparents had come. Another ubiquitous piece of graffiti was the National Front (NF) symbol, which you'd see sprayed in white on lampposts and the backs of young men's bomber jackets. A day wouldn't pass without hearing some bloke at the bus stop sniggering about shooting all the 'darkies'. Forty years after the war ended, not half as many people wanted anarchy in the UK as claimed to want fascism: the British National Party (BNP) and the English Defence League (EDL) are a pathetic shower in comparison with the destructive potential of the National Front in the late seventies, a time when British society had never been less economically unequal. The prospect of greater social and economic equality had no bearing on the feelings of those who believed Enoch was right.

For many of the adults I came into contact with when I was growing up, to be racist was not in the slightest bit shameful. No, to be racist was a symbol – indeed, the clearest sign – of their respectability. It tended to be people with better jobs, working at one of the car plants or in associated trades, who felt this way. You know the sort of thing. 'Only common people hang out with darkies.' 'Them Indians don't wash themselves. They hang around the streets all day doing nothing and taking all our jobs and houses.' If I ever want to feel really depressed, all I have to do is try to work out how many times in the first sixteen years of my life I heard the word 'Paki'. Never, ever at home. Outside the house – at school, at the bus stop, in the playground – ad infinitum. Sometimes it was used 'affectionately', as when a schoolmate would come back in September having been on holiday in Spain: ''Ave you seen 'er, she looks like a fookin' Paki!' As the years passed I tried hard to work out where this casual, endlessly repetitive racism came from and what it meant: whether it was pure ignorance, pure fear dressed as flippancy or pure belligerence. Not that there was anything pure about it. While the National Front emerged and, at least superficially, started to burgeon at a time when it seemed that working-class people had never had so much power, in the seventies many who regarded themselves as 'respectable' feared that Britain was on the verge of social collapse. The quadrupling of international oil prices in 1973 brought about a three-day week, power blackouts, and a deepening lurch towards unemployment and inflation that would last for the rest of the decade and into the eighties. Some chose to place their trust in those who promised order but who really wanted anarchy. (Some chose the NF, more chose Mrs Thatcher.) One thing this may have pointed to, and perhaps still does, was not a basic relationship between poverty and racism, but a more complicated one, revealing people's need to distinguish themselves, both in their own eyes and in those of others, and the lengths to which they might go to fulfil that need.

Working-class respectability was and is, at different times and for different people, both a positive strategy and a defensive one. Maintaining a belief in your superiority based on skin colour may be more to do with being terrified of what you might become were you to relinquish that belief. Would you just be scum then, like everyone else? Those who believed their position to be precarious in the seventies and eighties, whether it *was* precarious or not, held on to what they had in the fear that if they didn't hold tightly enough it would all slip away. 'Respectable' racism wasn't so much to do with the have-nots as with the have-a-bits. Those who had a bit didn't necessarily want more; they simply wanted to make sure they held on to what they did have. There was never a time when they did not feel in some way threatened: rarely in reality, but in existential terms, always.

When the first council tenancies in large numbers were offered between the wars, housing officers assessed prospective tenants for financial security, cleanliness and general attitudes towards the upkeep of their home and neighbourhood. It helped not to have too many children: not always because the houses on offer were small, but because of a lingering assumption that family planning showed restraint and therefore greater respectability. People were graded, sometimes with their full cooperation – in that they had to sign contracts stating they would not fall into arrears or hang their washing outdoors to dry – but often covertly, from housing officers' own notes made during and after interviews. The more respectable you showed yourself to be, the better quality of house you were allocated. Rougher-seeming, indigent types got flats and smaller, plainer houses. People worried about being housed next to 'the wrong sort' needn't have been concerned: in many cases, the social sorting process was taken care of by those housing them. Later on, when the council house-building programme accelerated, it was people who knew someone in the know – a housing officer, maybe, or at least a clerk in the same department – who wangled early viewings of the better houses. Later still, it would be those with nicer houses in the nicer parts of estates who would buy up their homes and add awnings, double glazing and other adorn-ments of respectability. They wanted to show to others how much they cared about keeping their corner clean, and that they had the means to carry it out.

But we're talking about other places, other times. Looking back, in Chelmsley Wood in the early eighties I could have counted on one hand the number of families who had bought their homes from the council. Thatcher's revolution – the property-owning democracy achieved through the Right to Buy – was a while off. What you had instead was a large number of rented houses that were treated by their tenants with as much respect, pride and attention as if they owned them. You also had rented houses that looked shocking in their lack of basic maintenance – implicating the council as much as the tenants who lived in them – and in terms of the things people were quite happy to do to their homes, such as write their house number over the entirety of the side wall in runny magnolia paint.

I started primary school in September 1980. Some of the songs I learned between arriving at reception class and entering the juniors included:

'Fuck, fuck, fuck, fuckability – that's the beauty of gas!'

'Stand in your dinner, your chicken or your rice (rice!)/When you've had your dinner, you can go and shag your wife (wife!)'

'If you go down to the woods today, you'll never believe your eyes/'Cos mom and dad are 'avin' a shag, and (insert name) is 'avin' a fag . . .'

Respectively, these playground chants were corruptions of a contemporary British Gas jingle, the chorus of 'Stand and Deliver' by Adam Ant, and the nursery rhyme 'The Teddy Bears' Picnic'. I learned them because it's what I overheard; it's how everybody spoke or sang, and reflected how everyone's minds seemed to work. (The kids', I mean, not the teachers'.) You might say the habitus of our reception class playground was a bit common. It wasn't a place where the forces of respectability held much sway over the urge to repeat something your big brother or dad had taught you to say the previous night because the sound of children swearing is hilarious. My idea of singing something cheeky was more of the 'Happy birthday to you, squashed tomatoes and stew' variety, though there was a boy a few years older than me who used to crease me up by saying every time we passed in the street, 'Ay Lyns, are you 'avin' a poo sandwich for yer tea?' Someone else's mum used to cackle, on being asked what was for dinner, 'Shit 'n' egg!' There was a divide already in place, dormant, waiting to burst forth. It wasn't quite as simple as whether or not you changed the words to television jingles; it was more to do with whether you were growing up to believe the lie that because you lived on a council estate you were thicker and coarser than someone who didn't.

That thing about the swearing. Why didn't I identify with it as something funny, something tension-releasing, when others did? The fact was, I just didn't think gas had fuckability. To my literal mind, it was nothing more than an excuse to say 'fuck', which, then and today, many people find hilarious. (Now I'm middle class, in the middle-class way I swear a lot when under pressure, but don't do it much for entertainment or emphasis.) When I first got to college, where people tended to speak much more primly, I started swearing copiously, just to – what? Prove a point? It probably had more to do with insecurity. I'm not sure, Richard, how it would have seemed to you. It may have been that, new to such posh company, I felt self-conscious. The consequence was that I acted to 'council-estate' type for a while, before my essential respectability eventually reasserted itself.

I can draw an outline of the landscape that shaped us with words such as Nice biscuits, pornography, underpasses, 2p bus fares: some of the earliest things I can remember. Nice biscuits we were given with a glass of milk at playschool. There's a fleeting memory of sitting in the corner trying to remain invisible while the other four-year-olds weaved around on trikes telling each other to fuck off. Pornography was another ubiquitous feature of our surroundings; the facts of life as a fact of life. Ripped-up pictures of disembodied fannies littered the pavement on the way to school and the bottom of the playing field; toilet doors were tattooed with spurting willies, phone numbers and the names of available girls. Long before you knew what sex was for you knew about Benny Hill, the video of *Lemon Popsicle* and the version of *Animal Farm* which has nothing to do with political allegory. An inherent feature of this early eighties landscape was a sort of dare-you-to-be-offended loucheness. If things seem bad now, the timbre of the culture then was easily as fixated on women as objects, as things to be chased and to be torn apart once they've been used. Dirtiness and seediness seemed to infiltrate everyday sights and exchanges: something which I tended to think of as wilful misremembering on my part until the revelations about decades of abuse wrought on children and young women by public figures including Jimmy Savile and Rolf Harris began to surface in the early 2010s.

There was porn also in the underpasses, the places we went to play, at least in daylight. We were actively encouraged to, as it was safer than playing in the street: one boy in my reception class had been run over and killed on the road nearest to our house in our first few months at school. Underpasses were refuges and escape routes, yet they also created a natural boundary beyond which we rarely ventured: it was that hard to pedal your trike up the other side, you'd usually keep to the half nearest your house. We were pretty much left alone to play outside, albeit in groups, from the age of four or five: free to take things in as we saw them, whatever it was we saw. It's the context in which you place those sights, those sensations, that counts.

The 2p bus fare? That was the fare for children, with adults paying 5p for any journey on the publicly-owned bus service in 1981. The West Midlands Passenger Transport Executive – how unwieldy and civic-minded that name sounds now – took up the idea of the Fares Fair policy from Sheffield City Council, which was then being run as the Socialist Republic of South Yorkshire by its leader, David Blunkett. The buses ran regularly, were cheap and got us around without fuss before deregulation made getting from A to B a matter of farce. It was still relatively unusual to have a car or a phone. We had a phone at home but no car, and every so often the mum of a girl I was at school with would knock on the door asking to make a quick call from ours, which seemed to run to hours.

I remember other things: being blanked by another girl's nan when we visited her in her British Legion flat after school one day; being invited into someone's home, not to have tea with them, but to sit on the settee while they had their tea. Later, when we were older, we'd be sitting on the stairs at school waiting for our classroom to be unlocked, reading the paper's gossip section, trying to see what we could out of the scratched Perspex windows. Humour, shame and yearning always were in league with each other.

Our family values were unspoken: they just *were*. The external environment, no matter how close it was to the front door, couldn't infiltrate it. At times the dichotomy was pronounced: no one in our house would ever dream of swearing, to the extent that I actually grew up thinking that swearwords were things that children had invented themselves and were only ever heard in the playground. If you'd told me before the age of, say, eleven, that they were adult words which children learned inappropriately, I'd have been stunned: I knew they were 'bad' and shouldn't be used, yet I didn't know why. To be aware of this claggy soup of profane wordplay and dirty pictures outside the home – when there was nothing like it in the home – seemed the normal way of things to me, yet the difference between the two sets of influences was vast. In turn, over time it made me a binary sort of person: prim and proper in a rough environment, coarse and chaotic in a posh one. What it also did was make me aware from a very early age that I was pretty unimpressionable: you could be your own person against the general drift of things, although it depended on there being a balance to what you took in.

Reading Paul Willis's *Learning to Labour* twenty-odd years later gave me a better insight into a phenomenon I had little chance of understanding while I was at school. I just couldn't get why the other kids played up. Why did they bother? What was there to gain from it? In another study,[1] published thirty years after Willis's, the social anthropologist Gillian Evans describes the way in which troubled children's response to authority is assumed to be pathological by their teachers, who come to believe that such insubordination is the children's own fault and therefore is barely worth attempting to change. Evans made her home neighbourhood of Bermondsey, south-east London, the subject of a study of how working-class children *become* 'thick', for want of a better word, as a direct result of going to school. Bermondsey is known for being pretty rough and for being the place that the *Big Brother* contestant Jade Goody came from. Goody, an abrasive but evidently sincere young woman, spun out her notorious appearance on the Channel 4 series into a career as a media personality with immense canniness and skill. Her initial infamy was notable for the way in which she was inaccurately vilified in both the popular and 'quality' press for being proud of her ignorance, an example of which was her belief that 'East Angular' was somewhere abroad. The over-riding tone of her 2008 autobiography is one of utter shame and anger at the education she received and at the upbringing which further hampered it, later illustrated by her insistence that her two sons should be educated at elite schools. (In a study of how working-class women are portrayed in the media, Bev Skeggs notes the responses of women in south-east London when asked about Goody's ubiquity. One describes her as 'my little ghetto rat made good, you know what I mean'.[2])

Echoing Willis's work with the school-leaver 'lads' in Wol-verhampton, Gillian Evans describes the refusal of many working-class boys, in particular, to engage with schooling as it is presented to them, as 'an oppositional stance'. They are not ignorant to start with: they choose ignorance in order to show how forcefully they reject being told what to do by someone who shows little or no understanding of their circumstances. Tunde, one child observed by Evans, is happy at home yet seeks out fights at school. He doesn't even do it to fit in: he's the insti-gator, the one who encourages the others to be disruptive, using his wit to propel them into a whirlwind of chaos which was regarded as typically mindless and therefore typically working class by a succession of mystified (and often temporary) teachers employed at his school.

'Tunde's school-based aggression is a situationally specific social skill,' remarks Evans. 'If we pathologise his behaviour we miss the opportunity to analyse, as a social phenomenon, the formation and effects of disruptive boys' peer groups at failing schools.' Many of Tunde's teachers believed his behaviour was so different from that of, say, the bespectacled whizzkid I encountered at the maths workshop, they barely considered him human. 'It is impossible for teachers to conceive of the idea that normal human children could behave like this,' Evans adds; 'disruptive boys must be other than human – more like animals.'

From the age of seven or eight, I read the paper every day before school: specifically, the *Daily Mirror*. The fact that we read tabloids in our immediate family determined the age at which I was able to appreciate what a newspaper is, to learn to read it, and then quickly to look forward to its arrival every morning. I wouldn't have been able to do that at that age had the papers around me been broadsheets. As the anthropologist Daniel Miller notes in his book *The Comfort of Things*, objects that have value to us help to form a bridge between ourselves and the people we love. The material stuff of our everyday surroundings – trinkets, clothes, printed matter – reminds us of people with whom we have things in common. Strange as it may sound, whatever newspaper or magazine we read represents just such an object. People identify with the paper they read to the extent that it can be used as a cipher, however crude, for someone's personal characteristics ('He's a *Guardian* type'; 'She's a *Mail* reader'). They may well become tomorrow's chip paper (or not, if you're in the habit of keeping old papers on days that seem significant, such as elections and deaths of notables), but what you read in them often remains imprinted on the mind as thickly as the ink on your fingers. And to a certain kind of mind, information is like a person, too: you have a primary relationship with it. You love it. Argh, the urge to get to the facts, to hold on to them all! They'll get you where you need to go. As a child, it seemed to me that, because it was likely there would be times in life when you might need to know something, the best course of action would be to try to find out everything. To the German critic Walter

Benjamin, writing in 1934, 'impatience is the state of mind of the newspaper reader':

> behind it smoulders the impatience of people who are excluded and who think they have the right to see their own interests expressed. The fact that nothing binds the reader more tightly to his paper than this all-consuming impatience, his longing for daily nourishment, has long been exploited by publishers, who are constantly inaugurating new columns to address the reader's questions, opinions, and protests. Hand in hand, therefore, with the indiscriminate assimilation of facts goes the equally indiscriminate assimilation of readers, who are instantly elevated to collaborators.[3]

Impatience, the least edifying characteristic of information junkies, is these days more readily associated with people addicted to the internet or to computer games. Benjamin accepts that the sources feel like food – 'daily nourishment' – yet notes that the relationship between feeder and fed is collusive. (The phrase 'Fact me till I fart', from the nineties BBC satirical series *The Day Today*, inevitably comes to mind here.) While growing up I colluded with the papers I relied on to give me a sense of the world outside, knowing they were offering up only one small part of it, but needing those offerings all the same. The idea that we all might die, unfathomably horribly, because of something called MAD – the Cold War nuclear doctrine of Mutually Assured Destruction – was so terrifying to me that I needed to know more about it; and yet the more I found out, the more frightened I became. The exposure was too early and – ironically for newspapers which even then I understood to be biased – too raw, too graphic, for me to comprehend without going bananas in the process.

The *Daily Mirror* and the *Sun* remained classic tabloids, classifiable as such mainly due to their 'dissident, ironic, mickey-taking quality', which Richard Hoggart identified as a hallmark of working-class communication.[4] The *Mirror*, however, reserved a stentorian boom for the most serious events of the day. Its headline for 10 December 1980 was 'DEATH OF A HERO'. It's hard to remember whether I would have been able to read that myself, aged four and a half, or whether my mother would have read it to me. What I do remember is sitting with my mum on the settee having our cereal on the morning of 9 December, my dad walking in from the kitchen, saying to her quietly, 'John Lennon's been shot dead', or something to that effect, and walking back out again. I knew who John Lennon was, and I knew that something terrible had happened, something which lunged hard at my parents' sense of rightness and optimism.

It did seem to matter, particularly to my dad, that there was a paper in the house at all times. At this point, around thirty years ago, newspaper sales had for some time been in decline from their peak in the early sixties, when three-quarters of the population read at least one newspaper and often two – a national in the mornings and a local in the evenings. In 1971, according to the Social Trends survey, 34 per cent of all adults read the *Mirror*; in 2010 only 41 per cent read a daily national newspaper at all.[5]

Our papers didn't leave the house – they were never taken on the bus or to the pub. The furthest they went was upstairs to the toilet, and at the end of their life each one became cat litter or sometimes papier mâché for a craft project. Looking back, I get a strong sense of the national newspapers we bought, in our household at least, actually talking to us and helping us to talk to each other. However jaded and populist they were – and we recognized them as being so – they provided reference points for changes and trends that were taking place in a socially volatile time. For all its respectable, ill-tempered working-class snobbery, Keith Waterhouse's weekly column in the *Mirror* always made my mum laugh because it was suffused with that mickey-taking tone and was based on situations she recognized: the Sharons and Traceys, supermarket cashiers who pretended that they were daft and that you were a pain, the fruit and veg sellers' signs that read 'potato's', and anyone whose middle name was 'Jobsworth'. Waterhouse didn't get on with the *Mirror*'s notorious proprietor, Robert Maxwell, and he took his column off to the right-wing *Daily Mail*. My mum didn't follow him there. We kept taking the *Mirror* but watched through our fingers, as you would an episode of *Dr Who*, as Maxwell's monomania took hold. It started looking more like the *Sun* every day: the girls on page five looking a bit less demure, and the content acquiring an extra film of froth.

The role of the local paper, by comparison, was to bear witness to the fact that, in the words of the geographer Doreen Massey, 'most people actually live in places like Harlesden or West Brom. Much of life for many people, even in the heart of the first world, still consists of waiting in a bus shelter with your shopping for a bus that never comes.'[6] To this day, this is a sentiment apparently often forgotten by editors of the overwhelmingly London-centric broadsheet newspapers, to which two examples from 2010 editions of the *Guardian* testify. First, on the sale of 'Lola's peanut butter cupcakes': 'We thought we were over cupcakes . . . how wrong we were. This is just too delish. And now on sale in Topshop for that perfect post-changing-room sugar slump.'[7] Needless to say, the generic Topshop branch invoked in that description was the fashion chain's flagship store in central London. Second, in a regular column about the life of a retired teacher in north London, the bohemian upper-middle-class suburb of Highgate was described as 'ordinary'.[8] This is nothing new, of course: the *Guardian* reporter Geoffrey Moorhouse, in his 1964 Penguin Special *The Other England*, illustrates much the same complaint with this quote from an unnamed periodical:

> I was eating a moussaka in Bolton the other day which (though nice) was made of potato, and it suddenly made me realise how little you can take aubergines for granted out of town.

'Town', of course, being London. 'Well, yes, indeed!' barbs Moorhouse right back. 'We do have trouble with our eating when we get beyond the North Circular.'[9]

Local papers served, and to a lesser extent still do, as a forum in which to complain and commiserate: not least about the actions of the council and other local institutions, but also about the actions of those who were deemed to be letting 'us' down by chewing up the streets with petty crime and rioting. Our estate, Chelmsley Wood, became synonymous in the eighties with the reporting of crime – domestic violence, fires in bungalows, the theft of toiletries – and the unpopularity of high-rise flats. Safe at home, much of this activity passed us by. (Crime levels, though they rose rapidly in the eighties, didn't peak until 1995. My parents weren't burgled until 1998, and then twice within a few months, in all likelihood by the same person.) My dad cherished the *Evening Mail* for its Spot the Ball contest, which I think he may have won once or twice; I read it for the Chipper children's club, which offered a £2 W.H. Smith voucher for every three letters its members managed to get published. (Once I got wise to this, I started writing in several times a week, on subjects as varied as 'my favourite pop group' and 'my favourite pop record', using the proceeds to boost my Lego collection.)

And there we were, in places like Harlesden or West Brom, waiting for the bus that never came. While we waited, we read the papers. In 'Culture is Ordinary', arguably his most famous essay, Raymond Williams outlines his belief that self-appointed 'thinkers' assign greater or lesser value to different aspects of our shared and continuous cultural landscape. He begins by taking a bus from Hereford Cathedral, where he 'had been looking at the

Mappa Mundi', just across the English–Welsh border, to the bus's terminus at the foot of the Black Mountains.[10] On the way, the driver and conductress are 'absorbed in one another' – platonically, we assume – as they have taken this journey, through astonishing disruptions in landscape, from city to country to pit village, so many times that they needn't look up and around. The historical-geographical culture of the borders absorbs and includes them to the extent that they don't need to notice it. Williams starts with the bus ride, not because 'buses are ordinary' or because he wants to show us how ordinary he is by virtue of using them, but because it appears to mark a journey in time and space between different worlds which, to him, are not all that different. It is only lack of time and the necessity of work that remove us from the Mappa Mundi, he states, not a self-willed removal from knowledge. We want to know, he says, and we will take buses – when they finally come – across borders in order to find out. Borders, in Williams's words, are there to be crossed, and their existence gives us a chance to recognize that there are different ways of doing things from the ways we have been taught.

For us, newspapers were the equivalent of crossing borders. The sheer variety and vibrancy of the popular press primed my curiosity about what went on in other places, in other people's lives. There's no way I can be sure that one came before the other – it may well have been that I was already curious, which led me to read newspapers, which in turn made me more curious. There was clearly a social origin – a class-conscious origin – to this, in the sense that I must have gleaned the idea that my parents regarded the *Daily Mirror* as more respectable than the *Sun*, and therefore a repository of more valuable, trustworthy knowledge. But one thing I am certain of is that reading both papers ignited a sense of political consciousness that has never left me. What they told me, long before I was able to put it into words, was that in the eighties the working class, as a recognizable social, economic and political grouping, was more fundamentally divided than it had ever been – and that these were not false, politically souped-up divisions but genuine differences in outlook between individuals that had built up over generations.

To comb over a year's worth of copies of the *Mirror* reveals that the twin obsessions of the paper in 1984, its light and dark meat if you like, were Princess Di and industrial relations. The tone adopted towards the former was a kind of deferential soapiness usually reserved for the genteel elderly; for the latter, it was that of men speaking bluntly to men – 'Now look here, fellas, do you want to keep your jobs or not? Then get in the room and bloody talk.' This was nothing new for the paper: in 1966 Richard Hoggart commented of its editorial tone that 'it has recognised certain attitudes which do exist in working-class life, has inflated them, and ignored others just as important but not so melodramatically usable'.[11] Indeed, the *Mirror* came in for a fairly regular kicking from Hoggart throughout the sixties, precisely because he felt it preyed ruthlessly on its readership's desire to get 'with it' – to assert their individuality in a time of economic and social progress – without having the tools to do so.

There were other highlights: one, a poetry column by Kingsley Amis, at the top of the cartoons page. Page three of the *Daily Mirror* dated 10 January 1984 jogs my memory more readily than page two, if only for the pop star-like status its main subject, the Princess of Wales, had at the time. Open the paper and the left-hand side is dense with news stories and the editorial column, 'Mirror Comment', along with an advertisement for instant window insulation. Page two's main story begins: 'Forty-three rebel pit winders who tried to defy the miners' 10-week overtime ban were suspended by their union leaders yesterday. They also face a wall of silence from three thousand angry miners who lost a day's pay yesterday when the rebels staged a 24-hour protest strike.' To the right, on page three, a pair of photos of Princess Diana on a skiing holiday with Prince Charles with the headline 'NOT SO SHY DI!'

The report reads: 'Princess Diana put on a mauve ski suit and a blue-and-white hat yesterday and stepped onto the slopes. And it was a different Snow Princess from last year – when she hid in her anorak and refused to be photographed. This year she was radiant in the crisp morning air at the start of her holiday in Liechtenstein.' It had the sort of detail that my nan, talking with my aunty Lil of a Sunday afternoon in the kitchen-diner while my dad and grandad sat in the other room watching *Grandstand*, loved unreservedly. They might have talked about the colour of the ski suit; about how different, how much nicer, Princess Di was than Princess Anne, who swore and was miserable. The pithead winders' walkout wouldn't automatically generate comment, not this far from Maerdy, though when asked both sisters would recall its reputation for intensive political activity. They could remember being told to sing 'Vote, vote, vote for Arthur Horner', in support of the Communist miners' leader and Rhondda parliamentary candidate, as they marched up Maerdy Road in 1933. 'But Labour were the party for the working class,' they would say proudly, not using the past tense with any pointedness.

I'm sure to this day that reading the *Mirror* made me aware of the roots and causes of the miners' strike, which lasted from March 1984 to March 1985. I always imagined it balancing the rightness of the miners' cause with the wrongful hubris of the mineworkers' leader, Arthur Scargill, and remained curious as to whether this was something I'd retrospectively associated with reading the *Mirror* at the time, when in reality my thoughts about the strike formed only much later, at a point when I was better placed to understand why it had happened.

I usually read the paper while I had breakfast, spreading it out over the table in front of the telly and looking at it over the Coco Pops while my dad got ready for work to a mixture of Radio 4 and local commercial radio. The week beginning on 9 January 1984 saw the *Mirror* cover the growing tension between miners, mainly those in the Midlands, who wished to preserve lucrative overtime shifts, and the NUM leadership, who had imposed an overtime ban lasting ten weeks following the appointment by Margaret Thatcher of Ian MacGregor, the Scottish-American former chair of British Steel, as head of the National Coal Board. The appointment of MacGregor, a noted opponent of strikes and strikers in his long career as an engineering executive, indicated that Thatcher had decided to do what she hadn't been able to in 1981, when her government, stumbling and unpopular, stood back from closing twenty-three mines. Having won the previous year's election with a majority of 144 seats, she saw a chance for her government to assert itself and its 'modernizing' agenda over traditional heavy industries.

By the 16th of the month, according to the *Mirror*, the 'rebel pithead winders' had 'caved in', giving 'miners' leader Arthur Scargill a boost by agreeing to back the NUM's overtime ban'. (The paper's tendency throughout the strike was to characterize the NUM's leadership, but not its members, as militant.) The following week, Neil Kinnock, who'd become leader of the Labour Party and leader of the opposition the previous October, authored a series of *Mirror* articles with the headline 'WHY I AM ANGRY', sharing page one on the first day of the series with 'The many faces of Boy George'.

'I am angry,' begins Kinnock's first piece, on 23 January. 'Angry at what is happening all over Britain today. Angry as a human being. And most of all I am filled with rage – justifiable, consuming, overwhelming rage – at what is happening to our young people.'[12]

The rest of the double-page spread promises: 'TOMOR-ROW: The Tory boot goes in', followed by 'The Family Crisis', 'The Age of Fear' and 'Ripped-off Britain' on subsequent days. The series makes clear the link between the clearly populist *Mirror* of the eighties and the more reserved campaigning style of the paper before it came into direct rivalry with the *Sun* from the late sixties onwards. Its tone of anger reflected the feelings of so many people in industrial areas – in South Wales, the north of England and the big cities – which continued largely to return Labour MPs throughout the eighties while the Conservatives won four successive elections on the strength of seats gained and held south of Birmingham. The assumption was made that *Mirror* readers not only knew what a 'pithead winder' was, but that they were working-class people who were directly experiencing fear and struggle.

I was, at this point, about to turn eight years old and living in a household which was at once interested in politics and deeply sceptical about its power to change things. The *Mirror* convinced me that change was possible: it and Frankie Goes to Hollywood, the outlandish Liverpool band whose single 'Relax' was banned in the spring of 1984 and whose second number one, 'Two Tribes', came packaged in a sleeve showing the number of nuclear weapons possessed by the Cold War nations. Within weeks of Maxwell's purchase of the paper in July of that year, perhaps fearful of its readers' strike fatigue, the *Mirror* organized a 'super children's gala' for miners' families, held in Blackpool and paid for by readers' donations and Maxwell's own (possibly embezzled) funds. A plane flew over the beach proclaiming 'Daily Mirror Welcomes Miners' Kids to Blackpool'. Three months later, the first *Mirror* bingo millionaire was announced. The winner, Maude Barrett, was immediately rechristened 'Our Maudie' and the story of her life – spent largely in poverty and domestic drudgery – was told by the paper's agony aunt, Marje Proops. I remember thinking at the time, *But surely this isn't news. This isn't about what's really happening.*

In the early months of the strike, though, before the bingo took precedence, the paper contained more extensive coverage of industrial and economic policy than would be conceivable in a mass-market newspaper today. It reflected a time when far greater numbers were unionized, working people for whom the idea of a shared workplace with shared struggles and goals, was more central to specific communities, particularly in mining areas such as those in South Wales, Scotland and the North-East. In 1984, there were a quarter of a million striking coalminers in Britain; today, there are fewer than 3,000 coalworkers in the entire industry. The *Mirror* could afford to present itself as the voice of non-militant organized labour simply because such a substantial demographic still existed – one, moreover, which was until that decisive year confident in its own voice. Even so, as the strike dragged on and as Maxwell's ownership made its mark on the paper's editorial tone, the *Mirror* took an increasingly exasperated line. Its front page on 3 November was taken up with the headline 'THIS TRAGIC FARCE – WHERE TO NOW?' It promises a 'full report' on pages two and three, with all other content relegated to a thin strip at the base of the page: 'Weekend TV 18 & 19; Benny Green 14, Pop 15, Stars 22, Win a £Million 23'.

Meanwhile, the voice of the 'affluent worker' – the automobile and light-industry workers who tended to live in the Midlands and South-East and who continued to vote Labour throughout the seventies, despite their individualistic outlook – was increasingly represented by the *Sun*. In line with its readers, the *Sun* got behind Thatcher in May 1979 and stayed there throughout the eighties. The National Coal Board, for its part, bought whole-page adverts in both newspapers in July 1984 to present its case, stating: 'HOW THE MINERS HAVE BEEN MIS-LED . . . 1. ABOUT THE STRIKE, 2. ABOUT WHAT THE STRIKE CAN ACHIEVE, 3. ABOUT THEIR FUTURE, AND 4. ABOUT THE PLAN FOR COAL.'

The British Steel Corporation, which was about to be privat-ized, joined the NCB on 30 August 1984 with an advert headlined 'A STRIKE LOOKING FOR A REASON', aimed at dockers and steelworkers who had just backed the miners, along with members of the TUC and the Transport and General Workers' Union.

At the same time, the *Mirror* was attempting the twin trick of trying to appear more like the *Sun* – in order to win back those who had defected – while reassuring its loyal readers that it would never stoop as low as its rival. The chief cultural differ-ence between the two papers, one might have argued, was that the *Sun* insisted on not taking anything too seriously – and woe betide you, Ordinary Joe, for being so uptight that you might want to read a paper that does – while the *Mirror* continued to trade on an idea of working-class seriousness and respectability. It's not necessarily the case that the *Sun*, with its tits-out policy, was calculated to appeal to a 'rougher' readership. It wooed readers away from the *Mirror* by appearing less stuffy, less wed-ded to an idea of the working class as a distinct social group, and therefore more forward-looking. It supported the Thatcher administration throughout its destructive project under a cover of light-heartedness and a cynical interpretation of its readers' desire for the good life. It was the *Sun* that invented newspaper bingo; the *Mirror* felt it had to follow.

In January 1985, the *Mirror* sent a 'campaign bus' around the country asking its readers what they thought of the paper. In Cardiff a salesman, John Wallbank, told its reporter that it 'should never, ever lower its standards' to look more like 'cheap tabloids'. A 69-year-old retired fitter called Harry Davies commented, with a typically south Welsh mix of pragmatism and Eeyorish stoicism: 'I've had the *Mirror* for years. I have only a couple of small criticisms. The £1 million prize is a mistake because it's too remote – you feel you stand no chance of winning. It would be better to have lower money prizes and more of them. Joan Collins seems to be in the paper too often. People get fed up of them.'

There would be less room for Joan Collins in the weeks that followed. On 4 March, the miners' strike ended, the NUM ordering its members back to work without the NCB having met any of its demands for miners' job security or the reversal of its programme of pit closures. The *Mirror*'s front page reported: 'The year-long pit strike finally petered out yesterday in bitterness, anger and despair . . . One Scots miner shouted at [Scargill] from only inches away: "We gave you everything . . . dead men, broken marriages, starving kids. Now you've sold us down the river."

Two days later, it featured a longer report from Maerdy, whose miners were the last to return to work: 'SOLID TO THE END: The men of Maerdy return to their doomed pit, heads held high. Their proud boast: "We never gave in".'

The *Mirror*'s reporter Paul Callan wrote:

> The 730 defiant men of Maerdy – not one returned to work during the dispute – were on their way back to their doomed mine, the last in the Rhondda. Their traditional solidarity – the village was nicknamed 'Little Moscow' in the twenties – had never faltered, and now they were returning with their dignity shining. 'We said we'd never go back, dragging ourselves like wounded animals. And we haven't.'

A year on, and the *Daily Mirror* was starting more to resemble the *Sun* : more foamy-mouthed headlines and italicized type for emphasis. A front-page headline from March 1986 stated 'BLOODY BRUTAL BRITAIN', with the subheadings 'THE CASE THAT HAS SHOCKED THE COUNTRY – VICARAGE RAPE: TWO CHARGED' and below, 'CHILDREN IN PERIL: SEE PAGES 2 AND 3'. 'The frightening truth about Britain's sick society was revealed yesterday – with the release of crime figures that will shock everyone. The statistics showed that sex attacks on children and rape cases soared last year. So what on earth is happening to us?' The Shadow Home Secretary, Gerald Kaufman, told the Commons: 'Since Mrs Thatcher came to power, total crime has gone up 41 per cent, violent crime 40 per cent, burglaries 54 per cent, and vandalism and criminal damage 76 per cent.' A series of *Sunday Mirror* features on youth disorder had the title 'BLOODY KIDS'.

The darkness at Thatcher's core is encapsulated by the infamous quote she gave in an interview with *Woman's Own* during the 1987 general election campaign: 'There is no such thing as Society. There are individual men and women, and there are families. And no government can do anything except through people, and people must look after themselves.' I'm aware now that these fragments of culture, picked out by a fervid and often frightened young imagination, barely represent the reality of what was happening to established communities at the time. (My husband, born in 1975 in the former shipbuilding town of Birkenhead, recalls from the eighties and nineties 'an atmosphere of total defeat'.) You sense this as a child when conversations between the adults around you tend to focus on money not as a means to a gentler life, but as something that must be scrabbled for. If this much has gone on cigs, that means we can't have fish for tea on Friday. If you want to drive a car, because you've learned from those in power that to use the bus is shameful, you'll have to work fifty-two weeks of the year and give yourself a duodenal ulcer in the process.

One of the most powerful passages in *The Uses of Literacy* sees Hoggart and his small siblings fighting 'like sparrows' for a small piece of their mother's only treat, 'a slice or two of boiled ham or a few shrimps', until 'she shocked us by bursting out in real rage . . . We got some, though we sensed that we had stumbled into something bigger than we understood.'[13] Although my experience of relative lack in the eighties was nothing like that of most children in the thirties, that sense of the fragility of having things – that the experience of daily life might go beyond just getting by – still stood. Fifty years after Hoggart, I bought two pens with the 20p piece I'd been allowed to *hold*, but not to *spend*, on their first day of issue in 1982. Spending the 20p on something we didn't even need caused such anguish in my mum that I've never forgotten it. The same goes for the time I slathered, rather than smeared, a piece of bread with butter 'to make it look like it does in the advert', causing her almost to cry at the evidence. I can see now that these acts would have upended her whole week's effort to budget, down to pennies, so that we could live without actually feeling poor all the time. She worked to build walls against that feeling: walls like sand that needed to be bolstered with constant shovelling.

Sometimes, for those of us growing up in the eighties, it felt as though there were two cold wars going on. In 1984, the bomb was permanently about to go off. I remember my mum and her friend Sue discussing an episode of *Threads*, the 1984 mini-series by Barry Hines imagining the aftermath of a nuclear attack on Sheffield, which had been broadcast on BBC2 the night before. They would have been cradling cups of pale tea on Sue's body-absorbing sofa, and I would have been sitting at my mother's feet, rather than playing with Sue's children as I ought to have been. They were recalling a scene in which a traffic warden staggers around shooting survivors of the bomb: 'The thing is, you would, wouldn't you? You wouldn't want to put your kids through that. You'd just shoot them.'

But that wasn't the whole story. In Liverpool you had Frankie Goes to Hollywood encouraging us to party as if it was, well, 1984, but to go out bloody fighting, just like the city they came from. 'Two Tribes' had a video which featured lookalikes of Ronald Reagan and the Soviet leader, Konstantin Chernenko, alternately wrestling and snogging in a boxing ring surrounded by baying men in suits. The producer of 'Two Tribes', Trevor Horn, recorded the song in a dozen different mixes, each on a separate 12-inch single. The cover of our copy, bought from the Woolies in Chelmsley precinct, featured a statistical break-down of the nuclear arms race: the number of nuclear-enabled warheads held by the US and USSR, the number of ICBM tests conducted by the two superpowers. There was never a darker time than this. (Though that may just be me: years later I asked my mum what she remembered of the Cuban Missile Crisis, as she was eleven at the time. She said she didn't really remember it at all.)

Hoggart might not have judged pop music so harshly had he not been writing at a point in the mid-fifties when pop music was essentially an unknown quantity and its possibilities still almost wholly unexplored. One of his accusations was that pop music, like pulp fiction, encouraged what he called a 'tail-chasing evasion of the personality'. Frankie Goes to Holly-wood didn't so much chase their tail as shake it; they didn't so much evade personality as flaunt every aspect of it. They made the personal – their gay-ness, their working-class-ness, their northern-ness – political without ever being remotely dull, and never underestimated the ability of a mass audience to cope with them as they were. Frankie simply assumed they could have number one singles like anyone else, which is what they did,

with songs that satirized the Cold War in a way that revealed its
terrible absurdity to an insomniac eight-year-old in Chelmsley
Wood.

In 1984 we had a boiling hot summer; everyone wearing
sleeveless T-shirts and jelly shoes. Most people with a Frankie
T-shirt – they were ubiquitous – had a knock-off from the
market which simply stated 'FRANKIE SAYS RELAX',
whereas the official ones, designed by Katharine Hamnett, had
messages which took up more ink: 'FRANKIE SAY WAR!
HIDE YOURSELF' and 'FRANKIE SAY ARM
THE UNEMPLOYED'.

What were you doing in '84, Rich? Were you being driven
around Wilmslow? Were your parents living the dream big-
style? Did you live in a mock-Tudor executive house? Tell me
more about it. That's the unknown country for me. Chelmsley
Wood was the unknown country for you, until you had the
misfortune to meet me and have to spend the next twenty years
listening to me going on about it. We're a right pair. You lived a
different eighties, the one that made sense to the people in
power. The idea of miners, and steelworkers, and dockers, all
fighting for their livelihoods, would have seemed a pretty distant concept to you, living in Cheshire.

I asked him one day recently whether this was true. 'The
eighties were like Shangri-la to my family,' he replied. 'They
were checking the share prices on Teletext on their new
tellies and couldn't understand why I didn't think that was
wonderful.'

Why didn't he think that was wonderful?

'Well, they all thought Scargill was a lunatic, Thatcher
was the saviour, and miners were evil because they punched
policemen . . . It just didn't make any sense because my family
was made up of really kind, generous people, and so when they

had these incredibly harsh opinions I just didn't understand it. It seemed out of character.'

That was perceptive of you, I said. Had they always been the same?

'There was this almost visible change after '79,' he replied. 'Whenever my family's gone through things from boxes from the fifties and sixties, you'd notice that anything delicate was wrapped up in the *Daily Mirror* . . . both my grandfathers had been dyed-in-the-wool Labour supporters but switched from the *Mirror* to either the *Daily Mail* or the *Express* in 1979 . . . they both desperately wanted to feel proud of Britain and being British, and both of them felt the Winter of Discontent was this huge blow to their sense of pride.'

That was a different eighties from the one I remember, though many people recall it more in the way that Richard's family did. In Britain at least, the other cold war, the class one, turned hot. This knowledge was at times viscerally present in our own household. I remember arguments about politics at Sunday dinnertime, a silent pall falling over the table. My grandad lost his job in 1981 but had already been made redundant once before, in the late seventies, before the Tories got in. My dad somehow held on to his job until 1995, when he was encouraged to retire, aged fifty. Like Richard's grandparents, both had become disillusioned with Labour for its inability to restrain the power of the unions at an already volatile time; my dad, for a while at least, believed Thatcherism had the answer. Had we lived further north, or had our family remained in South Wales, the story might have been different: neither of them spent years looking for work, finally being parked on to incapacity benefit; they never found themselves sliding around a landfill site looking for discarded copper piping to sell on; nor did they ever have to decide whether or not to become strike-breakers.[14] For whatever reason, such fates seemed closer, more likely, to me than they did to Richard.

We didn't have to live through these shattering experiences; we only had to look on and wonder what was happening to the country, never mind the world. Everybody was burned by it in some way, although in 1984 they also found at least one way to make reality a little more bearable. That year, Frankie Goes to Hollywood had three number one singles.

4.   Respectable in the Nineties

We took the war with us to secondary school. In 1987 we were treated to another general election, which the Conservatives won with another large majority. I remember that one well because on election day I was on a school camping trip in Wales, and I spent the rest of the trip crying: officially from homesickness, but quite possibly from despair. From September of that year I started taking the 97 bus to secondary school, a non-selective comprehensive opened in 1970 to serve the children of Chelmsley Wood. It had been built to take over 1,000 pupils, but by the time I started there it housed about 600, forcing the school to operate on just over half its original budget. When it was new, the campus must have looked like the sign of a spanking new social order: it had a swimming pool, a theatre-style assembly hall, a craft and technology block, thousands of new books, the works. By 1990, the year I turned fourteen, it looked old before its time. The school buildings, built to serve twice the number, felt like half-abandoned husks. (Small class sizes are not always what they seem.) The school as a whole felt fifty, not twenty, years old, with classrooms unused, walls unadorned with project work, nooks and crannies left uncleaned. In these ghostly rooms, from nine o'clock, we would have a lot of half-hour lessons during which nothing useful would be imparted or absorbed. As each classroom window was broken, by ball or by fist, it was replaced with a Perspex one, to be scratched with the witless tags of local massives and postcode posses.

We had a plain grey uniform: grey skirt or trousers, a

white – or once-white – polo shirt, a grey cardigan and black shoes. No blazers in case we couldn't afford them, and no ties. Cheap and practical, nothing we couldn't handle. (There's nothing like an inadequate uniform to remind you of your inadequacy.) Until 1987, the year I started at the school, there was a no-uniform policy in accordance with the school's founding principles, which were to encourage a sense of equality between teachers and pupils. It was believed then that uniforms represented hierarchy and conformity: not enforcing them was intended to be a step towards liberation. Pupils were not meant to feel inferior because of their social class, a fact of which they were reminded regularly. Back in 1970, I was later told by some of the school's early teachers and their former students, pupils were encouraged to think critically and to debate, in their everyday clothes, calling the teachers by their first names, learning a way of doing things they were assumed never to have encountered before. I was surprised and somewhat torn to hear this; it sounds fantastic and at the same time almost cruelly idealistic, as the liberating potential of such an approach could only have worked if every child in every school across the country had simultaneously been engaged in the same process. In 2001 I attended a reunion for the school's original intake, where the general feeling expressed by those in attendance – by then in their forties and frustrated to be struggling financially, doing jobs they didn't want their own children to do – was that they'd rather have been taught how to spell. (There was one notable exception: a man who went into factory management and attributed his enjoyment of the popular philosopher Edward de Bono's books to what he learned at school.)

It seems clearer in hindsight that the school's original determination to avoid replicating the hierarchies present in the wider education system and in society as a whole did little more than remind the children of Chelmsley Wood that they were working class and that was, you know, great, so the best thing they could do was to stay working class and be proud of it, regardless of the circumstances it might trap them in. Given that I wasn't there at the time, this may be a gross simplification. It may also show a basic conservatism on my part, one which reveals a kowtowing reverence for starched uniforms and decent grammar. Maybe. My feeling has always been that you can't do much about your oppressors without having access to the same tools that are used to oppress you. There's more than one way to look at those tools: whether to grab them or reject them; whether they make you a fuller version of who you are or a pale imitator of someone who's always known the rules from the inside. I felt then, as now, that there were some who would prefer it if rough diamonds were left unpolished, not out of respect for working-class culture but because of a desire of the privileged to have someone to pity.

Let's imagine a day in Year 9, at the turn of the new decade, in our computer studies class. At eleven in the morning, the teacher would be crying and her tallest pupil would be singing pop songs over the top of her quiet entreaties for him to stop. The girls would be comparing brands of hair mousse, bought from Superdrug on the way home the previous afternoon, and the boys would be going 'Arr no miss! OH NO! AH, MAN! Arr no miss! Look miss, he's torn me cowt! Arr God! Me pen's run ewt! I cor write enythin' dewn! Ah fookin' 'ell man!'

About six of us, out of fifteen, would be sitting in our chairs; the rest would be wandering around, picking pens up and dropping them again and feigning horror at their spatial incontinence.

'Arr miss, that means I can't do me work now!' There was this ginger kid who warmed his carton of free milk at dinnertime by nestling it in his crotch. At this point he would take pity on the newly qualified teacher, who would never have seen anything

like it in her bloody life, and ask her if she'd like to see his pet
snake. A decent chunk of every day would be like this, and
would have been like this since primary school. You would
learn to put up with it, like traffic jams. I'd at least be able to see
the trees outside and try to get through by breathing slowly.
We've got English later, I would say to myself, and that should
be better. Computer studies in fact involved a lot of writing
things down, rather than computing, for half an hour a week;
typically, we'd be about twenty-five minutes in when total
breakdown occurred.

The problem was that she was frightened of us, and this
would prevent her from giving any instructions with authority.
She may have been scared because she might have heard terrible
things about what went on in this school: that the children were
animals and you would never get through to them. She may
have wanted to better understand, even befriend, these deprived
children, who could probably teach her an awful lot about the
way the world works, or explain to her that such deprivation
would inure us to instruction by a figure from outside our limited realm of understanding. We didn't know how to get her to
teach us. All we could do was show her what would happen if
she couldn't control us. (I use the word 'we' in the collusive
sense: I would not be hanging my classmate up by his parka
hood, but neither would I ask for things to be different. I would
have chosen to believe that what was happening was inevitable
and that I could do nothing about it except silently wish that
everyone would shut up and do what they were supposed to do,
just for that half-hour, just to make it pass.)

The classrooms were locked on an average day until our form
teachers arrived at 8.45 in their cars from the suburbs. Those
of us girls who had shown up early would be sitting on the
stairs, pretending not to watch the boys playing football in
the stairwells, reading *Smash Hits* or fiddling about with

make-up from the precinct. By this time, in Year 9, we would have had months' worth of schooling wasted due to a basic incompatibility between teachers and pupils, the classroom and the lives lived outside it. Like the 'lads' of *Learning to Labour* and the Bermondsey schoolboy Tunde, we were told that we were uncontrollable and unteachable, and that we should have been grateful that we weren't growing up in the slums, as they had done. We would have been told more than once that we were insolent and moronic and destined for the dole queue: except for me, who would be told, in front of all the others, that I was different and ought to be regarded as a role model for *wanting to learn*. I can still remember the tall boy, Darren's, rendition of Kinky Afro, rolling around the classroom in a drunken approximation of the Happy Mondays' original hit: *Son, I'm thirty/ I only went with yer mother 'cos she's dirty/And I don't have a decent bone in me/What you get is just what you see, yeah*. Kids like Darren came into school when they felt like it, no more than a couple of times a week once Year 8 was out of the way. There were many others whose faces you would expect to see only once or twice a term. Maybe they had a point, and were clever enough to see the joke of school – the joke of the education they were getting – for what it was.

These boys had ancient faces, like wizened little Jamie, the protagonist of Bill Douglas's seventies trilogy of films about poverty and childhood in post-war Scotland.[1] They were raising themselves, having to do the work of adults – getting themselves up, feeding themselves, feeding the meter, sorting out their siblings – with the capacity of children. In that context school for them was meaningless. At that age I couldn't understand why they made it so hard for themselves. I felt for them, but at the same time couldn't even begin to understand them or the circumstances they lived in. They disappeared from sight because every time they became visible – every time they tried to be themselves rather than whoever the adults around them needed them to be – they were told they were nothing but trouble. (School is designed to teach you how to live as an adult in the adult world, but not how to survive being a child in it.)

For the rest of us, certain teachers made the difference between chaos and calm. They'd do this by letting you know that they knew you were human. For example, Mr B, the teacher who was later to warn me what to expect in sixth form, had a way of getting everyone to sit down and listen the moment he walked through the door of his classroom. He would stand poised, leaning back slightly on his desk with his hands clamped to the edges, as if about to tell us the most compelling story any one of us had ever heard. The stories he would tell, on an average day, would be about his own life, and would serve to remind us that he, too, had once been a working-class child. What's crucial is that he was able to do this without subverting that information for his own ends. One day he told us about how his mum, not having much time to make his packed lunch when he was at school, would peel two Dairylea triangles and slap them whole on to opposite corners of a slice of bread, leaving him to squidge them thin with the other slice when he came to eat them. It sounded like something that might happen to us, too. On another occasion, when I had turned up to class to find that my flask of squash had leaked inside my bag, he spent his break time helping me to lay out each juice-drenched page of my work folder on the radiator, mithering kindly as he went: 'Ooh, the squalor, the squalor!' There is something about the best teachers that makes their actions feel as loving as if you were a member of their own family. As a child you are at the mercy of adults. You need them to be that loving. If I don't remember things like that, it's hardly worth having a memory.

In spite of this, my chief memory of secondary school is this pervasive sense we all shared of having been condemned to a dump, yet assuming that there was no alternative but to put up with it. And yet that doesn't do justice to my experience in the whole. There was the fun we had raising money for charity, getting fired up by art and history projects, and a bizarre week at the end of one financial year when the school had to use up some unspent funds and we went on a coach trip every day of the final week of term. Sometimes, when plays were put on and Christmas concerts brought everyone together, our experiences of school couldn't have been bettered anywhere. The effect on our spirits and sense of self-worth of a really good sports day, for instance, was to make us feel we were as good as anyone else. There were also the significant – but significantly few – teachers for whom we had genuine love, whom we didn't really want to leave when it came to the end. Others were racists, snobs and martyrs, totally inadequate to the demands of the job. If they'd been doctors they'd have been struck off; luckily for them, they had this struggling, unpopular school to use as a refuge from scrutiny. I could shake my child-self for not knowing we could do something about it – that we could report them – for not realizing we could have them called to account. No one told us we could be powerful in constructive ways, only that we were destructive, and therefore powerful (the boys), or cooperative, and therefore helpful (the girls).

Looking back, I'm again struck by how atomized we were as pupils; how the prospect of forming caring friendships seemed laughable. We'd taken right inside ourselves a dog-eat-dog, siege-like survivalist mentality: not all of us, I must emphasize, but enough of us to determine the overall character of the school environment. We exploited each other – for money and grades, for lunchbox contents and goodwill – and fell out with each other, not just for a few days, but for years, over perceived slights. This exploitation was based on the simple fact that we hadn't been taught, or we had refused to learn, that it is all right for people to be different. We'd been taught about difference, just as we'd been taught about the difference between right and wrong, but we hadn't been able to take that knowledge inside us. Because the group had to be more important than the person in order to survive the institution of school, such knowledge couldn't be taken in for fear of causing a chink in the collective armour. As Paul Willis and Gillian Evans identified, solidarity was a matter of existential necessity. Girls would say to each other, 'You've ruined my life!', copying their mothers, who said this to them. Difference was not tolerated between children, as it was not tolerated between adults, because it was automatically regarded as threatening.

Given that we are talking about feelings here – the feeling of existential threat, the feeling of being sat on and limited by a larger collective body – it may sound unlikely, but I remain convinced that this was caused in part by an inability or unwillingness to think things through. One teacher I had who was extraordinarily good in this area – though he ought to have been unexceptional, and in other times and other schools may well have been so – was Brian Bowell, our classroom teacher in the second-to-last year of primary school. He took us seriously: not in the sense that he treated us like miniature adults, but in the way he acted upon his belief that we had a right to be heard, and that we were as much a part of society as any adult or any middle-class child, whose right to be heard – to form and express an opinion and have it interrogated by others – was taken for granted. Mr Bowell stretched our abilities to a degree that I'd never experienced before and never would again until sixth-form college. At the beginning of the year, he instigated two weekly institutions, the general knowledge quiz and the classroom debate. In hindsight, the reason these felt so special, so invigorating, was that both were vehicles for verbal reasoning and for testing abstract concepts, neither of which our previous teachers had paid particular attention to. One debate was on the necessity of nuclear power following the accident at Chernobyl in 1986; another was on greenhouse gases and environmental responsibility (again, this was 1986, years before learning about green issues became a standard part of the school curriculum). Faces that you had only ever seen looking stroppy or vacant were suddenly switched on: shyly at first, of course, given that we were being asked our opinions. Kids who grew up to have, shall we say, wildly variable fates talked clearly and articulately about what they felt was wrong with the world and what they wanted to do about it when they grew up. I never saw stronger evidence that you are taught how to be inarticulate, and you learn how to be ignorant, through what is withheld from you. Mr Bowell gave us a chance to talk and to reason before our ability to do so was allowed to wither from inattention.

Six years later, having survived secondary school – and there are always so many kids for whom eleven or more years of formal education seem barely to touch the sides – we were supposedly ready for the worlds of work or further study, but none which required any more brainpower than we'd arrived with. At the end of this process of dulling it was difficult to maintain the belief we had the power to shape our lives, if not the circumstances we found ourselves in. It was the kindest thing to do, really: it would have been dangerous to make children aware of their own power before being sent into the factories, vans, shops and caffs we were already headed for. The dissonance would surely have killed us. This was the way it went.

As a body of schoolchildren we were insulted by the education we received, in a half-empty school that was falling down, in a society which itself, in the late eighties and early nineties, appeared to be falling down. I remember the decrepitude of the buildings: not just the school buildings, but the closed shops, the abandoned pubs, the rows of half-destroyed garages abutting the terraced housing. I used to cheer inside whenever I saw something new being built, as I felt that it represented the coming – at last – of an end to the seemingly deliberate neglect of any environment the government did not care to identify with. We spent our formative years being insulted and we knew it. Individual teachers didn't insult us: the institution, the set-up, the joke of it, was the insult. Our experiences at school suggested to us that there are some children who want to learn and some who don't, and that if they don't, then they will suffer from their inattention some way down the line. I wanted nothing else but to learn. This pleased my teachers greatly, who channelled extra attention and energy into helping me to learn more, content in the belief that there are exceptions to every rule. There were many other pupils, particularly girls, who showed a strong but less desperate and obsessive desire to learn but who were helped to develop skills more suited to what was believed to be their obvious fate, which was to work in routine jobs for a few years before setting up home and raising a family. Some were ushered towards courses in subjects – like hair and beauty, like child development – meant for those whose entire worlds, they assumed, would be focused on the procurement of male approval and then on the bringing up of children. Whether they went on to do this is another story, but this is what they expected of themselves at fourteen, and what they were wholeheartedly invited to do. They were encouraged to put an end to other possibilities right there.

The key word here is choice, and the consequences of not having one. Whether you go, or whether you are sent. What this dichotomy brings to mind is the situation of my nan, a schoolgirl half a century before me, who was sent by her mother into domestic service at a time – just before the Second World War – when this industry in young women's labour was in steep decline from its late-nineteenth-century peak. She was packed off to a household in Carshalton, Surrey, in her mid-teens – without ever previously having left her home village of Maerdy – in order to become the family's breadwinner after her father's death, at the age of thirty-one, from illness resulting from a mining accident. Memory persists, and travels down through filial channels. My nan was never able to shake off the horror of the instrumentalism with which she was treated, although of course she understood that her mother was in desperate circumstances. After my great-grandfather's death they lived in a cellar and had little to eat much of the time. Her mother took in laundry, presumably from the wives of the mine-owners and managers, but it wasn't enough. I knew my nan to be loving but terrified of further trauma, which caused her to be closed to others in a way it took me many years to understand. The way she was dispatched – without choice, without ceremony, without question – undermined any belief she may have had that life was something you had any control over. Perhaps it's not surprising that fifty years later I should have felt so desperate for my own experiences to disprove that notion, only for that desperation to be intensified by the particular characteristics of the school I went to.

For two generations now, the state has presented ever more forcefully the idea that working-class individuals need to change in order to qualify as full citizens. In the words of the sociologist Val Gillies, the education strategy of recent governments can be summed up thus: 'For the sake of their children's future, and for the stability and security of society as a whole, working-class parents must be taught how to raise middle-class subjects.'[2] Gillian Evans's conclusion, meanwhile, is that working-class children start school and soon discover that they are not 'good enough'. While working-class parents tend to nurture their children according to an idea that their personalities are inherent, and therefore that it is neither possible nor desirable to change, school enters their lives at the age of five (or three, or two, depending on how 'deprived' you are) and demands that they change. Their personalities, the education system believes, are malleable, not fixed: they can be made to learn. Parents who don't collaborate in this instrumental, accelerated version of early development are seen as actively hindering their offspring's progress, while children themselves come to believe that they are useless in this new world of school if they refuse or are unable to change in the way that the institution demands.

As Evans notes, struggling families in poorer areas contain more than their fair share of children who are tired, confused and angry a lot of the time, which is why a school like the one I went to, unpopular and situated on a council estate with high levels of poverty, suffered far more from the effects of poor teaching than more popular schools in 'nicer' areas. Yet a lack of resources on its own cannot explain why someone like Tunde, the apparently 'out of control' child at the Bermondsey school documented by Evans, may be happy at home but still go crackers at school. To choose to endure or to reject something you have been told is your destiny requires using your strength in different ways: one pessimistic, one optimistic. You endure something in the assumption that there is no alternative, or that if there is one, it's not for you to have. You reject something – positively, optimistically – because you believe there is something better out there, even if you don't know what it is.

If you are prepared to behave – or, rather, if you refuse to misbehave, to be unaware of or to ignore the fact of class even as you are living it – then, as Evans writes, 'the inevitable result is that, at school, the working-class idea of the person is eclipsed and forced into the background of educated life'.[3] The

'working-class idea of the person' is that you are good enough –
you are lovable, you are worthy of esteem – just as you are. At
least, that's the *conscious* belief; your unconscious may well have
internalized a social hierarchy which deems you to be morally
and intellectually deficient. Put crudely, the 'middle-class idea
of the person' is that you are a project: you are nothing without
external input, matched with personal effort. The way this plays
out at school is that working-class children must, in order to
stay true to themselves, challenge those people and institutions
who insist on continuous self-improvement as a means of being
accepted into society. The state, operating under the guise of
neighbourhood schools, has sought to inform working-class
schoolchildren that they must reject the values of their parents
and community if they are ever to hope to be a part of society.

This process starts early, in accordance with notions of 'early
intervention' being imperative for children from poor families if
they are not to fail at school. Fifteen free hours of nursery care are
offered universally to three- and four-year-olds, but are extended
to two-year-olds as long as their parents qualify for certain state
benefits. While this has been heralded as a way for low-income
parents to return to paid work more easily, the consistent sub-
text offered by policy-makers – influenced by reports from
right-leaning think tanks such as the Centre for Social Justice –
is that working-class children need to be removed from the
malign influence of their working-class parents and educated
into middle-class norms as early as possible. The favoured theme
of education reports produced by the Centre for Social Justice,
established by former Conservative leader Iain Duncan Smith,
is that children are disadvantaged not by economic poverty and
inadequate local resources, but by the absence of a sense of personal responsibility in their household. An emphasis on personal
responsibility rather handily fits a template for economic growth
and social order based on a shrunken notion of state, or

collective, responsibility. The message becomes clear: 'You're going to have to become middle class if you want us to care about you.'

This is the great change that has occurred since I was at school twenty-five years ago: back then no one was expecting us to become middle class. No expectations of great change were foisted upon us. The assumption was that, given our backgrounds and the 'home' culture of the estate, we'd be doing well if we made it as far as the technical college. As I suggested earlier, this lack of expectation was double-edged, carrying with it the suggestion that some children aren't worth the bother. Without question, many things have improved in the intervening quarter-century: it's no longer borderline delusional for a working-class girl attending a non-selective school to aspire to go to university, though it may still be the case for certain boys. Girls from all social classes are now more likely to go to university than boys, a distinction which becomes more pronounced among the newest crop of first-generation university entrants. But how come a working-class boy, even now, is permitted to gain fewer good GCSEs on the grounds that 'he isn't academic', and be set up for a life of lower wages and less autonomy, when a middle-class boy, showing the same 'non-academic' inclinations, will be expected to pass them anyway and progress to university regardless? In 2013, the Labour MP Diane Abbott commented in Parliament: an 'emphasis on attaining core academic subjects is not, as is sometimes argued, contrary to the interests of working-class children'. Quite the opposite, she argued: 'Precisely if you are the first in your family to stay on past school-leaving age, precisely because you don't have parents to put in a word for you in a difficult job market, you need the assurance of rigorous qualifications.'

In the early nineties, the 'assurance of rigorous qualifications' was denied to roughly two-thirds of the population taking

GCSEs.[4] Without five passes at a 'C' grade or higher, you were more or less barred from taking A-levels – unsurprisingly, given the vast leap in difficulty between one and the other. A-levels were and remain an academic rite of passage for anyone hoping to go to university: they are a social marker in themselves. If there is any driving reason behind successive governments pushing to improve the GCSE pass rate since the mid-nineties, it is to ensure that more sixteen-year-olds progress to A-levels, without which an expansion in university numbers couldn't have happened. In its turn, a university degree is no longer so much a golden ticket but the basic passport to a decent life, without which you are denied entry. (And by the way, we think your parents are a bit scruffy.)

In such circumstances, children can be caught in a pincer movement between the needs of their parents and the needs of their teachers. It's more likely that a middle-class child will grow up in a nexus of academic support from their family, the education system and the state. They will also benefit from their parents' own ambitiousness, which arises from a sense of confidence and entitlement. A working-class child's experience of school is more likely to be fragmented and contradictory, and their potential to excel more likely to be compromised from being pulled in different directions by the needs of family, school and neighbourhood. A school can collude in girls' social and economic entrapment through the courses it offers; whereas for boys such as Tunde, the greater struggle is simply to be treated as human. By comparison, middle-class parents and their children's teachers are from the same class and therefore speak the same language to each other. Whether the symbols of social class are encoded in clothes or hand gestures or are made explicit through abstractions and vocabulary, they show to each other that they have similar sets of assumptions and the same broad understanding of the world: that it is good and just, and that you can be effective in it. They'll have the same broad set of desires for the child, and they'll understand implicitly what is required of the child in order to progress successfully and in order to reproduce the state of being middle class in the child. In the education system, as in the workplace, what's at stake for members of each class is represented by the conflict between individual advancement and solidarity with others. The irony is that the middle-class focus on doing well as individuals helps to consolidate the success of the group as a whole, while the relative working-class emphasis on solidarity can serve to increase tension and frustration between individuals.

Gillian Evans regards this process as one that takes place almost in spite of the institution of the school, with schools merely reflecting and containing the existing chasms between what is expected of working-class and middle-class people in society overall. Val Gillies, too, notes that 'the notion that middle-class children are bright, clever and possess potential is a common implicit assumption articulated by their parents, teachers and the children themselves ... [while for working-class parents] the attributes most likely to be proudly described were children's ability to stay out of trouble, get on with others, and work hard'.[5]

Given there was little likelihood of my ever getting into trouble, never mind getting on with others, all that was left was to work hard, which I did, applying myself to every aspect of life as though it were a work task. Listening to The Police at the age of five, with their talk of Belfast and 'ghosts in the machine', was an exercise in itself. You can take anything seriously if you try hard enough. Much later on, I would apply the same principles to creating a parallel universe to live in, which operated in the language of *Smash Hits* and *Top of the Pops*.

I'm remembering what Daniel Miller, the anthropologist, wrote about material things forming bridges between lonely – or potentially lonely – people and those they want to feel close to. Magazines, bright and accessible, can do that. *Smash Hits* was inclusive and collusive at the same time, encouraging its readers to regard pop music as 'utterly swingorilliant!!!', at the same time as sending up its inherent ridiculousness. The magazine developed a language of its own, making you feel warm towards it as though it were a friend, albeit one who couldn't look at a picture of Paul McCartney without rechristening him 'Fab Wacky Macca Thumbs Aloft'. One of *Smash Hits'* staff writers, Tom Hibbert, specialized in extracting revealing information from pop stars by stealth, notably via the question 'Does your mother play golf?' To him this was the best way of discovering (what he might have called) an 'umble pop servant's social origins. *Smash Hits* managed to maintain a consistent tone of irreverence without cynicism, in a way that seems at once refreshing and old-fashioned now. Its writers expected you to be in thrall to the excitement of pop music and pop stars but not to the extent that it killed off your critical faculties. It took a sort of common-sense approach to the celebration of artifice, and in that way it was respectable to its core. Flippancy and worthiness were regarded as equivalent evils. I don't know how I'd have got through my early teens without it.

What I remember most strongly about my time at secondary school is a feeling of isolation: typical teenage stuff overlaid with a reaction to what the sociologist Angela McRobbie describes as the 'hermetically sealed' nature of working-class culture in Birmingham. McRobbie cites a refusal to 'do things' – to find out more, to go beyond the very basics required – as a defining characteristic of 'the culture of working-class girls'. This became the title of a study she carried out at a youth club on another peripheral Birmingham estate in the late seventies, whose findings confirmed patterns of relating to each other and to the world that I recognize from my own early adolescence, fifteen years afterwards. The talk among girls in the club is of 'babbies', 'moms', misses, sisters and slags, while the social tone set by the group towards non-members is one of suspicion and hostility. The girls are old enough to sense that already they have come to be trapped by their gender and class, and respond to their invisible trappers by closing ranks.

'This feminine intransigence,' McRobbie observes,

> pervades every part of the girls' social lives and becomes a dominant mode of response to those outside their own culture . . . It is a sign of boredom and of dissatisfaction which is articulated in a policy of quiet non-cooperation. The girls take part in these actions by elevating out of all proportion a distinctly feminine ideology. They prefer fashion, beauty and 'female' interests to the team spirit of the club.[6]

But did my refusal to do what working-class girls were supposed to do create the conditions for me to become middle class? I would say yes, obviously, because it meant that I had no sense of group loyalty. The hard truth is that I lacked loyalty to the group because I felt they were completely wasting their time doing what they did, and I 'didn't mek it easy for meself' by trying to fit in. Although they would complain every day of how boring it was, doing what they did, they'd go and do the same thing again the next night and the next. It was just what you did; and indeed, it was another way of learning and being, most importantly a way of learning just how to be with other people without making a conscious activity out of doing so.

I didn't want to sit on the fence with the girls watching the boys do things; I wanted to do things myself. The gods who bestow privilege on those not born into it tend to favour those who have a knack for literacy. Usefully for me, as it turned out, doing things on my own most often meant doing something involving words. The many hours I would have spent 'each night out-of-doors, hanging about on the youth-club walls, listening to music' – with other kids, not alone – 'or watching the boys play football', as the subjects of McRobbie's study did, were instead absorbed by sitting downstairs with my parents, one eye on the telly, the other on my homework, or writing upstairs in my bedroom. There, alone, warm, I'd try to understand the racket that was being made on the John Peel show, or creak out essays, treatises and letters one thesaurus-researched word at a time. No siblings to barge in, no voices to intrude beyond those I selected. What social life I had was conducted entirely through pen and paper. At school I couldn't think of anything to say, whereas in this parallel universe I couldn't stop talking. From the late eighties onwards I'd been an obsessive fan of the Pet Shop Boys, who managed the feat of being regular *Smash Hits* cover stars (possibly aided by the fact that their singer Neil Tennant had once been its assistant editor) and a significant chart act without disguising the fact that they were middle-class men in their thirties who liked reading. Because of their popular appeal – they had three number one singles between the summer of 1987 and spring 1988, which Tennant describes inimitably as their 'imperial phase' – their biggest fans were teenage girls. They just tended not to be 'normal' teenage girls. They were the kind who wanted to marry a balding gay man rather than Jason Donovan, a chart rival who – back then – had all his hair and went out with Kylie Minogue. What united fans of the Pet Shop Boys was a sort of bookishness married to a sort of classlessness: we weren't of the right milieu to have followed Morrissey, for instance, whose absence from Radio 1's daytime programming was almost total. The Pet Shop Boys were, at least for a time, truly popular rather than being a cult act that had hits.

And yet. There was a class dimension to being a Pet Shop Boys fan, made more obvious in a way by the even greater popularity of Erasure, another not-conventionally-attractive keyboard duo. Erasure were, to put it coarsely, the working-class version of the Pet Shop Boys: they were brasher, more direct, and in Andy Bell had a far more entertaining singer, who essentially wore fetish versions of Elton John's cast-offs. Erasure were massive at school, whereas no one except me liked the Pet Shop Boys. (Perhaps you can see a pattern emerging here.) They encouraged singalongs at their gigs, while the Pet Shop Boys had the same set designers as the English National Opera. Erasure were vastly popular with middle-aged working-class women; by comparison, preferring the Pet Shop Boys was something of the swot's option. It was an incredibly respectable thing to do. It meant you *cared* – about what you looked like when you went to see them, what you sounded like when you sang along to them, your capacity for embarrassment, your ability to let go. There was, and remains, something a bit repressed about liking the Pet Shop Boys.

This didn't matter if you were a fan. We wrote to each other across whichever agonizing divide we were trying to breach, all from points of isolation. These days a social life unfettered by locality has been made possible by mobile phones and the internet. Back then, when there was one phone in the living room, and the possibility of instant communication with like-minded people was restricted to those with ham radio facilities, the exchange of letters – along with newspaper snippets, duplicate stickers, promises of meetings and other affirmations of *there being a point to it all* – was all there was. It became too important. If nothing came through the letterbox I flumped around teenagely for the rest of the day. Given how hard I'd always found it to make friends, a lack of dispatches from the outside world meant that my relationship to it always felt contingent and conditional, and that if I wasn't careful I could be swallowed up entirely by home. I had half a dozen pen-pals and a combative relationship with the Pet Shop Boys' fan club, whose organizers had difficulty grasping (or were inured to) the fact that the promise of an up-to-date newsletter was all that was keeping me from the adolescent psychiatric unit. I would write to them threatening to write directly to Neil Tennant's house (unfortunately for him, the inner circle of Pet Shop Boys fans, who formed part of my nutty pen-pal network, had his address) asking *him* why it hadn't shown up. Then, as you might expect, a few weeks later I'd receive a reply along the lines of: 'Please don't do that, it'll only wind him up.'

How pop stars cope with having fans is beyond me.

In the new year of 1989, a girl at school found my notebook sticking out of my bag, covered in quotes from a Pet Shop Boys annual I'd been given for Christmas. At my school, annuals usually had posters of Bros in them and word-searches made up of Top 40 song titles. Obviously, being a Pet Shop Boys annual, this one was different, containing, off the top of my head, a guide to Neil Tennant's collection of designer suits and a survey of Chris Lowe's contribution to the field of architecture (the keyboardist/trombonist qualified as an architect at Liverpool University shortly before becoming a pop star), which comprised part of a staircase in a Milton Keynes office block. Never was the rage to get to the facts sated so comprehensively by one modest publication.

A biggish crowd gathered, as if a scrap was about to kick off. I mean, if you find a diary, it's obviously going to have perving in it, which is worth ten minutes of anyone's dinner break. The girl started reading bits of it, haltingly, as if from a poorly translated instruction manual.

Oh, Seekers of the Truth! So you're all hip to British Marvel now . . .

[This suit's by] Comme des Garçons . . . most of these suits would cost about £500 . . .

Who gives a tinker's cuss for their reputation, I'm giving this one pop single of the week . . . [7]

'Tinker's cuss'. 'Seekers of the truth'. 'Comme des Garçons'. Whatever these phrases represented, the gathered crowd didn't find what they expected in them. There weren't any rude words (this is when I was still refusing to swear, on the grounds of refusing to do what everyone else did), so that was dull. Also, there were plenty of proper nouns that had no cachet in our environment (ones that would have done included Durex, Diadora, and Mills and Boon). They drifted away, probably bored to tears. There was nothing in there that could induce embarrassment, not on my part, anyway. I was proud that they didn't get it: 'it', presumably, being a secret language of taste and class that even I had only half a clue about. Writing random quotes on the sleeve of my notebook – a school-issue one intended for copying down verbs and pasting in our lesson timetable – was a cack-handed declaration of where I had wanted to be, to get to. Heaven was a place where people said things like 'tinker's cuss' and 'Comme des Garçons'. Sophistication is what I think I was after, even if it came across more like pretension in designer clothing.

The fact that the Pet Shop Boys had number one singles, million-selling albums and mass market annuals produced in their name now seems extraordinary: indicative of a time when it was possible to be sophisticated without apologizing for it. Yet their sophistication often went unnoticed because of the idiom in which they worked. In 1999, the Pet Shop Boys successfully sued the philosopher Roger Scruton for his claim, in a book titled *An Intelligent Person's Guide to Culture*, that they were representatives of a manufactured mass culture who didn't even write their own songs or play their own instruments. Suffice to say, he picked the wrong opponents. It was largely from their music that I learned, or started to learn, something like the 'unrestricted code' referred to by Basil Bernstein in his work on the effect of class on speech patterns:[8] not directly, but from something in between, a place mediating between the posh and the non-posh, the inaccessible and the (at least technically) accessible. Such places then included Radio 1. I remember one evening in 1991 listening to Annie Nightingale's request show, which was on at 7 p.m. on a Sunday directly after the Top 40 chart rundown. This is when I'd be doing my homework (twice over, in a way: one lot for school, the rest for the life I was planning). Nightingale reported that the Scottish artist and songwriter Momus had given her a self-printed business card bearing the legend 'World Famous Pop Singer'. Given he'd never had a Top 40 hit, she remarked, his claim 'had a lot of panache', before going on to play his song 'Nicky' – a rewritten cover version of the Jacques Brel song 'Jacky'. I can recall the priceless wryness in her tone as though I'd just heard her say it this morning. Of course, Momus wasn't at the time a world famous pop singer, and never did become one in the conventional sense, but it gave you hope that he might one day, and by extension hope that you could do the same if that was what you wanted. 'Famous writer' was what I wanted on my card. The privilege-bestowing gods like those who can use words, and they liked what I wanted to do. It suited them. It made their job easier.

I'm sitting writing this in Swiss Cottage public library in London, a kind of socialist paradise (it's linked by a little covered footbridge to the municipal swimming pool), surrounded by people silently engrossed in books, absorbed in the work of reading and comprehending the world and their place in it. I've always appreciated how light and free this space feels. There are no impediments to my using its resources. Though this library is in London, it reminds me a lot of the one around which I spent uncountable hours wandering, thinking and dreaming as a child. Both of them were built in the sixties, which you could tell not so much from the architecture – a sort of friendly Brutalism of blasted concrete and lovely polished wood – as from the anything-is-possible lightness of how it felt to be inside them. The library of my childhood has been demolished along with much of the nearby housing, but in my mind it lives and breathes like a ghost-home, partly as a testament to my mum and grandad's love of reading, which led them there every week, as habitual a part of their shopping trips as buying bread and putting bets on.

I picked up my first copy of the *NME* at Chelmsley Wood library in January 1989, not long before I turned thirteen. At the time the magazine was emerging from a period during which it believed itself to be a sort of music-themed version of the *New Left Review*, its writers finding any excuse to shoehorn a bit of continental theory into the weekly singles review. Luckily for me, the *NME* had started to accept that music which actually got in the charts had something going for it, and that people didn't necessarily want to know how the cow was killed before they ate the hamburger. By contrast, *Smash Hits*, which I'd been reading since I was eight, managed to celebrate the hamburger in all its toothsome glory without ever condescending to its reader-ship. Without there being both to consult – without the library to find them, without the record library to borrow records I'd never dare buy in case they proved to be unlistenable – there's no way I'd have been able even to edge towards an understanding of the possibilities of a culture beyond the purely popular.

Anyway, on the cover, this week in 1989, were New Order, a

band I'd only heard of because of the mutual appreciation society they'd formed with the Pet Shop Boys. It was because of the Pet Shop Boys connection that they had the odd mention in *Smash Hits*, which made them seem, I don't know, *plausible* for someone like me to listen to. Each of the band's four members was represented in a solo portrait, their features made psychedelically fuzzy and rendered in bright blocks of colour. The interview inside discussed how they had made their latest album, *Technique*, a record of deceptively samey songs influenced by their love of raving – as in dancing, not going mad – in Ibiza. I would be a teenager in three months, and not a word of it made sense to me; or rather, not a sentence of it. Both the writer and the subjects expressed themselves in ways so adult, so tangential and knowing, that I felt I had accidentally discovered something subversive. The magazine would need to be put away in case someone saw me trying to understand something it was not my business to know. (At this moment a scene in *Ethel and Ernest*, Raymond Briggs's graphic biography of his parents, comes to mind, in which his timid mother confirms to her husband and herself that 'it's not our place to know' what the word 'matriculation' means on their son's school certificate.)

It wasn't so much the *NME* 's in-jokes and verbal eyebrow-raising as their use of irony and abstraction which flummoxed me. I was used to reading material aimed at adults – I read my mum's *Woman's Own*, as well as the papers, as avidly as my own magazines – but I was unused to anything which encouraged you to read between the lines. While I was growing up it wasn't that nobody else I knew read, or wrote; it was more that what was being read and written served to differentiate boys from girls. Boys and girls I knew had already started to read a lot of what their parents read: boys, the *Sun* and books about the Second World War. Girls, Mills and Boon paperbacks and the *Sun*, only they would turn straight to Dear

Deirdre instead of the sport. Getting hold of the *NME* for the first time, even though it would be a long time before I actually understood its contents, meant more than just having something new to read. It was one of the best investments in my future cultural capital I could have made: another of those threads I'd grabbed unwittingly, making a connection between the world I lived in and another world of which I was barely aware: the thinnest thread linking the two for now, which needed reinforcing.

Everything changed in 1992. There was a degree to which I knew it would, because I would be leaving school; or more specifically, the environment of that particular school. One minute I was struggling for air, the next I felt as though I'd entered a large bubble of pure oxygen. I guess if you *want to learn*, and you go from a place where it seems that no one else does, to a place where everyone wants to, your daily life is going to improve somewhat. In some ways it was as simple as that. There must have been preparations – intimations – for the next part of my life, which I can't remember apart from the two pivotal facts of meeting Richard at the sixth-form college open day and, at the same event, being whisked away from a future defined by clumsy, working-class A-level choices towards one primed for passage into the middle class. English, politics and history gave me an elite-style liberal arts education by accident, the value of which, it turned out, was hard to put a price on.

There are certain details I remember: fragments of the nascent culture shock I was about to experience. (Too much oxygen in one go.) The first was that I didn't know there was a dedicated college bus that collected students at all points on the way from Sutton Coldfield, north-east of Birmingham, to the colleges at Solihull in the south, which passed through Chelmsley Wood at ten past eight every morning, taking kids to the technical

college. Instead I trudged my way through two winters of getting a bus at 7.30, arriving at the sixth form three-quarters of an
hour early, which meant I frequently fell asleep during lessons.
(This is an example not so much of lack of information as a
consequence of social isolation. I'd retained only a threadbare
relationship with my former schoolmates, many of whom would
have got this bus to the tech. Equally, because everyone I got to
know at the sixth-form college either drove in, got lifts from
parents or lived on the, well, Solihull-y side of Solihull, they
weren't in a position to tell me, either.)

Another thing that struck me straightaway at college was the
material people read during breaks. It was new issues of *Q* and
Empire, which even then cost two quid a copy, in fresh W.H.
Smith bags. *I bet they're on a tenner a week pocket money* is what I
thought: were they rubbing it in or what? I used to buy my copies of *Q* three months out of date for 20p from the kiosk in our
local Food Giant, which never sold one at full price. A graduate
of *Smash Hits* and *Number One* magazines, I figured that if
albums stayed in the charts longer than singles did, the information in *Q* – then, as now, full of interviews with major rock stars
rather than flighty pop stars – would never be too out of date.
Those who read these magazines discussed them in a level of
detail and with a degree of disinterested analysis that I found
almost disturbing. These were people raised on information.
They had been trained in – or had absorbed through osmosis –
the ability to look at things as if standing outside them. (In one
essay, Richard Hoggart recalls how the ability to argue a case
dispassionately, as opposed to just having it out with someone,
came to him only with difficulty once he was at university.)

The point is that at sixth form, I had initially no handle on
the skill of picking things apart. Used to being a freak, and not
used to the kind of volleying, reflexive, comparative conversation which characterizes middle-class interaction, I had an

incontinent desire for knowledge but couldn't work out how to put it to use. It was hard to express an opinion in the way I was accustomed to without sounding either ignorant or offensive, so for the first few months I tended not to bother, and preferred to listen, most often with a sense of pure exhilaration, to the sound of voices that weren't rejecting everything sight unseen. I asked Richard recently what his first impressions of the college were. 'It was astonishingly middle class,' was his recollection, though he immediately went back on himself and noted that most of his history set seemed to be the children of self-made men from Birmingham who'd done well and moved to the suburbs. Many of his classmates reminded him of 'that Harry Enfield bloke who goes, "I am considerably richer than yow". They were all very pleased with themselves because their house had a gravel drive with a third-hand BMW parked on it. They and their children seemed to think they were kings of the world.'

Get you, Rich! I don't remember so many people like this. Rather, it's the 'astonishingly middle class' aspect that has stayed with me. Richard recalled getting to know a lot of 'coppers' sons', whom he suspected had been drafted in for plenty of overtime during the miners' strike, whereas I met a lot of people whose parents worked in the more cuddly parts of the public sector. I met for the first time lots of people who were very friendly, sensible and earnest, people with an outlook I had never directly encountered before. They weren't merely concerned with taking the world and their place in it seriously, but with ensuring that everybody knew they did. Whether aware of it or not, they had been brought up to be 'nice': that is, to project an image to others of being pleasant and above all reasonable. In many cases, they were indeed the nicest and most reasonable individuals I had ever met. I mean, I'm not reading the news here; that's what being-middle-class-in-the-world is about. Darkness is managed or hidden.

The people I met were also very keen on 'issues' and 'cam-paigning', whether for wildlife conservation, for a boycott of Nestlé products on the grounds that they aggressively marketed formula milk in Africa, or – very commonly – for the legaliza-tion of cannabis. I was up for the first two but found the third dreary in the extreme. Because I knew very little about the habit-tropes of middle-class teenagers at this point, the constant going-on about cannabis did my head in. It smacked of phoney risk-taking, of getting 'out of it' because there was no pressing need to be 'in it'. (I never did loosen up in that respect, and didn't even drink until university. Within my respectable background, on the Welsh, lapsed Methodist side, there were hints of temper-ance; plus, the few months I spent as a Girl Guide in junior school were largely taken up with drugs education, which involved creating a folder of detailed descriptions of substance misuse and drawings of drug paraphernalia taken from a text-book. I haven't forgotten colouring in the nuggets of resin, and the syringe and the spoon.)

The broader point about that year, that September, was that I appeared to take to sixth-form college and its deceptively wel-coming milieu like a duck to water. That's the exact simile I used to one of my old schoolteachers when I went back to see them a few months later, the triumphant sixth-former in my new indie clothes. It felt easy because I was sure I'd got to my promised land, and it seemed that all it had taken to get there was to work hard and be prepared to cross the unofficial, yet highly visible border between estate and suburb. But within a month or two it was clear the experience was generating two conflicting sets of feelings. The first, absolute relief at being accepted by peers for the first time. The second, initially buried under the elation produced by the first, was absolute confusion. Did this mean I was now middle class? Did it mean I'd been middle class all along, and that had been the real reason I'd always felt like such a misfit? Christ alone knew. I couldn't get my head around it, even though at the same time I felt more comfortable in that environment than I'd ever done elsewhere. I'd only ever been able to be myself at home; now I could be myself anywhere. Well, almost anywhere. I still wasn't sure how wearing Doc Martens in Chelmsley Wood precinct was going to go. Not that I went there as much as I used to: mysteriously, the things I now wanted to buy – clumpy boots, broadsheet newspapers, Suede records – could be bought only in Solihull or in Birmingham, the great metropolis. (That's the irony, isn't it: it took the beginnings of a college education for me to become better acquainted with the city that generated – that *necessitated* – the estate I grew up on. Almost as if it required becoming urbane in order to feel properly urban.)

Another great point of confusion was realizing that the middle-class way of being was itself as self-similar and homogenizing as anything I'd known previously. It's obvious that each class has its tropes and its boundaries, its insiders and outcasts; that's what makes the social and emotional aspects of class more caste-like than if the the classes were purely representative of economic differences. It's a testament to their impermeability that I had no idea other classes – other milieus – operated in the same way as the one I had grown up in. There was an obvious degree of interchangeability: shellsuits from the indoor market became army surplus shirts from the flea market; trainers became Docs; the pop charts became the indie charts. With twenty-odd years' hindsight, it makes sense, of course, that a class positioned between two other classes might be the greater home for conformity after all. So the questions returned. Is this it? Do you have to pick a side and stick to it, even when there are bits of both that don't feel right to you? When something as total as your whole domestic and local environment has been shaped in one way, to encounter a world in which that environment might

have – would have – been shaped another way is wholly disori-
entating. That is when, and how, the breakdown came.

By the spring of 1993, after holding these two parts of myself
together for the first two terms, I found I couldn't do it any
more. In the first few months I'd been too caught up in novelty
and light-headedness to notice any disquiet; after Christmas,
when it became clear that I was struggling with the A-levels
themselves, never mind the place where I was studying them,
things got trickier. Travelling to college in the dark, I listened to
my Walkman on the bus louder every day as if trying to glean
the secrets of the universe, while reading the *NME* as if it were
the horoscope. One lunchtime, after a short college day, I went
into Birmingham to borrow records from the library. What I
remember is ordering soup in a café with my mum, having been
at sixth form that morning, and the next thing, curling into a
ball, crying. Later, being helped on to the bus back to Chelmsley
Wood, and all the old ladies tutting 'ah, shame'.

It wasn't as bad as it could have been: I didn't drop out or fail
any exams, even though, ever the dictionary swallower, I'd told
my history teacher that I'd found the course 'rather impenetrable'. Ooh no, much too controlled for that. But I did fall apart
inside, quite comprehensively, and expressed it through wither-
ing away, refusing to eat; bearing, in Hilary Mantel's words,
'smiling, skeletal witness' to the gap that had appeared between
the old life and the new one. Throughout this I tried doggedly
to penetrate the impenetrable: to do something effectively
impossible, which was to show myself and the world that if you
took enough exams, and passed them, you could glide seam-
lessly onwards and upwards.

The obvious thing would have been to leave college, it being
safer to go back to what you know, even if you can't hack that
either. I just couldn't. I'd had too much insight at that point into
how things could be. I kept going in, day after day, even when

feeling faint with derangement, in all probability because I couldn't countenance the thought of it not working out. Having spent the whole of my life up to this point being someone who *got on with it*, working and working towards a narrow, specific idea of liberation (liberation through education, essentially), I had no idea what else I could do. This didn't seem to matter quite so much to the people I was at college with, so I tended not to tell them about the state of my brain. It needed confidence — the ability to confide — to do that.

I have an image of that time of having set out blithely on an iceberg from the Arctic towards warmer water. Like a prat, I hadn't realized that what had been beneath me would melt, in all probability before reaching the tropical island where I assumed life would be easier. All that for bloody A-levels. They don't tell you that in the prospectus. That is one compelling reason why people drop out of education — they may do so at any stage, but particularly at the point where they have the opportunity to tell themselves *this far, and no further.* It is not that they are weak-willed or easily diverted: the education researchers Helen Kenwright and Jocey Quinn have shown that, in further education and at universities, working-class students drop out only after a period spent weighing up their options amid a combination of pressures, including financial, emotional, academic and social. The balance can be tipped in favour of leaving if there is too much dissonance between their old, or current, life and the one that appears to be within (or just out of) reach.

Over a period of about six months I somehow emerged out of the tunnel, I think simply by realizing that telling people what was happening was preferable to *not* telling them and having to drop out as a result. Richard responded by poking me in the ribs and singing the chorus to 'Nineteenth Nervous Breakdown' while eating a bag of crisps, which luckily for him I found quite funny. I realized that to make friends properly you have to tell them significant things about yourself, something I feel grateful to have realized at seventeen and no later. But what did the experience of sixth-form college itself teach me? Mainly, that middle-class ideals of self-denial, deferred gratification and restraint work only in a context of existential comfort and security. If you know your place in the world is reasonably secure and can be relied upon as a source of internal comfort, external or material comforts take on less importance. One of my favourite scenes of class-bound horror at the practices of other social groups comes in Zadie Smith's novel *White Teeth*, in which the upper-working- going on lower-middle-class pro-tagonist, Irie Jones, starts to visit an upper-middle-class household on a regular basis.[9] She can't get over the amount of cheese they have in their house. Whole cheeses plunked on bread boards for grazing on at leisure, and not a Dairylea triangle to be seen! People breaking off great chunks of it and waving it around, airily, while actually *talking to each other*! Of all the signs of this family's abundance and sense of entitlement that might have shocked her, it was the (probably smelly) cheese that knocked Irie sideways. It wasn't even that she'd never seen a whole cheese before; she'd just never seen an entire one sitting on someone's sideboard, rather than in a supermarket chiller waiting to be sliced off by the quarter. I can almost imagine my grandad tutting, 'Money meks money, dun't it?'

Money may to an extent dictate the choices you make, but having more can't explain the fact that you might, for example, spend it on a different kind of cheese rather than on larger quan-tities of the cheese you're used to. Economic and social mobility don't always go together, but the confidence brought about by knowing that you're comfortably off can only help to give a sense that all the riches of the cultural world are yours for the taking. Like Irie does, eventually I learned that most people do have to pick a side, even if they do it unconsciously. I didn't decide pragmatically to become middle class in order to access social esteem and higher wages. It happened that way because I happened to stay on at school. There is a sense in which you buy, or are sold, a one-way ticket. You can go back, but never again on the same terms.

PART TWO

Here

5. Snakes and Ladders

It is 2013, twenty years after the 'Nineteenth Nervous Breakdown' episode, and I'm sitting with Richard in a café opposite
Euston station in London a few hours before I give a talk at the
Royal Academy of Arts. It's fair to say our lives have changed a
bit since then. We are now both professional journalists, and for
fifteen years were relative neighbours in London. Until I moved
in 2012, we would meet up every month or so, in pubs or at my
flat in the East End, and continue the conversational see-saw
between politics and pop music that we began in 1992. Every
time we sit down and talk, the layers of time are peeled back and
I remember the way he always listened before speaking himself.
He always wanted to know what I thought. I think that if he
hadn't, I wouldn't be sitting in a London café waiting to give a
talk at the Royal Academy of Arts.

I get myself a cake and a latte – still quite tickled deep down
by the fact I can do this – and we give the current state of the
Labour Party a going-over, something we've been doing since
we first met. Imagine the water under the bridge since then. I
remember Richard nearly fainting with shock on hearing that
John Smith, their leader, had died in May 1994, and a couple of
months later, me ringing him from the settee at home in Chelmsley Wood.

'I'm dewin' it!' I yelled at him down the phone. 'I'm joining
the Labour Party!'

The cause of my excitement was Tony Blair. I'd just watched
him on the news making his first speech as leader, only fragments of which I still remember, but which I recall distilling

into this single sentiment: *he won't let us down*. Everything Richard had been telling me for the previous couple of years suddenly
made sense: there would soon be an end to endless Tories. In their
place would be socialism, and even better, a kind of socialism
that didn't involve being a schoolteacher and knitting your own
yogurt. There was something extraordinarily appealing about
that last bit. Indeed, looking back, it appears that the thing I
liked most about Blair, and the prospect of being a Labour Party
member with him as leader, was that he seemed smart, tidy and
modern. Respectable. The day I joined the Labour Party was
the day I joined the middle class.

After the Labour Party dissection we veer towards talking
about the copies of *Smash Hits* and Q we used to read. 'When I
was at private school,' remembers Richard, 'whenever I men-
tioned I liked pop music you could see fear in the adults' eyes,
almost as though they felt the vulgarians were at the gate.' Football was the same, he says, dodging the forkful of parsnip
cupcake I'm shoving excitedly under his nose. 'On our first day
we received a very big talking-to from an army major type,
complete with moustache and everything. He held a rugby ball
and said, "This to you is a football from now on. That round
thing you see around sometimes is played by common boys."'

In his experience, stratification led to casual assumptions. Or
was it the other way around? Richard received direct inculca-
tion in the supposed ways of the posh, a hoped-for inoculation
against being common, through his PE master's assumptions:
first, that only common boys liked football, and second, that
liking football would make you common. This is exactly what
Richard's parents – his father, in particular – intended. They
were desperate for him to make good properly, to enter the middle class fully armoured, which was why, Richard explained,
'they couldn't understand why I didn't think it was wonderful – "he goes to a posh school, he's passed all these entrance

exams, why doesn't he appreciate it more?" Failing the 11-plus scarred both my parents. The first thing my dad said when he got his big barn in the Midlands was "not bad for a boy who failed the 11-plus".'

There are countless other lives not lived. The one I am living now, I'm glad to say, makes me very happy, and I'm not particularly surprised at that because it's very comfortable. It's autonomous, reasonably stress-free. I'm living fully in the realm of an anointed class. There is always a sense of relief, a strong persistent voice that says, by turns, *Phew. We made it,* and *Phew, that could have gone horribly wrong.* Sitting here with Richard, the relief is palpable.

After sixth form and all the mental palaver it entailed, applying to university felt like the last hurdle. Naturally, it turned out to be the most confounding. I had a few choices on my UCAS form. You were allowed to have five, with which I covered the bases: home and away, university and ex-poly. Safe choices and wild ones. The only redbrick was Birmingham, which I put on there, along with Warwick, in case I bottled it and didn't leave home. I also put down Cambridge, and in doing so ignored Richard's earlier advice about the fact that the newer colleges took more applicants from state schools. Instead, I asked, and listened to, the staff member at college who I'd been told 'took care of' would-be applicants to Oxford and Cambridge.

'If you want to do English, why don't you apply for Christ's?' she suggested. I did as I was told. Christ's, as it turns out, took in among the lowest number of state-schooled undergraduates of all the Cambridge colleges. You might say this was reflected in my experience of being interviewed for a place there. I remember taking my Record of Achievement: a burgundy folder, issued by the Department of Education, in which all school-leavers were meant to insert their exam certificates and document extra-curricular activities for the benefit of employers and university admissions tutors. I was proud of mine; it was neat and well presented. It was respectable. It contained the evidence of my eight GCSEs, which included home economics and biology, my RSA Grade I certificate in word processing, and a personal statement detailing activities such as making cakes for Children in Need and collecting erasers. A letter must have been forwarded from the sixth form with details of my predicted A-level results, but apart from that I was flying solo in blissful ignorance.

I was informed that there'd be two interviews on the day, in the rooms of two different English tutors. The first you could prepare for, so I decided to talk about the essays of George Orwell, in particular those on everyday artefacts such as boys' weeklies and cigarettes. It went better than you might expect a conversation about literature to go between a seventeen-year-old from east Birmingham and a round-vowelled don who looked as if he lived off port. I remembered to say the things I could remember, and he nodded gamely. I couldn't at this point see any way in which I might be disadvantaged by a process in which face-to-face interviews are weighted against the evidence of written essays and exam results – although I do recall meeting my predecessor on the stairs up to the second interviewer's book-lined turret and snarling inwardly at the way she chirruped 'Good luck!' to me on her way back down. In the two seconds of our encounter I made a self-evident deduction: she was of the right sort, and I wasn't.

The tutor in my second interview of the day wore a cardigan and gave the impression he'd had enough. By way of a greeting, he opened a book of Wordsworth sonnets and, handing it to me, asked me to read aloud what was on the page before discussing it with him. I knew who Wordsworth was, having coveted copies of my mother's grammar school textbooks, one of which contained 'I wandered lonely as a cloud . . .', and tried to emulate the cadences of what little poetry I had heard being read aloud. I clearly remember sounding like someone attempting to translate from a language they'd never seen before; trying to shape my mouth in ways I thought might give the words the gravity they needed. The tutor started to snigger and, after thirty seconds or so, waved at me to stop. I knew I'd had it at that point. I can't remember if anything else I did or said made things worse or better, or indeed whether he ushered me out of the room to avoid further embarrassment. It was, after all, an easy way for him to dock an applicant from his list: *not up to it.* And that was it. Any illusion I might have had that you could climb a ladder without at some point falling off it – or being thrown off it – fell away at that point. Nobody, apart from Richard, had taken note of the number of missing rungs between that plucky, daft Record of Achievement and the requirements of the don in the cardigan. I realize now he couldn't be bothered to ask himself or his college why those rungs were missing.

I had another interview for university at the similarly elite University College London. Again not having the first sodding clue what I was doing apart from knowing how to get from Birmingham to Victoria Coach Station without bothering my parents (this in itself is a life skill), I joined a group of sixth formers who were being given a tour of the quad and campus in advance of their interviews. When we paused in a corridor to admire the embalmed body of the college's founder, the utilitarian philosopher Jeremy Bentham, a girl the same age as me remarked with mock enthusiasm: 'Fuck me, it's Jeremy Bentham!' To which my inward reaction was *Who the fuck is Jeremy Bentham?* I wasn't sure whether to express amusement or sympathy at the sight of this corpulent figure, his yellow waxen 'head' (replaced after the real one was stolen by students) lolling slightly in its glass box. I decided it was probably best to find it, and him, hilarious: almost as hilarious as the two-hour lecture on Beowulf we were invited to attend that afternoon. Is it a fair question to ask why I hadn't heard of Jeremy Bentham or had no familiarity with Old English? You could ask any one of the teachers we had over the course of twelve years of compulsory schooling why such information wasn't imparted. I was a voracious reader, a curious and attentive finder-outer, yet nothing I'd read had yet led me to those reference points. The potty-mouthed student seemed to know who he was, so I assumed that I ought to as well. Looking back, I can't really see how I'd ever have found out who Jeremy Bentham was by the age of seventeen without having received a fundamentally different sort of education.

General knowledge has its class parameters like anything else: I'd stumbled into elite rooms without the required passwords, only to be found out when asked for them. Needless to say, I wasn't offered a place at Cambridge, but I did receive an offer from UCL, which I didn't take up. Instead I accepted a place at Queen Mary and Westfield College, also a part of the University of London, but one whose entrance hall didn't have intimidating waxworks of people I didn't recognize. Queen Mary – which at that time was accepting people to study English with two 'C's and one 'B' at A-level – was pitched just right for someone like me. It wasn't the reach-for-the-sky choice, but neither was it the choice of someone who'd given up on the idea of doing right by yourself, of trying to take the chance you'd been given as far as you could. It was the *respectable* choice. Once I arrived at Queen Mary, I met boys from Stepney Green, Grimethorpe, Halifax – places with, at one time at least, fiercely autodidactic cultures of their own built up over decades of collective organization and stability – who, after going home for Christmas and being told that they were losing their accents, caved in to family and peer pressure and abandoned their courses. When the New Year came round, they stayed put and stayed local.

For every one like them, though, there were others who were fulfilling their own and their parents' dreams. The culture of Queen Mary allowed for these kinds of difficulties and differences, and in so doing resembled far more closely the dream that some of us have of all children getting a good education – one which equips them both to function well in the society we have and to take part in building the society we hope for – regardless of their origins. In contrast to that ethos, selection in secondary education and later at elite universities is geared towards reserving the best education for those well primed to pass certain tests. These may be tests of intellectual ability, of someone's ability to wing it on the day, or of society's ability to maintain a large – but not *too* large – middle class.

Today, social mobility still occurs in a context of educational, cultural and social inequality, creating new generations of 'uprooted' and 'anxious' individuals whose success is presented as evidence of a classless society. The reality is that they remain the exceptions to the rule, rather than examples of meritocracy in action. Time and again we return to these uncomfortable grammar school graduates (and drop-outs, for that matter), many of whom wrote to Richard Hoggart in the years after *The Uses of Literacy* was published. (' "So others have felt as I have", etc', is how Hoggart characterized the tone of their relieved correspondence.) You don't have to have been on a scholarship or a grammar school boy or girl, or to have been from that generation, to see a kindred soul in his archetype of a nervy, intense individual, 'emotionally uprooted' by education from their original class, who has yet to find a home in their new, socially elevated grouping.

A process of detachment from their class of origin in circumstances such as these begins early on. As Hoggart writes of the 'scholarship boy': 'He has to be more and more alone, if he is going to "get on". He will have, probably unconsciously, to oppose the ethos of the hearth, the intense gregariousness of the working-class family group.'[1] Most grammar schools may have been abolished, but the scholarship boy's experience continues to ring true for anyone who has been educated out of their original class. I was there; now I'm here. Though I've 'got on', there is a part of me which feels – and has always felt – appallingly lonely. Early on this manifested itself at school, in my stubborn refusal to like what everyone else liked, in my insistence on liking the things I liked instead. To this day, this isolation feels to me most evident in how I'm terrified of lacking knowledge and somehow being caught out and having my ignorance exposed. To ward off this fear I've marinated myself in information – facts, history, words. I find this comforting. I have mastered the formal language and got it to work on my behalf. But I can't get away from the basic fact of having risen out of – and not with – my class, or whichever micro-class I started out as part of.

I realized I was hardly the first – or the last – to feel that way when I came across a book called *Breakthrough*, a 1968 collection of accounts by writers, academics, artists and other notables of their experiences of social mobility, usually through education. It's very much a book of its time in that its editor, the academic Ronald Goldman, had recognized the existence of many individuals like him who had been socially mobile through education, yet whose collective testimony highlighted the rarity of their experience. Such a book wouldn't get commissioned now because of a widespread – and in itself quite dangerous – assumption that social mobility no longer exists at all. Most of the writers in *Breakthrough* undertook their lonely journeys before the Second World War and therefore prior to the changes brought about by the 1944 Education Act, which created a system of large-scale grammar schools, secondary moderns and vocational technical schools. One account, by the celebrated Cumbrian landscape artist Sheila Fell, describes the gross, unwitting intensity of being an only child: the things you learn too quickly, before you're ready, in the presence of adults, and the things you don't learn in the absence of peers. You learn all of the adult things and none of the childish things, so that when you grow up you are already old, yet at the same time somewhat unworldly. She grows up in an idyllic dyad, mother and daughter, with her miner father often away working. The mother and daughter sit in their remote home sewing and pressing flowers together until Fell is beckoned to art college in Carlisle, and then to the Chelsea College of Art. Cumberland is no longer her home. Instead, it becomes her subject, one to which she returns repeatedly and obsessively: a soft blanket of familiarity.

Then there is Jane Mitchell, a classics scholar at Reading University, who grew up in Glasgow with one half-brother thirteen years older. She went to Oxford in the mid-thirties on 'a substantial grant from Glasgow Corporation'. There, she at first 'felt abysmally ignorant, but I listened and learned, followed up references to unfamiliar authors and pondered on unfamiliar value-judgments'.[2] Unlike Fell, her links to Glasgow become more distant the longer she spends in the south, which causes lasting filial awkwardness amid a sense of liberation.

Hoggart is in there, too, commenting on the exam-induced nervous breakdown he suffered during his transition from Hunslet to Leeds University; as is Dennis Marsden, whose account of growing up 'respectable' in Huddersfield informed his later work with Brian Jackson on *Education and the Working Class*. 'I didn't make many friends,' Marsden recalls of his time at Cambridge on an 'exhibition' – an open scholarship – from his grammar school in Huddersfield. 'Yet how quickly all those very large Public Schoolboys called Charles or Miles or Giles or Jeremy struck up an acquaintance and hailed one another loudly across street and quad!'

His father was a millworker of keen intelligence whose 'shy

personality', in Marsden's words, had been subject to 'bruising and blunting . . . by the rough world of the mill'. While Marsden experienced an escalator-like trajectory from grammar school at eleven to Oxford at eighteen and a career as an academic, his father 'never got away from that world or even that particular mill' – a fact which Marsden senior (and, I don't doubt, Marsden himself) found 'unbearable', announcing to his family on occasion that 'If Ah'd known then what Ah know now, Ah'd have thrown meself in t'cut [canal].'[3]

Marsden, like Hoggart, felt 'vertiginous' at the speed with which he ascended the social ladder through education, a sensation he put to productive use in his research with Jackson. The pair concluded that any working-class child who succeeds in an education system that favours middle-class children 'may become a puzzled and insecure adult'. For those born in Britain between about 1940 and 1960, this was a less uncommon experience than it had been for either Marsden or Hoggart, born a generation earlier, as the infant welfare state provided opportunities for social mobility in relative abundance. It needed professionals, technicians, administrators, nurses, doctors and teachers, while the shift from heavy industry to light industry and communications required fewer people to get their hands dirty. In addition, labour shortages and an abundance of overtime made it possible for many individuals to achieve economic mobility without having to exchange one class for another. In spite of Harold Macmillan's stated goal of 'a property-owning democracy', home ownership had not yet come to be fetishized, so it was not yet considered unreasonable to earn good wages and still want to live in a council house.

But for those born after this period, those who came of age from the late seventies onwards, no such bounty was in evidence. A political hardening against working-class interests combined with a prolonged economic crisis which began in the late sixties and continued until – well, did it ever end? If you moved from the working class into the middle class after this point, such mobility was arguably now less likely the result of social change and more a case of bloody-mindedness. This didn't mean an *end* to social mobility; merely that opportunities were fewer and those who weren't well primed to take them were blamed for lacking initiative by those who were doing very well out of the Tories.

There are two deleterious myths about social mobility, one presented generally from the right of the political spectrum, and one from the left. The former is that individual social mobility has no costs, only benefits; the latter that social justice and social mobility are mutually exclusive, and that for social justice to prevail, the wish for individual social mobility must be sublimated to the valorization of your whole class. The existence of a 'golden age of social mobility', which ended in 1979 if you hate Thatcher or in 1997 if you hate New Labour (they abolished the 'assisted places' scheme which allowed some children from low-income backgrounds into fee-paying schools for free), is also overstated. In reality the picture is mixed: the general rule is that social mobility was, and is, experienced by large numbers of individuals within a structure that keeps a much larger number in their class of origin. Upward social mobility is more common than downward because it is generationally harder to lose middle-class privileges, once you have them, than it is to gain them. A family may rapidly lose money – through repossession or bankruptcy, for instance – but its members can't lose knowledge already gained, qualifications already earned, expectations already entrenched, half as quickly. This is something which members of the middle class tend to overlook or underestimate, and which causes them to work harder than they probably need to in order to retain those privileges.

No government wants to tell its voters, at least directly, that

they should know their place. Social mobility, therefore, is presented as both the central problem of class inequality and its
solution. If the problem of class is depicted as one in which not
enough working-class children get to become middle-class
adults, it can be made into something that can be sorted out by
pulling a few policy-making levers. The 'education' lever –
ping! The 'cycle of poverty' lever – ding! The 'we've talked
about it so that means we're doing something about it' lever –
bing! And within a generation, the classless society has been
created. Except, again, there's Hoggart's empty coffin. That's
not to say that government has no role in creating the conditions
for higher levels of movement between classes. If we look at the
recent history of social mobility, both as it's been experienced
by individuals and as a phenomenon affecting the wider culture,
it's possible to see how those levers can to an extent be made to
operate in favour of those previously unfavoured. Many of these
levers have been education reforms. The raising of the minimum school-leaving age to sixteen in 1972 was the first step in
ensuring that fewer youngsters left school without qualifications.
The establishment of the Open University a few years before
made further study more accessible to those who hadn't immediately progressed to university, while a degree itself has been
transformed from a minority pursuit into something undertaken
by around 40 per cent of all young people. When government
decides to invest in people – as, for instance, did New Labour
with the Education Maintenance Allowance (EMA) – it can have
transformative results. Sixth-form students told the House of
Commons Education Committee that the EMA provided not
only practical help to stay on in education, but gave them a sense
that the government recognized and cared about those from
low-income backgrounds, which in itself had a 'massive' impact
on their motivation.[4] (The EMA was abolished in 2011.)

Periods of economic growth and recession have respectively

widened and narrowed job opportunities. Government policy has also meant that, at some times more than others, it has been easier to achieve mobility through the mechanisms of well-resourced state education, full employment and universal goods such as the NHS. (I make this observation as someone who believes that a strong welfare state supports, rather than infantilizes, people.) Significantly, though, if you were of working age in the fifties and sixties, you had a chance to escape the poverty associated with being working class, without necessarily having to leave behind the people and culture of that class.

The clearest starting point for surveying social, as opposed to economic, mobility is not the introduction of free schooling for all at the end of the nineteenth century but the 1944 Education Act – widely known as the Butler Act after its creator, the Conservative education secretary R. A. Butler – and its implementation by his Labour successor, Ellen Wilkinson, after the war. On appointing Butler in 1943, Winston Churchill reminded the incoming President of the Board of Education of his task. Butler recalled being told by Churchill: ' "You will move poor children from here to here," and he lifted up and evacuated imaginary children from one side of his blotting pad to the other; "this will be very difficult." '[5]

For the generation before mine, the chance to go to grammar school was given to 'the brightest quarter' of eleven-year-olds in the country. In theory, grammar school places were awarded regardless of class; in practice, allocations were deeply biased towards those from middle-class backgrounds. You had to pass the 11-plus, of course, which immediately slanted the odds towards children who had quiet rooms of their own at home in which to work and prepare for exams. If you passed the 11-plus, you had to have parents who could afford the byzantine uniform requirements of most grammar schools, which sought to emulate public school appearances through an insistence on

stripy ties, different hats for different seasons and expensive
blazers. Grammar schools were fewer and therefore often further away, necessitating long journeys and more spending on
bus fares. Even if they could afford it, parents of such children
needed to be able to see the point in spending all that money.
Should you have passed those first hurdles, you had to fight your
corner as the only kid from your primary school to have got as
far as grammar school. You could say to yourself: 'I am representative of my class, we are learners just like everyone else, and
now we have the chance we are here to learn.' Or you could say:
'I am representative of my class, this school bears no resemblance
to the life I have outside it, and I shouldn't be here.'

The historian David Kynaston has examined the influence of
the Butler Act on Michael Young's part-satirical, part-polemicial
1958 book *The Rise of the Meritocracy*, about a future British society in which intelligence-testing and educational hot-housing
produce a new elite based on 'merit' as opposed to inherited
position, but ends up replicating the injustices of the old hierarchy. Kynaston weighs up what it meant to be a 'classic
meritocrat' in the late fifties: to qualify on these terms you had
to pass 'the triple historical test of (a) being born in 1933 or later,
(b) being working class and (c) going to grammar school as a direct beneficiary of the 1944 Education Act and using that
education as a ladder for further advancement'.[6]

Dennis Potter, the television playwright and coalminer's son,
passes Kynaston's test; the celebrated photographers Don
McCullin, David Bailey and Terence Donovan don't, on account
of the fact that their success was achieved without the aid of the
11-plus. Instead, in common with most British people whose
living standards and (to a lesser degree) social status improved in
the twenty-five years after war ended, they didn't get much
beyond elementary or secondary modern schooling. What actually helped people the most – the mechanism by which most

escaped dire poverty in the postwar period – was not the reor-
ganization of compulsory education, since academic excellence
was still deemed possible only for the 'brightest'. It was a combination of factors, the most obvious being full employment,
which gave workers better pay, greater choice and more chances
for advancement (because they didn't have to remain stuck in a
bad job for fear of not being able to find another one). There was
also the continued popularity of night school and other forms of
non-compulsory education, such as the Workers' Educational
Association and university extra-mural departments; and the
fact that the basic security provided by the welfare state allowed
parents to relieve their children of the grinding poverty of their
own childhoods. Together, they formed the conditions for high
levels of economic and social mobility in the three decades or so
after the war.

The unusual degree of success achieved by grammar school-
educated public figures – such as Potter, Joan Bakewell, Melvyn
Bragg and Alan Bennett, all of whom not only passed their
11-plus but went on to study at Oxford or Cambridge – also
led to a perception that grammar schools acted as a mass catalyst
for bookish working-class children to enter the upper-middle
class. The reality for most working-class kids who went to
grammar schools is that they did better than they would have
done had they gone to secondary moderns, but not nearly as
well as their middle-class counterparts: working-class grammar
school graduates were 'both overqualified and underqualified'
for the range of jobs that was open to them.[7] Very few made it to
university; equally, few were trained in practical skills that
would help them to get work. Leaving grammar school before
the sixth form was overwhelmingly common among children
from unskilled and semi-skilled backgrounds, with middle-class
children at grammar schools five times more likely to go to university than their working-class counterparts.[8] Those who left

at fifteen or sixteen often entered clerical employment, though this often resulted in a working life as routine and poorly paid – if not worse paid – as if they had gone into skilled manual jobs or trades. The third pillar of the tripartite schooling system proposed by Butler in the 1944 Act, technical schools, never truly materialized: only a few hundred were built, in comparison with the 1,200 state-run grammars and 3,800 secondary moderns that existed at the end of the fifties.[9] (One clear beneficiary of the technical school experiment was David Jones, from a lower-middle-class background in south London, who worked as a commercial artist in his teens before turning himself into David Bowie.)

Having said all that, the fact that fully one-quarter of secondary school children were educated at grammar schools in this period was bound to have some effect on the wider culture. Because the offspring of the upper middle class continued to be educated at fee-paying schools in great numbers – 8 per cent of children attended private schools in the mid-sixties, when the middle class was smaller than now, compared with 7 per cent today – there was a degree of scope for children of the upper-working and lower-middle class to move up a rung or two by dint of grammar school expansion. One great benefit of mass social mobility, in so far as it existed in the thirty years or so after the war, was that individuals who were caught up in that difficult process could console themselves, perhaps even each other, with new books, plays and films – and, later, bands and records – that seemed to mirror their experiences and give them reference points from which to make sense of them. In the 1963 film version of Keith Waterhouse's novel *Billy Liar*, Billy Fisher's father tells his errant son, born circa 1945 and now clerking unsuccessfully at an undertaker's, that he 'should be grateful' for having had the chance to get as far in life as he has. 'And don't I know it! When I passed the exam for the grammar school the first thing you said was how are you going to pay for the uniform! I should be grateful, that's all I've ever heard!'[10]

From the late fifties, beginning with *The Uses of Literacy* in 1957, Alan Sillitoe's *Saturday Night and Sunday Morning* in 1958, the film of John Braine's novel *Room at the Top* in 1959, and Shelagh Delaney's play *A Taste of Honey* in 1960, members of the working class could see themselves represented in ways that for the first time went beyond caricature: young men and women were shown in possession of interior monologues and mixed-up motives. Not all these figures were socially mobile, but what all of them shared was a sense of freedom, brought about by rising wages and shorter working hours. Alan Sillitoe, born into an indigent Nottingham family, left elementary school at fourteen having failed his scholarship exam twice. His definitive anti-hero, Arthur Seaton, no more wanted to be middle class than to be like his 'dead from the neck up' parents. If you were Arthur, you could have a good time and stuff the rest of it. What's the betting he would have voted for Thatcher? Whether in spite or because of his hard-knock start in life, Sillitoe was a man after Seaton's heart. He fought against soppy notions of collective sentiment, believing that the role of literature was instead 'to give the feeling of individual dignity that mass communication, by its own definition, is unable to transmit'.

Members of the first 'mass' grammar-schooled generation, however, did perform an important service beyond their own betterment. Those who entered public life were prominent and (just about) numerous enough to serve as a visible reminder that working-class people weren't thick. They included working- and lower-middle-class writers such as Waterhouse, Stan Barstow (author of *A Kind of Loving*) and Arnold Wesker (*Chicken Soup with Barley*). One sign that working-class experiences were being noticed and valued for their own merits, and not for how they could be shaped to middle-class tastes, was how autodidacts such as Colin Wilson – author of *The Outsider*, an idiosyncratic non-fiction book about misfits in art and literature – and Sillitoe were also swept to prominence in this tide. What characterized these writers was a strong sense that, though their work was disparate in style and origin, they were working class without having to represent the working class. None of them tried to ingratiate themselves with middle-class readers; equally, they were unsparing in their portrayals of working-class lives. They had the confidence to present their characters in the whole without worrying too much about airing dirty laundry.

The frankest in this way is Delaney, perhaps because she was the least compromised by the 'vertiginous' ascent enjoyed by many of her male peers. Waterhouse zoomed off to London as soon as he got the chance, as did Sillitoe in a more roundabout, bohemian way. (Waterhouse stayed within shuttling distance of Soho and Fleet Street, while Sillitoe lived abroad before settling in Notting Hill.) Both *Billy Liar*'s Billy Fisher and Arthur Seaton rail against their parents for their docility and conformity at opposite ends of the working class, but Josephine, the pregnant fifteen-year-old heroine of *A Taste of Honey*, can't bring herself to condemn her flaky mother, in all probability because she knows she is headed that way herself. In spite of all, she finds a way to express her belief that she is 'an extraordinary person' – in her best friend Geoff's words, 'bloody marvellous!'

Perhaps the ultimate fictional 11-plusser isn't Billy Fisher, Kingsley Amis's eponymous 'Lucky Jim' or even Joe Lampton, the hero of *Room at the Top*. It's Ken Barlow, the long-standing *Coronation Street* character played by William Roache, who won a scholarship to Manchester University, qualified as a teacher and then seemingly caught the first bus back home. Over five decades, Barlow has been seen to suffer as the hard-won, elaborate syntax of his educated 'code' – along with his literary pretensions and his anguish about the state of the world – is forced along the tramlines of terrace life. You can tell he often hates it, but loyalty as much as cowardice has kept him there through a dozen changes in profession. In the very first episode of *Coronation Street*, broadcast in December 1960, he is seen looking uncomfortable and ashamed at the presence of a sticky HP Sauce bottle on the dinner table while having tea with his parents. His – slightly – elevated position in relation to his neighbours suits someone whose tetchy disposition means he could never have tolerated being a small fish in a big pond. He has held court on the cobblestones and in the Rovers, a man whose 'book-learning', to use a Hoggartian phrase, is as much respected as begrudged. If Hoggart, in *The Uses of Literacy* and his three volumes of autobiography, managed to create a sort of non-fiction Proust, the collected writers of *Coronation Street* have succeeded in telling a convincing whole-life story about the merits and limits of social mobility in much the same way as François Truffaut did in his series of films about Antoine Doinel. Even then, from 1959's *Les quatre cents coups* to *L'amour en fuite* in 1979, we find out only about twenty years' worth of Doinel's bullet-dodging course from borstal to bourgeoisie; Barlow's deracinated adventures have so far featured on *Coronation Street* for nearly six decades. As recently as 2008 he attempted to write his own *Bildungsroman* of class confusion in urban Lancashire, holing up in a box room which, after a few days of whiskey- and cigarette-fuelled creation, was described by his mother-in-law, Blanche, as smelling 'like an anchovy's jockstrap'.[11]

The opening up of grammar schools and other selective schools to a slightly larger minority of zippy, restless working-class children had a significant effect on wider culture in other ways. While it's hard definitively to distinguish cause from correlation, I believe there are visible signs that the sense of opportunity – of success as against failure – afforded by passing the 11-plus affected the development of British pop music from the early sixties to the early eighties; signs which can be traced alongside the social and political changes that were taking place at the time. Three of the Beatles went to grammar school: Paul McCartney and George Harrison to the prestigious Liverpool Institute, and John Lennon to Quarrybank High School. Only Ringo, the poorest of the four as a kid, wasn't primed in this way for relative success. Bowie went to technical school, while countless of his contemporaries, including Lennon, Brian Eno and Bryan Ferry of Roxy Music, Pete Townshend of The Who, Rod Stewart and Ronnie Wood of the Faces, Ray Davies of the Kinks, and most of the Rolling Stones (ex-grammar school boys), attended art school. Later, the Sex Pistols' Glen Matlock went to art school, too, while all of Joy Division and all of The Smiths attended grammars – except for Morrissey, who went to a secondary modern and never let anyone forget it. Many of these individuals already came from the upper end of the working class and the lower-middle class, a good indicator of how they avoided the dead end apparently presented by secondary modern schooling. However, in these instances I think it's safe to describe pop stardom as a form of social mobility, given the limitless horizons it presents for travelling the world, meeting people from different walks of life, and for using the money and time off afforded to adopt some of the habits of the leisure class: fine wine, good food, art as a hobby or creative sideline.

Writing in 1967, the journalist Kenneth Allsop noted that 'today's prole pop stars . . . have achieved a novel condition of classlessness by staying themselves, without capitalising on the "charm" of being a colourful peasant, as they move relaxedly between embassy receptions and the cosmopolitan soirées of high bohemia.'[12] Those 'prole pop stars' reacted in different ways to their new condition: Bryan Ferry married into the aristocracy and sent his sons to Eton, while the children of the self-consciously 'ordinary' McCartney went to the school nearest to their home in Sussex, a non-selective comprehensive. Culturally, however, both were able to enter 'high bohemia' without particularly changing who they were. The Beatles expressed an extraordinary degree of confidence in their ability to widen what popular music could include in its parameters, and therefore in the ability of their listeners to take in, to cope with, new ideas. They didn't hog their discoveries; rather, they invited everyone to share them.

By the mid-sixties, Labour's education secretary Anthony Crosland was making plans for the replacement of the tripartite system with non-selective comprehensive schools for all eleven-year-olds. (Crosland privately made the notorious statement that he wouldn't rest until he'd abolished 'every fucking grammar school' in the country.) He worked on the proposals with the social scientist and education reformer A. H. Halsey, who supported a comprehensive system on the grounds that he believed all schools could be as good as the best grammar schools. Unlike the upper-middle-class Crosland, Halsey, the socially mobile son of a King's Cross railway worker, later changed his mind. In 1981, just over a decade after most grammars and secondary moderns were replaced with comprehensives, he wrote that comprehensives had instead created a situation in which all schools were nominally the same but within which the slights of class simply reproduced themselves. Halsey feared that in his work with Crosland he had accidentally aided the development of 'a huge hidden curriculum' in which a majority of pupils – as with secondary moderns – absorbed 'a sense of their own relative incompetence and impotence – a modern, humane and even relatively enjoyed form of gentling the masses?'[13]

In the sixties the 'hidden curriculum' at working-class schools comprised CSEs in practical skills such as woodwork and pottery. By the eighties and nineties they had been replaced with the mechanics and hair and beauty courses I hated so much at school. The evidence seems to suggest that comprehensive schools in themselves have not hindered social mobility, compared with the tripartite system, and have certainly saved millions of children from the anxiety and unfairness of the reductive 11-plus exam. But I wonder whether Halsey was also talking about the covert programme of damage executed in schools by teachers convinced of their working-class pupils' low ability and, inadvertently, by working-class parents reluctant to push their children any further than their 'natural' abilities would take them. The historian Selina Todd interviewed dozens of people from working-class backgrounds – many from the first generation educated under the 1944 Act – about the attitudes they held towards their experience of education and in particular how it had affected what they wanted for their children. Noting that 'children born in the forties were almost twice as likely to gain formal qualifications as those born in the interwar years', Todd records that many, though by no means all, of her baby boomer interviewees became socially mobile through education. Christine Elliott, a Coventry woman interviewed by Todd, had two daughters who both failed their 11-plus in the fifties. Elliott had grown up during the Depression, suffering a nervous breakdown aged nine brought on by her family's poverty. She tells Todd that she 'just wanted (her children) to be happy' rather than to strive for qualifications, but that's not all there is to it. She also feared that education beyond the secondary modern level – the level achieved by the majority – would lead them to 'think they're better than everybody else . . . if you went to university . . . you thought you was better than the other people, but you weren't no different'.[14]

Instead Elliott's daughters benefited from the abundance of routine work the city provided in the fifties and sixties, which downgraded the importance of qualifications as a prerequisite for employment, though Todd also notes that in 1959 Her Majesty's Inspectors of Schools complained of 'not sufficient provision of post-compulsory education' on offer in Coventry to meet demand.[15] The level of education Elliott's daughters received was ultimately decided for them by their mother, who sought both to protect them (by wanting them to be happy first and foremost) and to protect herself (by avoiding 'losing' her children to education). To be sure, jumping through hoops for advancement was no one's idea of fun, especially if the experience of arriving at grammar school – wholly entitled to your place there – revealed new degrees of snobbery and ostracism to which you'd had no previous exposure. Howard Blake, the son of a Coventry bus driver, 'realized [he] was working class' only when he entered grammar school; Ann Lanchbury, also from Coventry, 'truly can't remember any (other) girls that lived on council estates' at her grammar school.[16] The extent to which experiences like these put off working-class scholars is made visible by the fact that relatively few actually made it as far as the examinations which would have rendered – in their instrumental way – their discomfort worthwhile.

If, however, you felt kinship with Hoggart's 'scholarship boy', there seemed to be few other options than to carry on traipsing joylessly up the social ladder. He sees a distinctive loneliness in the working-class scholar, manifest in 'an unusual self-consciousness before their own situation'. In adulthood, he deduces that the *déclassé* meritocrat 'is at the friction-point of two cultures: the real test of his education lies in his ability, by about the age of twenty-five, to smile at his father with his whole face and to respect his flighty young sister and his slower brother'.[17]

In July 1961 Hoggart was pitched against fellow scholarship boy Enoch Powell in a BBC radio debate titled 'Social Equality – The Class System'. Though the two men had reputations for seriousness, Hoggart was clearly the more mild-mannered and plain-speaking of the two. Powell, the austere classics scholar, only child of a Birmingham headmaster, called 'the 11-plus "as near as we can get to equality of opportunity"', and accused the ambivalent Hoggart – you can almost imagine Powell's spittle-flecked tirade – of holding 'a class grudge'. Hoggart, for his part, replied that the people he had known back in Leeds 'lived in a society where they knew they would get the dirty end of the stick most of the time, and they'd built up a whole lot of very good defences . . . it was claustrophobic, it was narrow, it was limiting, especially for the budding abstract thinker, but at the same time . . . you could grow as a person'.[18] The idea that all working-class children passing the 11-plus would go on to become, well, austere classics scholars or the like was, he continued, simply Powell's wishful thinking: what was foremost in the minds of their parents was that 'Our Jimmy' would be going on to a steady, renumerative 'white-collar job'.

The idea of my taking the 11-plus, floated by our primary school headmaster, came and went virtually without comment. I don't remember there being a great period of weighing-up, of examining what was on offer, on anyone's part, but then I can imagine that my parents didn't want to place any unnecessary stress on me by making too much of a fuss about it. The 11-plus was by that time no longer a demarcator of where everyone at a particular school in a particular community was headed. Divorced from the tripartite system, the exam once again became something that odd (in every sense of the word) children were singled out for, almost as though there was something wrong with them, which could be ameliorated by intense adult scrutiny followed by a three-hour exam. I remember having only the vaguest idea of what it was and what it represented, which dented my ability to make an informed decision. I don't recall feeling any disappointment at the time, possibly because I was never taken to the school – one of the King Edward VI schools in Birmingham and, although I was aware it was meant to be special, wasn't able precisely to grasp at the time what was special about it. Going there would have meant two buses there and two buses back every day. It would have meant a much earlier dislocation from Chelmsley Wood, a much earlier beginning to the psychological disruption that eventually came at sixteen, which in all probability wouldn't have been good for an eleven-year-old of nervous disposition.

I have no idea how much chance I would have had of passing the II-plus, let alone anything else. Yet that name has followed me around for nearly thirty years. *King Edward's* this, *King Edward's* that. I don't know a single person from my estate who went there; though I knew plenty who were bussed or driven to comprehensives outside the estate with a better reputation, and even one or two who went to private schools; but never *King Edward's*. Yet since I became a journalist, and particularly since I wrote a book, a number of strangers familiar with the names and ways of Birmingham schools have assumed that it's where I went, and that I couldn't possibly be doing what I do now had I not gone there. They've assumed that I was on an assisted place, that I won a scholarship, and generally that I was on an educationally assisted path of upward mobility from early childhood. Surely, they reckon, there could have been no other way to get from *there* to *here*.

Crosland and Halsey, among other influential Labour figures, believed that selection was both egregious in itself and inimical to the social growth which ought to accompany economic growth. What was, or could have been, the alternative to phasing out grammar schools? Critics of the comprehensive school system, which from 1974 replaced the split system of academic grammar schools and vocational secondary or technical schools which had stood since 1945, believe that it kicked away the only ladder that existed for working-class children to achieve social mobility in large numbers. Supporters of comprehensive schools, on the other hand, claim that they were an important step towards reducing the influence of social class on children's educational attainment. There are two broad truths to consider: one is that the attainment of sixteen-year-old school pupils *in general* has improved dramatically in the four decades since comprehensives were introduced, particularly since the introduction of GCSEs in 1988, which merged the old two-tier exam system of CSEs (Certificate of School Education) and higher-status O-levels. While fewer than 10 per cent of sixteen-year-olds gained the equivalent of five A*–C grade GCSE passes in 1970, around two-thirds do now. The second is that, in areas that have retained their grammar schools, such as Kent and Buckinghamshire, poorer children – those who qualify for free school dinners – do far worse at GCSE level than those in all-comprehensive areas.[19]

As someone who went to a secondary modern school in all but name *within* a comprehensive system, but who might have benefited in some ways from a grammar school education, I find it hard to be a cheerleader for either side. Those who publicly celebrate comprehensive schooling are often those who did well in it; I can't help feeling they *would* say that. That ungenerous instinct in me coexists with an understanding of the facts. Grammar schools *do not* help school pupils as a whole, and in fact, where they operate, actively damage the attainment of poorer children. Going to a grammar school might have made a difference to my education, but *only* mine. I'd have been 'rescued', 'lifted', 'chosen' – singled out at the expense of others, however you slice it. The same would have applied had I gone to any school with a majority of middle-class rather than working-class pupils. The writer Heather McRobie has said she doubts that she 'got into Oxford for any reason other than the fact my highly successful, middle-class state school may as well have been a fee-paying school, in terms of both the socio-economic background of the students, and its singular obsession with getting us into Oxbridge'. Tellingly, given my own experience of the Oxbridge hoop-jumping test, she notes that her own interview for Oxford 'felt like a cosy chat, even though for many other, brighter, candidates, it may as well have been in a foreign language, whether or not their interviewer made references in Latin'.[20]

Few who believe in comprehensive schooling as an ideal are certain, if they are honest, that it exists in practice. The comprehensive project was developed out of a sense of injustice at the fate of those children who were, on the results of a single exam geared towards middle-class assumptions of abstract rather than applied knowledge, consigned to a second-class education. But the dismantling of the tripartite system from the early seventies onwards produced a revolt from middle-class parents for whom grammar schools had worked disproportionately in their children's favour. Instead of a mass middle-class exodus to the private sector, a process began whereby affluent parents started to hog newly comprehensive schools for their offspring according to their catchment area – through buying properties closer to certain schools – and their existing intake. Rather than bringing about a greater mix of social groups and academic abilities through a single-tier system, ingrained assumptions about the insubordinate and disengaged 'nature' of working-class children made comprehensive schools arguably even more class-ridden. During the seventies and eighties, as schools became more divided according to the social class of their pupils, teachers' and parents' existing perceptions of different schools and their pupils' ability did not change: rather, they were reinforced by the fact that the performance of schools became ever more defined simply by the socio-economic circumstances of their intake, as opposed to their intake *plus* academic selection.[21]

When Labour took power in 1997 on the platform of 'education, education, education', a further tier of complication was added to the school system with the introduction of academies and school specialisms. The aim of academies was to introduce a degree of private funding – and, it was assumed, expertise – into a sclerotic, underachieving state sector in order to improve the performance of secondary schools in poor areas. The idea was to blast schools in poor, usually urban, areas with resources and a sense of there being a 'fresh start' for their pupils. The results were drastically uneven, often depending on the areas in which academies operated. Some of the earliest, such as Mossbourne Academy in Hackney, east London, achieved stunning GCSE results from its first intake, while others – notably those outside London and outside inner cities – struggled to improve on the results of their predecessor schools. Indeed, while the gap in attainment between poorer children and affluent children has narrowed since 1997, much of that narrowing is accounted for by the turnaround in the exam fortunes of schoolchildren in London alone. (This seems to be related to factors including the improved performance of children from ethnic minorities; the fact that outstanding teachers are easier to recruit in London and the South-East; and a specific education policy, the London Challenge, which promoted collaboration between schools and emphasized access to arts and culture for London pupils.) Outside London, especially in the north, the gap refuses to narrow.[22]

Professor Diane Reay worked as a primary school teacher for the now-abolished Inner London Education Authority before moving into academia and researching the effects of social class on individuals' education. Asking what a socially just education

system might look like, she notes that, through the tools of setting and streaming, even those middle-class children attending
socially 'mixed' comprehensive schools continue to be educated
apart from their working-class peers.[23] Following a move away
from streaming in the seventies and eighties, education reforms
from the early nineties onwards prioritized target-setting and a
rigid attention to 'results' which, since 1992, have been publicly
presented in the form of school 'league tables', designed to aid
parents in choosing a school for their child. This political preoccupation with 'consumer choice', which the introduction of
academies did nothing to arrest, has only entrenched the advantages of those who are aware of a greater range of choices, and the
significance of those choices, and who are best placed to make use
of them. Reay argues that the end result of a choice-based system
is that 'the working class have largely ended up with the "choices"
that the middle class do not want to make'.[24]

Today, there remain 164 grammar schools in England, whose
pupils are disproportionately middle to upper-middle class and
whose resources and connections – as with the 7 per cent of the
school population who are educated privately – allow those
pupils to obtain a disproportionately high number of places at
elite universities. In 2012 every one of the top ten schools in the
country with the highest proportion of pupils going on to a
Russell Group university was a grammar school. By contrast,
there were 330 schools and colleges that didn't send any of their
pupils to a Russell Group university.[25]

Nevertheless, in Labour's last term of government, from
2005 to 2010, there was an enormous increase in the percentage
of young people from low-income neighbourhoods going
into higher education at eighteen. In 2010, the Higher Education Funding Council for England reported 'substantial and
sustained increases' in the numbers of young people from the
poorest areas entering higher education from the mid-2000s

onwards. Moreover, in spite of a vast increase in tuition fees from 2012, this upward trend has continued. The supposed working-class aversion to debt (always overstated, in any case, since few working-class households have ever managed to sustain a reasonably aspirational standard of living without the aid of hire purchase) was finally overturned by the need to take out five-figure loans for the same degrees their mostly middle-class predecessors attained for free. Although these new working-class students tended to attend universities that were formerly polytechnics and colleges of higher education, rather than more prestigious institutions, this still translated into better pay and a degree of social mobility for many who, without a degree, would never have had access to professional or white-collar jobs.

In 2009, the Million+ consortium of new universities reported that, while only 8 per cent of students at the twenty-eight member institutions had professional parents, 17 per cent had found professional jobs three years after graduating.[26] More recent findings by the Resolution Foundation – a think tank that conducts research into the social effects of a low-wage economy – suggest that economic mobility, measured in terms of how many people experienced growth in earnings that took them from the lower to the higher end of the spectrum, increased in the 2000s compared with the nineties, but only for those with higher qualifications. This trend has also continued: the better qualified you are, the more you earn, to the extent that a degree has become all but essential in order to earn above-median pay.

The Conservative – Liberal Democrat coalition, which took power in May 2010, put improved social mobility at the centre of its rhetoric, asking the former New Labour health secretary Alan Milburn to continue the commission on social mobility and child poverty he established at the end of Labour's time in power.

At the same time, the coalition allowed universities to charge much higher fees – up to £9,000 per student per academic year – partially to replace government funding for teaching, while also restricting funding for further education – the alternative, non-A-levels route by which many working-class students progress to university. Not only that, but Labour's Education Maintenance Allowance was 'redirected' towards a 'pupil premium' for disadvantaged secondary school pupils. The result is that the existing, if tacit, class-based hierarchy in British education has now also become an explicit economic hierarchy, in which those with the most money get to progress the furthest and to attend the most prestigious institutions.

The most recent wave of university expansion, which began in the year 2000 when higher education colleges were permitted to apply for university status, disproportionately benefited working-class students, not least because it normalized the idea of 'staying on' at school. Then again, there's 'university' and there's 'uni'. I've never got on with this casualized and truncated form of the original word. It suggests a lack of respect for the institution of the university, or at least a refusal to respect or measure the weight of it. It suggests that in order to be incorporated into 'the real world', the very idea of the university has to be simplified in order to be made manageable. Rather than stepping up to the 'elaborated' multisyllabic breach, this new and widened cohort of students was encouraged to chop it down to fit the 'restricted' code they knew. There was a great deal of meeting in the middle: rather than extending the research-intensive, highly academic model of Victorian and sixties 'plate-glass' universities, the newest wave of universities – formerly polytechnics, colleges of higher education and teacher training colleges – have tended to pile it high and sell it cheap, marketing themselves as distinctly 'local' institutions which will give you a degree without trying to force you out of your class comfort zone.

Of course, there are students who have always stood out and who are able to tolerate the internal dissonance of attending a middle-class university as a working-class student. But while the new universities go out of their way to smooth over the cracks of class for those who are used to fitting in, the redbricks – institutionally, at least – prefer to deny that such a problem exists outside the minds of their prospective students. Diane Reay and other educational researchers have noted that in the UK working-class students 'tend to choose a university with which they feel comfortable, where there are "people like us" '.[27] This applies equally to middle-class and working-class students, meaning that the former are more likely to choose 'old' universities and the latter, 'new' ones. This has the effect of entrenching the existing advantages of middle-class students, who are more likely to choose established universities, and limiting the potential advantages of working-class students.

At 'Eastern', a college of further education selected by Reay and her colleagues for their study, it wasn't possible to compare like for like with more established institutions. The degrees taken by the working-class students interviewed at 'Eastern' are in performing arts and childhood studies, rather than in chemistry, engineering, law, history and English, which their other working-class interviewees are studying at universities of varying prestige. In comparison with 'Midland' and 'Southern', two Russell Group institutions chosen for their sample, 'Eastern' and 'Northern' provide a setting for degree-level study which, they found, is characterized by an emphasis on continuity rather than change, and which allows working-class students to feel they are accepted as they are without offering them the chance to become familiar with things, habits and people beyond their existing experience.

This often involves carrying over from school into higher education a sense – a stance, maybe – of not-botheredness, that working-class disdain for 'keenness' still serving to keep the group members in line with each other. Working-class students at these colleges quickly learn to keep quiet about loving their subject. 'I really don't want to be the clever one or the swot,' says Kylie, a history student at 'Northern' who finds that she fits in 'socially, totally' but not 'academically'. On her upcoming Masters course at a Russell Group university she expects, conversely, she'll 'fit in fine academically but won't fit in at all socially'. At 'Southern', by comparison, students come in three dispositions, according to a working-class law student: 'geeky, geekier and even more geeky'. Working-class students at 'Southern', he felt, were used to standing out at school on account of their swottiness, and therefore were prepared to stand out again on account of their class.

So tightly bound is social class to the education system, I would argue, that higher education in particular has the potential to cause deep rifts within families and peer groups if it doesn't equally benefit all members. I'm reminded here of individuals I met at university who dropped out, essentially to avoid changing and therefore upsetting their families. The place they came from was too fragile – too traumatized, perhaps, by generations' worth of deferred dreams – to accommodate change. Another working-class student at 'Southern' told the researchers that she had learned not to mention anything pertaining to university life when visiting her mother back home: 'It's just like, don't go there.' The instruction, the injunction, is to pretend that nothing has changed by 'going there': the only way she can maintain good relations with her family is if she doesn't 'go there' at home, and indulges their discomfort by not talking about her experiences at university. The potential for offence is felt in both directions: in order to remain equal in the mother's eyes, the student and her mother must remain on the same experiential and educational plain. But not only has 'Southern', the elite institution, accepted the student on the basis of her intellect and potential – assumed neither to be deficient nor warped – she has accepted *it*, for what it can offer her. She learns from her mother that she was meant to say 'no' to all that. Her potential wasn't simply contained and thwarted by outside forces: it was contained from within.

In this way we can see a form of double-think in action. Ignorance and fear of the outside world doesn't develop in a vacuum: to keep those you love close to you requires keeping them within the world you know. The consequences of advancement may mean good news for the individual but bad news for the family and the neighbourhood. It may require bearing yet more loss as one more member sails away on her ship of freedom. There is a strong sense of emerging from a state of ignorance in which it is possible to labour for a lifetime with little fruit. Women who were not sent away begged each other not to leave, to stay and help the others to survive, which risked bitterness between sisters, mothers and daughters when there seemed no other option but to go elsewhere to make a life. With every departure came a loss of the meaning and hope that comes from being with others. The flourishing of individual potential was seen as harmful to the collective, and that is the problem we are discussing here.

If there's one definitive experience that has left a chip on my shoulder that I can't quite brush off, it's that encounter with the dismissive don at my interview for Cambridge university. It's a stupid thing, given the life I have now, but what it did was expose – to reflect back to me, even though I was well aware of it underneath – the inadequacy of my secondary education. It made me feel totally second-rate, and of course I hated that. At school we really weren't supposed to feel that way, and yet the sheer paucity of resources – the crumminess of the buildings, the lack of trips and materials – seemed to tell us that we were, even when we weren't directly exposed to the abundance of resources at other, better-placed schools. We just *knew* there was something lacking. If a brittle self-belief had got me as far as that interview, it was pulverized in that short, shameful encounter.

There is this idea I keep coming back to, one of stunted mobility, caused by the structure itself impinging on the consciousness of people who are desperate to get out of the box in which they've been placed. Education hasn't liberated them from it; opportunities that others have seized have not been grasped. This has nothing whatsoever to do with stunted intellect. As Hoggart implied of the socially immobile 'carousel' existence which he knew and resented from his childhood, it's in the interests of institutionally powerful people to tell you that you're thick and that it's too late to do anything about it. To reverse this confidence trick, you have to force yourself to believe in a greater part of yourself than you actually do. You may feel infinitesimal in comparison with the forces that constrain you, yet you have to tell yourself that there's a rope you can grab on to which won't fray – or be yanked away by an invisible hand – when you give it your whole weight. This is the paradox of trying to achieve social mobility through the education system, which is nothing more than a finely tuned replica of the larger social system it serves. I would never discourage someone who is attempting to do just that, of course, aware that it may be their only tangible, navigable chance of getting out of the box. I'd say, *Go for it. Get out.* When I say navigable, I mean it in precisely the dogged, ladder-clambering way you're meant to approach social mobility. It's supposed to be a triumph of the will, as is illustrated by the many clichés used in newspaper-speak and political rhetoric: as a 'bright but poor child' on a 'tough estate', you 'do the right thing' and 'get on your bike' to places

of greater opportunity without waiting to be 'lifted out of poverty'. Richard Hoggart saw the fundamental shakiness of the
social escalator through the prism of the lonely scholarship boy;
Halsey through the 'gentling' – the 'hidden curriculum' of
diversionary, non-academic courses – offered to those who have
never been expected to go very far.

6. Drive a Knife in the Wedge and Twist It

There was a time in the late nineties when it seemed as though my premonition on the settee – when I called Richard during Tony Blair's inaugural speech as Labour Party leader and told him I'd seen the future of socialism – had come true. For a short while I believed that Blair and John Prescott, his authentically northern deputy, would see us right, and that somehow, together, all of us, we would restore the promise and glitter of a country that the Tories had spent eighteen years grinding into the earth. I remember in 1999 travelling into central London on the tube one Friday evening, probably heading to a gig in a sticky-floored hellpit or perhaps, now that I had a job in the media, going out for a better class of pizza: one with a charred, as opposed to a cheese-stuffed, crust. The train stopped at Bethnal Green, where in the fifties Peter Willmott and Michael Young (author of *The Rise of the Meritocracy*) had based their study of extended families in the East End.[1] A pair of young working-class women, aged no more than twenty I reckon, got on and spent the next few stops passing between them a bottle of Moët champagne, treating it as only a *relative* luxury. *Yeah, we've got champagne*, their tiddly nonchalance said. *So what? It's Friday.* I felt like cheering them on as they drank. *Get in! This is bloody it*, I thought. We can all drink champagne now and no one can stop us. Respectability be damned!

Labour's election victory in 1997 remains inescapably linked in my mind with youth, with good times, perhaps because I had just turned twenty-one when it happened. Labour had the feeling of a government that would encourage us to live out our dreams, with its blessing and support. If the spirit of divide and rule had won in the eighties, a divide-and-rule doctrine continued in the nineties under a different guise. In the mid-nineties, New Labour's ideological spine was of a piece with the individualism of the eighties; it sought to dress up the blunt Conservative language of 'you're on your own, mate' with a sophisticated, positive-thinking lexicon based on that persistent meme of 'livin' the dream'. To feel discomfort about constant change, an emergent feature of globalization, was to be inherently right-wing; yet equally, to believe in the strength of collective public institutions – such as unions, such as entirely publicly funded health and education systems – was unhelpfully Bolshevik. The sociologist Anthony Giddens – architect of the Third Way, a sort of anti-ideology ideology which underpinned New Labour policy – saw the future as a fantasy compendium of unlimited choice that could be unleashed for everyone subject to the removal of a few pesky socio-economic barriers. There was much to be said for the way New Labour encouraged a sense of diversity of opportunity, as opposed to mere equality of opportunity. It allowed people to think that they might be able to do something different with their lives, and perhaps encouraged a sense of agency.

Not everyone thought this was wholly a good thing, among them the social theorists Ulrich Beck and Zygmunt Bauman. Beck, who died in 2015, was a German sociologist who believed that class and social solidarity had had their day, and that the individualism which had taken their place 'condemned' people 'to be the authors of their own lives'. Bauman, a Pole working at Leeds University, advanced the yet more pessimistic theory that across the world millions of individuals, cut adrift from traditional notions of class and geographical belonging, were surplus to the requirements of capital, making it virtually impossible for them to create stable, meaningful or purposeful lives.

I first started reading up on sociology a couple of years after leaving university. I was working at *Heat*, a weekly magazine which set out offering a pithy, relatively critical review of pop culture but which, in the face of poor sales six months after its launch, turned rapidly into a celebrity pictorial specializing in publishing photos of pop stars and television actors surreptitiously picking their noses or scooping their dogs' mess outside branches of Starbucks. Although I didn't register this at the time, it now seems clear that the success of *Heat* in its second incarnation, a few years into New Labour's period in power, was utterly in accordance with the times. The aim of showing Liz Hurley, say, getting out of her car wearing tracksuit bottoms, was to narrow the distance between those photographed and those looking at the photograph, in so doing making it seem feasible that anyone could become a film star. The idea that 'real' people could become celebrities, while celebrities could be proved to be 'real', was strengthened once Channel 4 launched the reality show *Big Brother*. At the same time that previously unknown people became famous through appearing on the series, *Heat* sought to illustrate that famous people were, in its words, 'just like you and me!'

I must stress that I wasn't reading sociology books while working at a mass-circulation magazine in order to annoy people (I found plenty of other ways to do that, such as trying to mention Proust in every preview of *Coronation Street* I wrote). It was more the case that I liked both: Bauman and Barlow, if you like. The desire to like both – to enjoy both 'high' and 'low' culture – was a marker of my burgeoning cultural capital, and something I'll come back to later in this chapter. But I found the developments at *Heat* unsettling, not least because it had started out as just the sort of magazine – essentially *Smash Hits* for adults – I wanted to read. There was clearly some sort of levelling intention in the 'just like you and me!' mantra; but it was levelling in the wrong direction. The second half of *The Uses of Literacy* focuses on what Richard Hoggart saw as a deliberate, cynical slackness in the way 'matey' magazines and pulp fiction communicated with their working-class readership. He writes of 'persuaders' who wanted you to believe not only that you were as good as everyone else, but *exactly like them*, too. The coming of mass literacy, he argued, was a singular opportunity to raise public debate, to include everyone in the acts of discrimination and decision-making. Hoggart feared that the opportunity was being squandered in an attempt to get everyone to 'join the club'.

What if you didn't want to be in the club – didn't want to be famous, didn't find film stars particularly impressive? Did it make you a snob? While working at *Heat* I did begin to feel like a snob for wanting the magazine's frames of reference to be more than the four main TV channels and who was in the charts, and especially for wanting it to return to its more critical, or at least fair-minded, origins. After an incident involving my refusal to give a dodgy Robbie Williams album more than two stars, I eventually stopped writing for it and spent a few years as a freelance writer, including several months working on a TV supplement that came with the *Daily Mirror*, titled 'We Love Telly!' (I don't think even Hoggart, an expert at mimicking the demotic tone of popular reading matter, could have come up with that one.)

I did love telly; no problem there. I had a large one at home at the time. Yet here, again, I quickly fell into a position of not being sure whether I was an insufferable snob or whether I just 'had standards'. The problem this time was chavs and pikeys, or rather the keenness of some staff members to use the terms 'chav' and 'pikey' in reference to things and individuals they wished to deride. In the land of telly-loving, everyone was 'just like you and me', unless they were 'pikeys'. Someone would come back to the office from their lunch hour with a Top Shop necklace they feared was 'a bit chavvy'. The wrong font on a feature made the whole page look 'pikey'. Everyone seemed to have 'gyppo' neighbours with ASBOs and rabid dogs who 'brought down the area'. At times it felt like working in a bus shelter, waiting for the bus that never came, with no choice but to overhear an unending drizzle of classist chat.

The *Mirror* was a paper I'd associated since childhood with a tangible sense of decency. As naïve as I may have been, I never expected its staff to feel such a need to define their respectability – their similarity to the paper's 'decent' readers – through the use of such terms. However, this was 2004, and chav-bashing was all the rage. There had by then been four series of *Big Brother*, the second of which had led to Jade Goody becoming infamous for her ignorance and in so doing made it all right to denigrate people regarded as common, because they were thicker than the rest of us.

The belief that an amoral, intellectually stunted and socially isolated 'underclass' of people exists in highly unequal countries such as the US and the UK has proved magnetic to newspaper editors over the last thirty-five years. Significantly, the idea became entrenched in tandem with the coming of mass unemployment, a side-effect of seventies industrial decline accelerated – some would say deliberately – by the aggressive promotion of *laissez-faire* economic and industrial policies on both sides of the Atlantic. In the eighties and nineties the American social scientist Charles Murray wrote extensively about his theory of an 'emerging underclass' of people in both the US and the UK who did not work and seemed immune to the concept – or, perhaps, *his* concept – of respectability.

In an interview in 2005, Murray expressed the opinion that 'these people' – those he has identified as holding an entirely different value system from that of the majority of people – 'have

never been socialised and they simply don't know how to
behave, from sitting still in classrooms to knowing you don't hit
people if you have a problem. It is very difficult, almost impossible, to take these people now and provide basic conditioning.'[2]
(A characteristic feature of such pronouncements is the use of
the phrase 'these people'. 'These people', over there, are not and
cannot ever be people like us.) Although Murray – as you've
probably already worked out – is a confirmed right-winger, the
views he holds are echoed at least in part in Britain by politicians
from across the party spectrum, including the Labour MP Frank
Field, whose desire to uphold a particular vision of working-class
respectability leads him to denigrate those who fall short of
that vision. In 2005 he recommended that households with a
record of anti-social behaviour ought to be sent to live in 'sin
bin' containers under the motorway.[3] With Graham Allen, a
companion on the Labour backbenches, Field is an active advo-
cate of 'early intervention', an approach to government spending
based on the conviction that the poorest and most isolated individuals in their constituencies – Nottingham North and
Birkenhead, respectively – are by definition unlikely to raise
children who can fulfil their personal and economic potential.
In order to remedy this assumed deficit, the state or the voluntary sector is compelled to intervene with behaviour-changing
programmes centred on parenting, employability skills and the
promotion of individual responsibility.

It so happens that Nottingham North and Birkenhead are
among the poorest overall of all 650 parliamentary constituencies, containing very high numbers of long-term unemployed.
Birkenhead has experienced something close to total economic
collapse since the decline of shipbuilding in the seventies:
Cammell Laird shipyard, for instance, employs less than a tenth
of the number who worked there at its peak. Many who do have
well-paid jobs work away – in overseas security, the merchant

navy and the army – due to the dearth of such jobs locally. Nevertheless, the ideology of the times prefers that we characterize – 'pathologize', the professionals would say – the reactions that some individuals have to their social abjection as evidence of their inadequacy as individuals. The 'early intervention' narrative succumbs to the idea that there are jobs available in such places, it's just that the people living there can't do them, and that their children are potentially too damaged to do anything other than repeat a 'cycle of poverty' created by an economic system that allows poverty to persist across decades.

Other public figures and bodies commonly identified with compassionate social action rather than blanket condemnation have fallen into a specious trap of equating poverty with brain damage. In 2008 the now-defunct charity Kids Company, founded by Camila Batmanghelidjh, ran a newspaper and public transport advertising campaign claiming that the brains of neglected and brutalized children were deformed and smaller than normal brains. The Advertising Standards Authority upheld the complaint that the campaign was racist by implication in its use of an image of black teenagers in hooded tops assaulting a well-dressed white man. The charity, which folded overnight in August 2015 amid claims of financial mismanagement, funded a 2008 study by the Institute of Child Health which aimed to show that the brains of some of the children who used its services had been physically changed by their experiences of poverty and neglect. This is somehow well intentioned, yet risks reinforcing every known stereotype of poorer people while flaunting a body of research that has been shown to be variously flawed and biased. For instance, in March 2014 the Early Intervention Foundation invited the American psychiatrist Dr Bruce Perry to address its supporters. During his talk he showed them film clips of a 'neglected' Ukrainian woman crawling on all fours, unable to speak, and a slide purporting to illustrate the difference in size and shape of a 'normal' brain and a 'neglected' brain.[4] What he didn't mention was that the 'neglected' brain had been subject not to the averagely grim experience of familial poverty, but to the sustained and wholly anomalous institutional neglect of being raised in a Romanian orphanage in the era of Ceauşescu.

Shortly afterwards, Perry's claims were refuted by the American philosopher John Bruer, author of *The Myth of the First Three Years* ('the first three years' being the period in which a child's brain is seen by early intervention advocates as being most susceptible to damage through neglect or under-stimulation, and therefore the latest point by which any state-aided remedial programme needs to have commenced). 'We have to avoid this implicit assumption that growing up in poverty damages your brain – irreversibly,' he wrote, while adding that 'there are things that can have a considerable impact on changing whatever it was that occurred earlier in life'.[5] Such things might be a solid, consistently good state education for all children; solid, consistent support for families to earn enough money to prevent their household from swimming in and out of poverty; even, perhaps, solid, consistent state support for individuals throughout their lives, regardless of their circumstances.

Supporters of early intervention are in one way desperate to emphasize their loathing of social inequality, yet at the same time seem just as keen to make exceptions – freaks – of humans caught at the wrong end of the balance of power. Field in particular maintains that he is motivated by wanting the best for his overwhelmingly working-class constituents, while the former Conservative leader Iain Duncan Smith was motivated to set up his think tank, the Centre for Social Justice, after visiting residents of the Easterhouse housing scheme outside Glasgow and convincing himself that family dysfunction was the chief cause of poverty, and not the other way around.

Tabloid journalism for its part has always relied upon the assumption that the institution of the family, of the household, cannot be attacked or defended from ideological positions, simply because it is too fundamental to most people's lives. The left says that home is a dangerous place without state support. The right says that home is where it begins and ends, and the state should have nothing to do with it. There's so much room for diversity that there's little point in making appeals from broad ideological standpoints. This is left to the broadsheets. Instead the red-tops tend to rely on an assumption of 'decency' and 'dignity' on the part of the reader which can be played upon mercilessly when shocking, yet uncommon, cases of abuse and neglect within the family are brought to light.

This playing on the assumption of decency was taken to a frenetic level following the retrieval by police of Shannon Matthews, an eight-year-old girl who went missing from her home on the Moorside estate in Dewsbury, West Yorkshire, in February 2008, and was found hiding under a bed in a relative's house three weeks later. She had been hidden there by her mother in the hope of gaining a large sum of reward money. The case was covered luridly by the red-top papers and the *Daily Mail*, which featured an early exposition by Conservative Party leader David Cameron on Britain's 'broken society' – and more thoughtfully, though with no less detail, by papers such as the *Guardian* and the *Daily Telegraph*. A reporter for the latter, Neil Tweedie, linked the circumstances of Matthews's trauma with the wider socio-cultural hounding of people who live on council estates, most of whom are in work and for whom family life is generally no less stable, if under far greater pressure, than for those in more affluent areas. Other writers, beneath the cloak of respectability supplied by membership of the 'quality' press, found little reason to reflect, still less to try to understand.

Consider this paragraph on the case from a piece by Christina

Patterson, a columnist for the *Independent*, some eighteen months after Karen Matthews, Shannon's mother, was convicted of forced abduction and perverting the course of justice:

> You'd have thought that after seven pregnancies Karen Matthews might just about have worked out the connection between sexual intercourse and the screaming blob in the Morrisons bag, but perhaps someone needed to spell it out. There were, however, 22 agencies involved in supporting Matthews and her extremely complicated family. Short of moving in and wiping the babies' bottoms themselves, it's slightly hard to see what more they could have done to enable her to keep the children she continued, at regular intervals, to spew out.[6]

There is no compassion in evidence here; no attempt is made to grasp the painfully iniquitous conditions in which such cruelty is inflicted. (It came to light during the trial of Karen Matthews and Shannon's stepfather, Craig Meehan, that they had used Morrisons carrier bags on their younger children when there were no nappies in the house.) 'Spew', 'blob', that deliriously sarcastic 'slightly': no sense of the damage done other than the damage reported on. It's more recklessly condemnatory a piece of writing than any published on this case in the *Daily Mail*, a paper more routinely associated with hatred of disorderly lives. The *raison d'être* of the article is to communicate the writer's moral distance from and superiority over the column's subjects, and to agitate similar feelings in the reader rather than encourage any degree of self-examination and reflection on the society we live in. There is something wicked about its glibness, as wicked in its way as the actions being discussed.

Then compare this with an essay about the revelation in 2010 that Jon Venables, one of two ten-year-old boys who were convicted of the torture and murder of the toddler James Bulger after abducting him from a Merseyside shopping centre in 1993, had apparently suffered a breakdown in the years following his release from detention and had repeatedly breached the terms of his parole by returning to the Liverpool area, from which he had been banned for life in return for being supplied with a new identity. He was later charged with possession of pornographic images of children.

'I've been thinking all week about Jon Venables,' begins this diary piece. The author, Andrew O'Hagan, continues in this preoccupied tone:

> Outside, buses pass in quick succession, the passengers reading their newspapers and seeming very sure of something: 'Once Evil, Always Evil,' says the *Mirror*. I keep thinking of Meursault, who didn't know why he did it, who didn't see the size of the damage, who wasn't able to opt for survival, with the sun beating down and explaining nothing.[7]

O'Hagan's article wasn't published in a newspaper but in the *London Review of Books*, a fortnightly literary magazine. But the author of the *Independent* column, a former literary editor, could equally have opted to invoke Meursault, the narrator of Albert Camus's novel *L'Étranger*, in this tale of alienated lives rather than impale her subject on a spike of invective. In the piece on Venables, O'Hagan goes on to confess that he, too, had maltreated and sometimes injured other boys, not to mention cats, while growing up on a housing scheme in the west of Scotland in the seventies. The *Independent* columnist builds high walls of disgust and self-congratulation between herself and the objects of her ire; O'Hagan composes his thoughts with restrained anger as opposed to indignation, because he can see essentially no difference, bar the grace of God, between himself and the murderer Venables. 'I am human, and consider nothing that is human alien to me.'[8]

Michael Donovan, the toothless forty-year-old who was

found to have harboured Shannon Matthews in his flat in Batley
Carr for twenty-four days while most of the West Yorkshire
police force had been seconded to nearby Dewsbury Moor to
look for her, appeared to lack Charles Murray's definition of
'basic conditioning'. He either colluded with or was hood-
winked by his nephew's partner, Karen Matthews, to hide her
daughter. During his trial and subsequent imprisonment the
Sun described Donovan variously as a 'bug-eyed beast', a 'freak'
and an 'oddball'. Ashraf Dadhiwak, a newsagent in Batley Carr
who spoke to a reporter from *The Times* when Shannon was
found, showed greater insight: 'He is a loner who used to come
into the shop with his two daughters. He did not look as if he
was all there, if you know what I mean. He looked ill to me,
certainly not healthy, and had the appearance of someone frightened of something.'[9]

That a forty-year-old British man, in 2008, might have no
teeth, suggests a sickness in the society rather than in the person:
the sickness of being unable or unwilling to give dignity to all
its members. The importance of 'character' was invoked frequently in this debate. Character might mean having something
behind the eyes. It might also mean giving the impression and
revealing the substance of sentience. But it doesn't go anywhere
towards suggesting that any individual who fails to develop
'good character' might have done so in an environment that has
been subject to relentless, and in some ways deliberate, social
and economic damage. In other words, there's a reason why
things like this happen in Dewsbury, Haringey and Doncaster,
and not in Guildford or Weybridge. To seek to understand why
is not to excuse or explain away the acts of individuals, or their
responsibility for them: to borrow a phrase from Zygmunt Bauman, 'Society can (and does) render certain choices less likely to
be taken by humans than others. But no society can completely
deprive humans of choice.'[10] Bauman's point is echoed by the

novelist Hilary Mantel in a 2009 essay about her early career as
a social worker, though the fact that she began her working
life in the seventies suggests that family problems apparently
arising out of social dysfunction did not begin with the onset of
Thatcherism:

> On Manchester high-rise estates I had seen the sour human com-
> edy enacted: dad pickled in alcohol, mum a nervy chain-smoking
> wreck, son a 'young offender' caught up in a spiral of petty crime,
> pregnant daughter banging on the doors of the nearest psychiatric
> unit. Ah, the 70s: what a golden age![11]

In another piece by Mantel, published after of the death of
'baby P', nineteen-month-old Peter Connelly, at the hands of
his father and another man resident at his family home in
Tottenham, north London, the writer maligns her former
colleagues, who wilfully ignored the extent of abuse in their
clients' households because they could not bear to pass judgement on people they assumed to be so unlike them as to have an
entirely different set of values:

> Aspiration was a middle-class trait, they thought; the working
> classes preferred to muddle along. The privileged had their
> ethical standards, but it was unfair to universalise them. The
> workers had their own amusements, bless them, and should be
> allowed their vices.[12]

Much of the coverage warranted by these cases in the national
press focused on the apparent moral bankruptcy of Britain's
workless 'underclass' (though Craig Meehan worked as a fish-
monger at Morrisons and Michael Donovan had worked in IT
before suffering a breakdown). Attempts made by the mainstream British political parties to interpret the needs of 'the
white working class' – regarded as a sort of racial subset in itself,
and characterized by an inherently noble, if socially rather

backward, stoicism – is a classic example of how social stratification leads to the warping and splitting of a common language.

'Once Evil, Always Evil', said the *Mirror*. Bearing in mind
that, as of 2011, 5.1 million working-age adults in Britain had a
functional reading age of eleven or below, it's always possible
that tabloid newspaper text is produced with the express intention of making it understandable to the largest possible number
of people, with an unintended consequence of this being that
overall literacy is never improved by access to this particular
form of reading material.[13] Nobody who's had a minimum of
eleven years' compulsory schooling should want to read the
Daily Star, a paper with minimal useful content which presents
no challenge whatsoever to your intelligence; something must
be going wrong somewhere in society, somewhere in the process of education, in order for that to happen. Most of those who
now read the *Star* would once have read the *Mirror*.

If 'culture is ordinary', as Raymond Williams stated, then
why should parts of it be so alienating to different people who
belong to the same national culture, depending on where they
stand in the social structure? The problem of no longer wanting
to read the *Daily Mirror* – of finding that it no longer in the main
speaks a language that I can relate to – may be a purely personal
one: a trifle in the larger scheme of things. The paper is still the
third most read of the paid-for daily titles, selling around 840,000
copies a day as of October 2015 against the *Daily Mail*'s 1.5 million and the *Sun*'s 1.8 million. Yet it seems to be a title utterly
torn between its past and its present, and perhaps torn between
its desire to appeal to an inquisitive and engaged working-class
audience and a suspicion that such an audience can no longer be
relied upon to be either. My concern is: if you live in a social and
linguistic environment where any broadsheet might as well
be published in Greek – until you acquire the cultural and
educational capital to tune into its, by turns, Olympian and

self-consciously demotic wavelength – how will you now find print news reporting that is not based on the assumption that you are an imbecile? There is a sense that the *Mirror*, perhaps alone among the tabloids, is painfully aware of the difficulty of communicating to a mass audience in such a climate. It's like the child in class who wants to put his hand up without attracting the derision of his friends, and so does it in such a way that he gives the impression that he's showing up the teacher rather than seeking his approval.

The rich and powerful, it appears, get to make the rules; meanwhile, the poor and powerless become convinced that they have no influence whatsoever on how those rules are made, yet invoke them in order to make others feel subordinate. This, you might say, is nothing less than an expression of wilful ignorance in a society that places a punishingly high premium on self-policing, self-regulating behaviour. The French sociologist Loïc Wacquant describes this phenomenon as 'punishing the poor' – the act of actively criminalizing those at the bottom for making bad decisions from a severely limited pool of options, decisions which themselves are influenced by social injustice and the sense of hopelessness it causes.

In their study 'Living Inferiority', Simon Charlesworth, the sociologist Paul Gilfillan and the epidemiologist Richard Wilkinson argue that the quality of social relations in working-class areas has deteriorated with the decline of industry there, and that relationships between atomized, unemployed or insecurely employed men are now characterized by violence or the threat of it.[14] They argue that, during the postwar era of virtually full employment, the dignity of having work gave men better opportunity to develop a sense of fairness, solidarity and honour. I'm only partially convinced that having work – any work – automatically made men's lives better before that point, or that irresponsibility and nihilism among young working-class

men did not exist. The poet and novelist John Burnside testified
to his experience of growing up in the sixties and seventies with
his violent father, a steelworker migrant from Scotland to England: 'He'd discouraged me in everything I wanted to do,
because of the climate of fear he lived in. Trust nobody; don't
aspire above your station; you're poor so you're there to be hit
and if you get used to that, you'll be fine. Just drink some beer
and beat your wife up now and then.'[15]

The authors of 'Living Inferiority' go on to compare the
experience of one of their interviewees, an unemployed man
who becomes anxious and ashamed in the presence of a
middle-class woman, with 'descriptions of ranking behaviour
in chimpanzees'. (I have to say that encountering such a stark
comparison in the sterile confines of an academic paper made
me feel a bit queasy. Setting aside this comparison, there's also
the fact that you can be made to feel ashamed of who you are no
matter what your status, if in a particular situation your face
happens not to fit.) The authors continue: 'When working
people say "having nothing" is stressful, it is because it is linked
to, and emerges from, an experience of being nothing, denied
even self-respect.'[16]

I don't doubt the significance of the authors' work or the
importance of their arguments: it's crucial to be clear when
describing the deleterious effects of social inequality, 'how deep
it goes and what it does to people'. Yet there's a danger in using
such comparisons: the desire to restore someone's humanity by
bearing witness to their suffering might yet end up compounding that suffering. Can you truly be 'denied' self-respect, given
that the prefix 'self-' suggests it has to be generated from within?
If it turns out that you can, isn't having your experience of social
relations compared with that of low-status chimpanzees another
way of denying someone self-respect?

What the authors indisputably make clear is the importance

of the relationship between status, confidence and social capital: each adds to the other as your social esteem improves, and correspondingly diminishes if it declines – through, for example, being made unemployed. A man without work loses status and confidence, which in turn makes social relations with individuals of higher status tense and awkward. The professional woman, unknowingly basking in her high status, projects an aura of confidence which in turn makes social encounters easier. You can almost imagine her taking him to task like a problem child: 'I'm nothing to be scared of! I'm as ordinary as you are. *Honestly.*'

We are no longer an industrial society in which most people are working-class, doing low-skilled jobs. We are increasingly a knowledge-based society in which pay and social esteem are gained chiefly from doing technical and professional jobs for which you need qualifications. No matter that society would cease to function if every manual and service worker simultaneously took the day off: it is easier to pretend that such people and the jobs they do are dispensable, because surely any old chimp could do them. I'm reminded here of school, of my schoolmates' insistence that everything was a fucking joke, that you were bound to get lied to and what was the point? It felt to them that there was no point in protesting overtly, that their intelligence was being insulted. It felt better to pretend the intelligence wasn't there in the first place, or at least to divert it into mischief. They knew what was waiting for them once they got out there. A woman interviewed by the *Guardian* in 2009 gave her opinions on what caused elite universities in places such as Bristol, her home city, to attract and educate so few students from working- and lower-middle-class backgrounds. 'It's partly down to intelligence,' she told the reporter, safe in the knowledge that she was communicating with someone of similar means and therefore a like mind. 'It's not that the universities are necessarily elite. The children of intelligent parents are more likely to be bright and pushy themselves.'[17]

The late Chris Woodhead, a former chief inspector of schools, also believed that middle-class children do better at school because they have 'better genes', and felt that any attempt to raise the attainment of working-class children is unlikely to bear much fruit due to the simple fact that their teachers are working with damaged, dunderheaded goods.[18] The possessors of such opinions, defending personal success by farming out failure to others, reveal a lot about themselves in the process. The ability of the average-but-privileged to regard themselves as 'better' may go some way towards explaining why unprivileged students disproportionately avoid elite universities even when they have the grades to apply for them, a tendency which reinforces the hoarding of cultural and social capital as surely as a thirty-foot wall around Oxford. No wonder it has become a crime to be thick, or more specifically, to be thick and poor at the same time. Just as you can be socially immobile as long as you're middle class, you can be as daft as you like as long as you have confidence.

But was this always the case for people who find their way towards areas of culture that were previously unknown to them? The Northumbrian writer Lee Hall's play *The Pitmen Painters*, like his screenplay for the 2000 film *Billy Elliot*, grew out of a true story, in this case that of the Ashington Group of artist-mineworkers whose paintings came to the attention of critics and collectors in the twenties and thirties. 'The basis of the script was my own experience,' Hall recalled. 'I grew up in an environment that had a suspicion and distrust of any intellectual activity, of any attempt to be objective about life or art. That conservatism, that philistinism within the working class, was at the root of *Billy Elliot*. And it was reinforced by the philistinism of the Thatcherite years.' The pit village's closely knit social structure – though limited like Hoggart's carousel, it bound individuals into the community through its workplace – worked to the miners' advantage. The leanings that some mineworkers had towards seriousness and self-help found expression in their enrolment of tutors from the Workers' Educational Association to teach classes in art appreciation, at which they first encountered the work of Cézanne and Picasso. 'They were aspirational about high art,' insists Hall:

> They not only felt entitled, but felt a duty to take part in the best that life has to offer in terms of art and culture. That 50 years later I could write *Billy Elliot*, a story about the incomprehension of a mining community towards a similar aspirant to high culture, seems to me some sort of index of a political and cultural failure. We've got this divide, that existed for the Ashington miners and is still there today, between what one lot of people seem entitled to in terms of culture and another lot aren't. There's this terrible lie perpetrated by those who sell us this rubbish that only certain people can have access to great culture and the rest don't need to know about it and wouldn't like it if they did.[19]

In the seventies and eighties, following mass redundancies in the heavy industries, thousands of laid-off manual workers returned to education, many of them studying politics and sociology in an attempt to understand how the collective power they had marshalled as union members in the seventies could have dissipated so swiftly. With their new qualifications a significant number became teachers and social workers; others became self-employed, making a living of their own choosing, which didn't necessarily pay any better than their previous work but offered more autonomy. Hoggart, for his part, regarded as 'anathema' the idea that adult education might be offered solely in order to acquire qualifications. As he saw it, you didn't seek to improve yourself solely for the reason that you wanted a better

job – although the broadening of your employment prospects
was a useful by-product of such an activity. You did it because
you wanted to live as full a life as you could, and valued the
sense of calm and relief that came from being quietly absorbed
in a task. The desire to live a full life can of course be included in
the definition of social mobility: not automatically upwards, but
the widening and broadening of mobility in all kinds of spaces,
including the mind. It's an expansion of personal freedom,
which is inevitably restricted by barriers to the fulfilment of
that desire.

What Lee Hall describes as a 'suspicion and distrust of any
intellectual activity' is surely evidence of self-preservation, the
expedient of rejecting something before it rejects you. Get in
there first and you don't get hurt, or so you tell yourself. Yet,
when repeated over generations, suspicion can curdle into a habit,
then a creed, making any attempt to wriggle out of its iron jaw
twice as difficult. The work of Mike Savage and other social
researchers at Manchester University reveals a class-and-cultural
landscape of 'omnivores' and 'refusers'.[20] Those who are better
educated tend to be more confident, and because of that confidence they tend to enjoy a wider range of cultural products.
They enjoy pop *and* classical music, British food *and* foreign cui-
sines, concerts *and* walking, sport *and* art. Just as Bernstein
distinguished between working-class use of only the 'restricted'
language code and middle-class use of both restricted and 'elaborated' code, the well-educated are aware of the divide between
what's perceived as 'high' and 'low' culture, but enjoy and make
use of both. Those who are less well educated tend to have less
confidence. They not only stick to what they know but forcefully reject the value of things they don't know about: for
instance, liking chart music but 'hating' classical music, dislik-
ing 'foreign' foods and so on. In this way there's a link between
the cultural choices of those in the 'dislikes and avoidances'

groups, who tend to be older and have fewer qualifications, and the political choices reflected in voting for the United Kingdom Independence Party, Ukip, perhaps even the British National Party (BNP), or by abstaining. It's another vote of no confidence, if you like: having no confidence, either in oneself or in a socio-cultural-political system dominated by those with confidence coming out of their ears.

The essential cultural divide between the classes, however, is not between specific choices but between how many choices we are permitted, and permit ourselves, to have. I was ignorant of great parts of our cultural and artistic heritage for many years. Ashamed of that ignorance, I took on the role of 'refuser', affecting a lack of interest in the things I didn't know about. *This far, and no further.* Classical music was rubbish, I thought, Shakespeare was nonsense, and travel was overrated. I colluded in perpetuating my own ignorance by denying the value of any aspect of culture from which I felt distanced. To embark on the Sisyphean task of educating oneself into the dominant, posh, culture – of which this book inevitably forms a part – not only requires you to know that it's there in the first place, but also to not feel terror and shame when confronted with its power.

The American writer David Brooks describes highly educated 'bourgeois bohemians', most often working in journalism, academia and the creative industries, as forming part of a new industrialized-world elite.[21] This, he says, is because the accumulation and application of knowledge have become valued over almost all other economic activity: knowledge is a hoardable commodity, like gold or oil, and can be withheld from others who need it but who both lack the means to accumulate it at the same rate and constantly find that they apply it in the 'wrong' way to satisfy this new ruling class.

The point is that education can be both a tool and a shield against the 'symbolic violence' – to use Bourdieu's phrase – of class discrimination. While there will always be working-class jobs that need to be done, there is no reason why the people doing them at any given time should always remain in the working class. It's right to argue, of course, for a high minimum wage and a greater level of respect for those doing jobs disdained by the new elite, but the question is: should they spend their lives doing the same thing in order to fulfil a political need for the existence of a static, immutable – and therefore easy to patronize – working class? In this particular sense, New Labour's social legacy was a positive one: its very pragmatism allowed many working-class individuals to think of themselves differently. They no longer needed to assume the part of a 'heroic', 'downtrodden' mass, because it was assumed that everyone wanted to become middle class.

But therein lies a whole other can of worms. That same Third Way pragmatism which encouraged individuals from all classes to become 'authors of their own lives' came down harshly on anyone who strayed too far from respectability as it was newly defined. You could author your own life as long as it was the right sort of life: one which chimed with socially conservative notions of individual self-reliance and self-betterment, of keeping your head down and your nose clean. During the New Labour years emphasis grew on productivity, on the importance of making a contribution – defined in flatly economic terms – to one's society and community. As in other rich countries, the pursuit of knowledge for its economic and socio-cultural worth rather than for its own sake was encouraged, to the benefit of middle-class people like me. The love of a Labour government for its voters became distinctly conditional.

Savage concludes that 'it still makes sense to see Britain as having three fairly strongly culturally bounded classes, with a large working class', and that the dominance of elite cultural forms, in terms of the resources they attract and the power they confer on the individuals who both use them and make use of them, persists. The difference now is that cultural capital has a value in itself, improving the social capital of those who possess it – particularly among what he calls the 'established middle class', who use their love of culture to amass relationships across a broader spectrum of people and places than those who are less interested in cultural pursuits. The initial results of a mass online questionnaire, 'The Great British Class Survey', developed by Savage and his colleagues and hosted on the BBC website in 2011, seem to back this up.[22] A strong tendency is revealed for the intensely privileged – those rated as part of the 'elite' or the 'established middle class' according to the survey categories – to regard themselves at once as both 'posh' and 'ordinary'. They are aware of their status and yet at the same time are at pains to point out that they 'work hard' for it. To deny the power of cultural and social capital is normal, possibly because if what you 'choose' to do is only the same as what everyone around you also 'chooses' to do, how can you possibly be part of a tiny elite?

This is how privilege becomes truly concentrated – through the systematic denial of the way social and cultural capital works by the very people who are hogging it. Such blanket denial serves to convince members of the middle class that, generation after generation, they have to tighten their grip on the advantages they have because they are always at risk of losing them. This is the logic of the argument that anyone who isn't extraordinarily rich and privileged is part of 'the 99 per cent' and must, therefore, automatically have more in common with the working class than with the elite. All this claim succeeds in doing is to sharpen middle-class elbows and entrench the instinct to hoard social and economic goods that you've convinced yourself are hard won and easily lost. The reality is that, while the middle class has been greatly enlarged in the last two generations by an expansion in white-collar, professional and managerial jobs, it is largely composed of people who have convinced themselves that they are a step away from penury. This involves a remarkable act of middle-class doublethink, based on a simultaneous desire to identify with and to distance oneself from the working class. You have to do a job to pay your bills, therefore you must be working class. You are often overdrawn, therefore you must *definitely* be working class (a common misperception among middle-class people is that working-class people have the same access to favourable lines of credit, such as cheap or free overdrafts, as they do. The reality is quite different.) And yet . . . your child can't go to that school over the road, because, well, the kids are *different* from yours. Your child must have access to the cultural resources you expect and deserve, and which you assume working-class schools, parents and children lack. You must be and yet you *mustn't be* part of the masses. You identify when it suits you.

The fact is that 99 per cent of people do have to do a job in order to pay the bills, but by no means does it put 99 per cent of people, never mind 99 per cent of the jobs they do, in the same boat. Power accrues more fiercely the closer to the top you are, and to deny this fact is an act of what Bourdieu termed 'symbolic violence' towards those with less of it. Those with more power in society include all those who are employed full-time, permanently, in jobs that do not wear them out and kill them early, who are paid above the median (one in every seven working people pays the higher rate of income tax) and who are afforded social status and acceptance on the basis of the work they do.

For the solidly middle class this is hard to admit; still less to accept. This is most readily expressed through estimation of one's place on the income scale. Research on economic inequality and its social ramifications has shown that those near the top of the earnings scale consistently underestimate how well-off they are in comparison to others. In 2009, the TUC created a 'Middlebritainometer' allowing wage-earners to input their income and find out where theirs lay in relation to the average.[23] It showed that richer people believed themselves to be far closer to the average than they really were. Those earning £35,000 a year, which in 2009 put them in the top 20 per cent of UK earners, placed themselves 26 percentage points lower than their actual position.

Assumptions like these predominate in the accounts given to the sociologist Will Atkinson in his 'search for the reflexive worker', a rigorous test of Beck and Bauman's assertion that individuals are now free – or are condemned – to float through life on a bed of their own decisions, no longer hampered by the time-honoured anchors of class and place. Atkinson's extensive interviews with working and middle-class people about their working lives reveal that there is still an overarching class structure which hugely influences, though without wholly determining, individuals' trajectories throughout their education and subsequent career. There remains a strong and structured class bias to how people 'get on', which underpins their decisions to embark on the escalator of economic and social mobility, how far they feel entitled to ascend and, of course, whether they can get on it in the first place.[24] They may not even want to, regarding as insulting and deferential the very idea of climbing a ladder away from their roots towards a supposedly elevated position. More likely, however, is that they have less – far less – confidence in their own intellectual abilities.

Working-class respondents tended to report to Atkinson that they were 'not very academic'; that school had been 'boring', a 'pointless waste of time' and generally irrelevant to the lives they had been raised by their parents to emulate and expect. When they failed to progress in jobs, or kept changing jobs, they felt they had only themselves to blame, yet recognized that an implicit bias towards middle-class models of achievement had put them at a disadvantage at school. Hannah, an administrator from an upper-working-class background, resented the academic focus of the school she went to on the grounds that 'I just got the impression that they just wanted the ones [who] were really bothered or . . . the kids that keep their heads down and do well, which I suppose is what you should do when you're at school but not everybody does.'[25] This often led to their acceptance of routine jobs in adulthood, blaming themselves for not working hard enough or for being 'tearaways' when they should have been studying. By contrast, middle-class interviewees told Atkinson that going to university had been 'a natural progression', and 'normal' in their family and peer group. No one from this group questioned their academic ability, which both reflected and brought about a level of confidence that enabled them to take greater risks – and enjoy greater rewards – in the world of work. A true Bourdieuan, Atkinson values social and cultural capital as being on a par with economic capital: while financial stability is the obvious bedrock from which less tangible resources are acquired, once they have been acquired within a family they tend not to be mislaid in transmission to the next generation. This creates a 'glass floor' for children of middle-class families, which effectively prevents them from falling into the working class even when they do relatively poorly at school.[26]

As for me, I continued to live the dream. I was on the right side of New Labour's rewritten history: a young woman in the first mass cohort of university-goers, who didn't have to pay fees, whose grant paid the rent (even if the extras had to be financed with shifts at Greggs), and whose family's 'white-collar leanings' made it easy for me to adapt to a world in which knowledge, and its hoarding, counted for everything. I soaked up the excess like a cat bathing in cream. While this was happening, it became acceptable to denigrate people who fetched up on the wrong side. The perceived faults of those at the bottom of society have been ever more emphasized as inequality has widened. It's become easier to believe that those at the bottom haven't succeeded in society because they aren't clever enough to do so. As more people have done well at school, not doing well at school looks more like personal failure – neurological failure, even – because 'everyone knows' how to pass exams. If you're at the bottom it's because you either haven't tried to better yourself, or you have tried and were too dim to succeed.

The case of Kids Company – a charity which set out to help the most vulnerable children in society, but whose founder, it has been claimed by staff and clients, created a culture of dependency on cash payments and gifts rather than enabling people to realize their own wishes – is apposite in these conditions. Thanks to the dedicated efforts of journalists, a previously submerged story has come to light of how Camila Batmanghelidjh may have blinded donors, trustees, media and high-level politicians alike with an extraordinarily atomized view of her clients' needs.[27] She talked little about structural failure except in the context of social services, and tended to speak of the poverty endured by her clients as being a result of their parents' inability to care for them, rather than in terms of joblessness and low pay. Kids Company relied on a particular interpretation of neuroscientific arguments to explain why its clients needed help. This suited the agenda of politicians who believed that intervening in the lives of individuals was preferable to, and indeed more politically valuable than, making great efforts to reduce social and economic inequalities.

You ask yourself what this means for society, when the powerlessness of one class in relation to another mutates into a person's power to hinder the progress of others. Nothing is done if not done together; and if we refuse or are unable to work together because the classes have ossified into groups that don't trust each other and don't meet, does that mean an end to progress? The more polarized we become by advantage and its lack – the less 'average' each of us becomes – the more thoughtlessly we will walk into traps of advantage and disadvantage, abundance and poverty, trust and suspicion. This is how the cynics win: by picking apart the unifying threads of culture and society and insisting there are some people who never belonged, who never wanted to belong, in the first place.

7.   Who's Respectable Now?

As you've probably worked out by now, I'm terrible at letting people just be themselves. I remain hidebound by the sort of working-class respectability which wastes time nervously looking around and upwards for approval, long after acquiring as full a complement of middle-class life clichés as it's possible to have. I make a big deal out of all the everyday things I do – from avoiding Tesco's to recycling assiduously – as though the universe depended on my making a statement about them. I'm obsessed with my small children's dietary intake and limiting how much television they watch, even though I know full well that they're already middle class and virtually nothing I do will alter their middle-class trajectories through life. They are learning from me the urge to tinker with the lives of other people who never asked to be tinkered with, who merely ask to gain access to the tools to do things their own way.

On the other hand, I resent the idea of feeling guilty about my own socially mobile route through life, even though I feel guilty about it in practice. It is what it is. I can't help my current class habits any more than I could my original ones. I'm clearly confident to a degree in the middle-class world, because I've shown no desire to lose my accent or, indeed, to change fully the person I started out as being. This can partly be attributed to serendipity: I've always loved words, and it turns out that being useful with words – even when I say them in a Brummie accent – is highly valued in the society we live in. It doesn't pay especially well, but – and I say this with emphasis – that doesn't prevent me from being middle class, or from enjoying a middle-class lifestyle (the frugal version at least, which assigns talismanic qualities to a diet based on porridge, pulses and mackerel, and which makes a very big deal about one's neighbourhood having 'great public transport links'. Once I got to university and discovered lentils, I always knew I'd be able to afford to eat). Without that lapse in my respectability, without that ability to let go, if only slightly, I wouldn't have been able to become a writer, with the irregularity and occasional impecuniousness it entails. The desire for autonomy has always won out over the desire for security, though it's easy to say that when you are confident that the place you're going to gives you the greater chance for both, compared to the place you came from. To borrow a line from the novelist Geoff Dyer: 'Basically from the age of eighteen onwards, in one way or another, I became a member of a sort of leisure class.'[1]

So, since we're all supposed to be middle class now, it must be impossible to be both respectable and working class. To be respectable, in politicians' terminology, is to be 'aspirational', 'hard-working', to 'play by the rules'. Governments spend entire political terms in election-mode panic, with the single object of convincing working-class people that they're middle class and middle-class people that they're working class. That way, everyone is kept on the edge of their seats by the thought that either they'll be rich tomorrow (if the Tories get in) or poor tomorrow (if Labour get in). The political landscape has merged from red-blue-yellow into muddy brown. That's not to say that there are no significant differences between the parties in government; more that none of the parties has any idea how to anticipate the needs of an electorate that no longer acts – if it ever did – as a mass, yet seems still to require the comfort of identifying as one.

The socially immobile majority, who left school at sixteen or before and who have 'worked all their lives', as opposed to

having had 'careers', enjoyed the benefits of working-class affluence for as long as it lasted, which is to say until unemployment
began to rise, first slowly, in the seventies, then drastically, in
the early eighties. The economist Avner Offer notes that inequality increased in part *because* of the growth of further and
higher education, as it increased both the advantages of the well
educated and the disadvantages of those without education;
especially, in his words, 'those older men whose valuable "learning by doing" human capital had become obsolete and who were
too inflexible to retrain'.[2] Films such as *The Full Monty* and
Brassed Off showed working men who were prepared to retrain,
as strippers and children's entertainers respectively, but whose
resilience was tested by the belief that a cruel political trick had
been played on them.

Anyone who failed in the long term to find a job was subject
to this process, with catastrophic effects. Between the mid-
seventies and the mid-nineties, the difference in life expectancy
between the top and bottom social classes grew from 5.5 years to
9.5 years: at the regional extremes, men in Calton, a very poor
ward of central Glasgow, can expect to live to fifty-four; men in
Chelsea, west London, to eighty-two. From the early eighties
onwards, young men found it almost impossible to get regular
work if they'd left school without qualifications. The postwar
rule of thumb, whereby you could leave one job on a Friday and
start another the Monday after, had ceased to operate as unemployment rose following the economic crises of the early seventies.
Around the age of nine I saw the oldest brother of one of my
primary school classmates jump from one YTS placement to
another: one week, he was our classroom assistant; the next, a
labourer for the council replacing the smashed-in window of
our dinner hall. Yet the aimlessness of a life bouncing between
dole and short-term work was to some extent curtailed by the
fact that physically so much more had to be done then than now

in order to survive. The prospect of social ascent was exchanged
for sideways mobility, because the financial security on which
upward mobility depends had collapsed for many people. House
moves – regular and sometimes clandestine if conditions became
too bad or the rent couldn't be met – required similar feats of
exertion, conducted on foot rather than by taxi or in a mate's
van. Nowadays, cannabis, the internet, computer games and the
odd bit of fishing – for its peace and stillness rather than for
food – help to kill time, if not the idea that time is still something that needs to be got rid of, killed.

Once you're near the bottom, there's only so far you can fall.
It is dangerous, not to mention naively hopeful, to think you
can climb easily out of a world from which no one you know
has managed to climb. A distressing series of quotes from young
people in an unidentified 'northern town', in response to questions asked by the Social Exclusion Task Force in 2008 about
their 'aspiration and attainment', reveals a flat landscape scattered with chasms into which they simply assume they will fall.
'I want to be an electrician,' says one, 'but I am going to go to
prison . . . I don't want to. That's just what's going to happen.'
Another shrugs: 'There's no point in trying, because I am no
good at anything.'[3] Others point out the injustice of being told
not to put your postcode on your CV, as it's 'the wrong one'.
Not only that but your teachers seem to have given up or never
cared much in the first place.

There are a number of reasons why you're more likely to hear
a young person in, say, Blackpool or an estate outside Doncaster,
than someone in Bracknell or Tunbridge Wells state that 'there's
no point in trying' because they are 'no good at anything'. It's
part of the baggage of coming from a place that is isolated – or
has become isolated – and has too few decent jobs to go around.
This is where a substandard quality of education, housing and
transport collude to strike down individuals and areas that are

already disadvantaged. The main issues at stake are an under-supply of housing in the south and an under-supply of decent jobs in the north, which effectively makes housing less affordable for people all over the country, but for different reasons according to where you live. Access to decent housing, and the means to pay for it, underpins the basic quality of life for any individual; not only decent in material terms, but decent in how well it is integrated into the social fabric. A political emphasis on home ownership has sought to make those who rent from the council or from housing associations – rather like those who took the bus instead of drove cars under Thatcher – feel ashamed of the way they live. From being the aspirational choice, accessible only to those viewed as sufficiently respectable, social housing has had its worth diminished by negative propaganda.

At the same time, even good housing does little to improve your life – and in many ways can be detrimental to it – if situated in the wrong place, either for your individual circumstances or for the needs and whims of industry. The author James Meek, in a 2014 essay on the politics of housing, noted that social housing policy has travelled in but one direction since 1979, towards the removal of the state from housebuilding and from making rents affordable to those on low incomes.[4] In general economic terms and not just in housing policy, there has been a further trend of managed decline north of Birmingham. There has been no significant effort to rebalance the economy away from London and the South-East towards areas where people may want to stay, because of family ties and good-quality housing, but feel they cannot because there isn't the work to keep them there.

Much interwar and postwar council housing is solid, spacious, with front and back gardens. Such housing, often on the peripheries of large towns and cities, spent much of the eighties and nineties empty, or 'hard to let', due to the disappearance of employment and a downward spiral of low demand and

economic decline. Hull, Nottingham, Leeds and Liverpool, for
instance, are replete with large outer estates, giant Bournvilles
without the linking purpose of a nearby workplace. Those who
kept their jobs moved away to owner-occupied estates; those
who didn't, in many cases, got stuck. The outer wards of Nottingham, containing estates built to house workers at local pits
and textile factories, are among those in the country sending the
fewest young people to university. Most estates are no longer
half-empty but still suffer from geographical isolation and,
increasingly, the effects of Right to Buy combined with those of
Buy to Let, where former council homes are bought by private
landlords who are unconcerned with maintenance or neighbourhood stability. Most council tenants may be in work, but
receive such low wages that they cannot survive without housing benefit.

The geographer Danny Dorling notes that across England as
a whole there are plenty of houses with many spare bedrooms,
but because they tend to be owned privately and inhabited by
the well-off, the government doesn't consider them 'spare' in the
way that they feel free to regard bedrooms in the social sector as
'spare' and therefore liable to be sanctioned.[5] In London, against
an opposing trend elsewhere in the country for once-grand family homes to become nurseries and care homes, mini-mansions
which were converted into flats mid-century are being turned
back into single family homes, with multiple en-suites, live-in
nanny quarters and two-storey basements to house the gym,
wine cellar and cinema.

Dorling, who has been researching housing and demography
for over twenty years, points us to what we already have, rather
than what we could have. He exhorts us to look after what is
already there: a stock of mostly well-proportioned, secure, safe
homes which, if well cared for, have shown themselves to be
capable of housing families for hundreds of years. (Even prefabs,

built to last a maximum of twenty years, have in many cases lasted three times that long.) They just happen to be in the 'wrong' places; places where there is too little work or, for certain people, none at all. The task, then, is not so much to get people into houses that aren't currently there, but to get the availability of housing and the availability of education, jobs and transport matched up so that homes are not made redundant at the same time and on the same scale as people are. Dorling's is a distinctly humanist plea, relating security of shelter to security in other areas of life: financial (earning enough to pay your rent or mortgage, with a bit left over), geographical (living where you would most like to live, rather than where you have to) and emotional (being able to support and be supported by family and neighbours). In Liverpool, where there are 22,000 people on the waiting list for social housing and 11,800 empty homes, it's harder to combine these three aspects than in many other, better-off places. Large areas of housing in the city have been subject to repeated clearances over several decades. The most recent of these waves of disruption was the Pathfinder Housing Market Renewal scheme, New Labour's apparent solution to the fact that house values in many parts of northern England and the Black Country had collapsed.

In towns of waste – marked by the waste of assets, the waste of human potential – it is harder to imagine against all immediate evidence that it's possible to live anything other than a scrabbling, scrappy kind of life. In areas such as east Lancashire and South Yorkshire there have been surges of electoral support for marginal right-wing parties such as the BNP and more recently Ukip. In the mid-2000s, when the BNP looked to be on the verge of a significant electoral breakthrough (as did Ukip in the run-up to the 2015 general election), public figures in the mainstream of political and media life asked why 'the white working class' – the loosely defined yet clod-like mass that was assumed to be supporting this regressive movement en masse – were so dissatisfied with their lot that they would turn to fascism to express their displeasure. At around the same time, the philosopher Julian Baggini's book *Welcome to Everytown* documented an everyday life and language in Rotherham (the South Yorkshire town containing S66, the 'most average' postcode area in England) permeated with casual racism. 'Almost everyone used the word "Paki" . . . as though it were just another adjective, like tall or Italian.'[6] While living in S66 Baggini hears the word used so liberally, and by such a large cross-section of people, that he concludes it is a place where the word has lost its power and can therefore be used without the intention to offend or shock. He extrapolates from this that not everyone who uses the word 'Paki' is necessarily racist; perhaps, even, that to suggest otherwise is itself a slur. Based on my own experiences of hearing that word every day and the contexts in which it was used, it's impossible to agree. Just about everyone knows what that word means; to pretend not to know is to feign ignorance, something which just about everyone is capable of doing.

The closest I've come to identifying a source for this obsessive attachment to the language and symbols of fascism is when reading about *ressentiment*, a curdled, inward-turned but outward-directed form of resentment experienced by individuals near the bottom of social hierarchies. The term was first used by Nietzsche at the end of the nineteenth century, and was later further developed by the moral philosopher Max Scheler, who defined *ressentiment* as a sort of compounded resentment, or resentment-as-martyrdom, the result of being found wanting in a society which promises entitlements to all yet delivers them unequally. The British sociologist Vron Ware, in an essay linking *ressentiment* with the way in which middle-class commentators and gatekeepers (the BBC, for example) unwittingly create 'races' out of classes, notes that Scheler believed 'the condition can entail a kind of pleasure inherent in self-pity or victimhood, and . . . does not necessarily expect or want a remedy'.[7] Were a 'remedy' to present itself to people who regard themselves as victimized – say, in the form of a governing party that promised to prioritize white applicants for social housing – the search for something or someone else to resent would not end.

We live in a society in which it is possible to benefit greatly if you are well educated, socially skilled and adaptable to change. The problem with resentment, born from class anger and low social status, is that it begets stubbornness and a desire to keep things as they are. It's impossible to thrive in a society built on change, however you feel about it, unless you are able and equipped to accept responsibility for shaping your own life in circumstances you have little control over. It's important in this area to make a distinction between stoicism and martyrdom. Both place the inevitability of suffering at the centre of human experience. From the latter viewpoint, joy and contentment are fleeting, whereas pain can be relied upon as a daily torment, so familiar that it becomes a comfort. To be fearful and resentful is a choice; in some cases a structured, reactive one, yes, but not one that goes away with an increased pay packet. It's both a denial of the qualities that lead to dignity and a stab at dignity, and therefore complex and contradictory. In other words, all too human.

Yet it remains the case that public figures – political commentators and politicians among them – try to make a moral cause of working-class individuals having been 'driven' to the far right or Ukip by their experiences of bad housing and unemployment. In the process, the idea that working-class voters – like their middle-class counterparts – in fact made a conscious decision to vote Ukip, or embrace the English Defence League (EDL) and their like, risks getting lost. What's obscured in such arguments, in other words, is the sense that working-class people have agency. For instance, in *Chavs* – an important book which rightly argued against the 'demonization' of working-class people – the political journalist Owen Jones wrote:

> The rise of the far right is a reaction to the marginalization of working-class people . . . Karl Marx once described religion as 'the sigh of the oppressed creature': something similar could be said about the rise of the far right today.[8]

You can detect in Marx's quote, and Jones's apparently approving use of it, a clear sense of the working-class person as noble wretch, driven to shameful acts because he knows no better. What's absent is any suggestion that far-right parties, most notably the BNP, rose to relative prominence from the mid-nineties onwards because people – individuals – voted for them. Implicit in this quote, too, is a sense of automatic cause and effect: that because working-class people are marginalized, they vote for fascists, and if they do so it's because they aren't listened to by more acceptable parties.

It's beyond question that the far-right appeared to 'rise' in the late 2000s, gaining a few dozen council seats and a place in the European Parliament. This grim trend caused a great deal of hand-wringing in public life. A series of BBC 2 films on 'the white working class', delicately titled 'White Season', appeared to exonerate this entirely made-up racial grouping of racism on the basis that they hadn't had enough attention paid to them by BBC 2. So obsessed became the BBC with its desire not to overlook these perceived grievances that it started sending television crews to peripheral council estates in order to look for evidence of racist activity. Researchers for the Joseph Rowntree Foundation reported that tenants on Scholemoor, an interwar estate in Bradford:

had confronted a BBC team who turned up to film a piece on the rise of the BNP on Scholemoor. They requested evidence from the BBC for their claims and when the team was unable to provide any, they escorted the crew from the estate, asking them to carry out proper research before they portrayed Scholemoor as a BNP area in future (the BBC crew has not returned).[9]

A 2011 edition of BBC2's *Newsnight* contained a film on the activities of the EDL, which included a visit to its Chelmsley Wood 'branch'. (Chelmsley Wood had a BNP councillor, George Morgan, between 2006 and 2010.) Yet support for the BNP collapsed between the 2010 general election and the 2012 local elections without the needs or the voices of working-class voters becoming any more central to mainstream political debate. Matthew Goodwin, a psephologist and expert on right-wing electoral politics, notes that fewer than 26,000 votes were cast for the BNP in 2012, compared with more than 240,000 in 2008, with voter share in each ward it contested declining to 8 per cent from over 18 per cent in 2006. This tallies with a rise in support for Ukip, a party which also seeks to conflate respectability with anti-immigration sentiment, yet manages to appear less racist than the BNP.[10]

Voters in Chelmsley Wood replaced Morgan at the earliest opportunity with a representative of the Green Party, yet there has been remarkably little commentary on the tendency of the downtrodden white working class to be driven into the arms of environmentalists. No one ever mentions the legions of well-housed, well-paid people – working class as well as middle class, and by no means always white – who consider themselves superior to others based on their skin colour, or the countless badly housed, badly off people who are no more driven to fascism than they are to veganism.

It's certainly possible to argue that, in spite of their number members of the working class always have been on the margins of political concern. The warped equation of respectability with racism *does* have something to do with class and power. Not that I'm remotely inclined to make excuses for anyone who acts on that equation, consciously or otherwise and regardless of their class position. But is it really the case that people would stop being racist were they to become richer? There are many reasons why people wanted to vote for the BNP until 2010, and any number why Ukip has gained similar popular ascendancy since the former's collapse. It partly comes back to the conviction held by so many of the adults I knew while growing up: that everything's a joke. A cruel, unfunny, dispiriting one, but a joke nonetheless. Politicians, decision-makers, anyone who does things behind your back, they're all in it for themselves and not for you. It's a weak defence, a miserable expression of hurt. Researchers interviewing residents of Castle Vale, a Birmingham council estate close to Chelmsley Wood, on their perceptions of ethnic minorities in Britain 'identified some key recurrent emotional themes: resentment; betrayal; abandonment; loss; defensiveness; nostalgia; unfairness and disempowerment'.[11]

The key word in that statement is 'emotional'. It comes back to that sense of grievance, which the resentful racist points at as something apparently tangible, rather than at a power structure so overarching that it can't be pinpointed accurately. It's the conviction that someone else is having a better life than you, and that they have some secret key – whether it be the colour of their skin, their apparent difference, their ability to manage money and negotiate 'the system' – which ensures that you cannot ever hope to have as good a life as they do. It's easier to blame a person than a thing. Easier to stay in your place and construct a worldview from there than to take a step outside and find out where your real place is in relation to others. Some people are ignorant through circumstances, but others are just cynical, and feign ignorance or revel in it to disguise their basic fear of things that are unfamiliar. How does that get to be the case?

In her book on the British working class, the historian Selina Todd suggests that economic inequality is a primary cause of racism on the part of working-class individuals, and regards current political rhetoric as fuelling anti-immigration sentiment rather than representing a misguided attempt to respond to what is heard by politicians on countless doorsteps. 'In a country where no major party talks of ending economic inequality,' she writes, 'but all talk of the need to control immigration, race has become the only legitimate means by which white working-class people can claim their right to some of the goods and services they help to produce.'[12]

This is a statement that has to be made with great care, and in full awareness of the fact that it suggests that the main political parties actually help to *create* racism, rather than merely fuelling a pre-existing tendency, whether shamelessly or cluelessly, in the chase for votes. While it's certainly the case that economic inequality (almost as much as social inequality) divides people without them necessarily realizing it, to suggest that 'white working-class people' have only the language of race to express their grievances both legitimizes that choice and ignores the fact that people are perfectly capable of nurturing such grievances without the aid of government propaganda. Perhaps it's a personal failing on my part to assume that someone who even remotely considers voting for a far-right party is simply a racist git and needs to be told so, rather than someone whose mind would be changed by constructive engagement with non-racists or by the simple expedient of having more money. I don't know. The experience of growing up in a local culture where casual racism was virulent hardened me somewhat. It also made me quite sure that, while *ressentiment* has a socio-economic root, the point is that it is felt and advanced by

individuals, often those whose sense of existential threat means
that they spend inordinate amounts of time trying to force
people to agree with them. The end result is a local culture in
which – as Baggini found and as I experienced – racist language and expressions of racist thinking are utterly embedded
in everyday exchanges, even among people who are otherwise
'all right'.

Matthew Goodwin, writing about Ukip's potential appeal
among older working-class voters, observed that the real driver
of Ukip support, particularly from former Labour voters, was
'social and cultural', rather than economic. Indeed. Labour's
electoral response to Ukip in the 2014 European elections was to
cast it as a nasty Thatcherite party that would steal your money.
'Such a response is not surprising,' he wrote; 'it is rooted in the
old Marxist belief that support for nationalist parties is driven
by economic insecurity and encouraged by capitalists who
would prefer ethnic over class conflict'.[13] Yet here's a thing: if it's
exposure to capitalism that makes people racist, then surely they
would have been less racist when Britain had its twenty-five-
year social democratic flowering after the war? Not so. Even in
times when working-class people have been more politically
visible, racism has had some sort of expression. Think of the
1958 race riots in Notting Hill, which occurred at a time when
working-class living standards were starting to rise. And
when dockers marched in support of Enoch Powell, in 1968,
working-class people had never been as well paid or found it
as easy to get a job. (Harris Beider, an academic specializing
in issues of community cohesion, notes that opposition to
large-scale immigration has been a majority opinion since 1964,
regardless of who is in power or how well or badly the economy
has been doing.[14])

In 1969 the social worker and journalist Jeremy Seabrook
resided in Blackburn and wrote, in his characteristically revolted

tone, of the way in which local inhabitants obsessed and fanta-
sized about the lives of people from India and Pakistan who had
moved to the town to work the night shifts in the mills. Seabrook's white neighbours were dispossessed people, for sure, but
no more dispossessed than those who'd crossed the world and
left their families to do the shifts that were hardest to fill. The
sheer negative power of what his interviewees say, not in spite of
but *because* of the fact Seabrook has given them a voice – still
shocks. When talking of the new arrivals, it's all about how 'the
Pakistans' dine on Pal dog food (a 'fact' told and retold to
Seabrook with particular relish), and how they don't wash, and
there are seventeen children to a house, and *they* don't wash, and
they shit in the middens, and they get all the social security,
and they get the best houses. It's about respectability and the
apparent absence of it in people whom they've never even spo-
ken to. Seabrook gets his interviewees to pour their hearts out:
hearts which turn out to be dejected and abject, and in many
cases filled with bile. Sitting in the front room of a Blackburn
terrace house, listening to a group of neighbours attempt to
outdo each other in moral indignation, he observes that, once
the group has – finally – exhausted the trope of 'the Pakistans'
sleeping in eaves by the dozen, it is as though they have taken
part in a kind of warped, destructive confessional.[15]

Four decades later, in their deep study of lives and attitudes
on three Norwich council estates, Ben Rogaly and Becky Taylor found similar expressions of fear and loathing among some
residents they interviewed:

> CHARNELLE: If we go over there we get shot. That's what
> annoys me. If we go over their country.
> BT: Like which country?
> KELLY: I don't know. Some country you get shot, don't you?
> 'Cos you're white.

BT: Do you?

CHARNELLE: Yeah. And they come over here and say that
we're racist, and they be racist to us.

BT: Has anyone ever been racist to you?

KELLY: Not that I know of. 'Cos they speak in their language,
don't they? You can't really tell.[16]

There's a risk inherent in recirculating such views: it may well be
the case that Charnelle and Kelly are deliberately winding Taylor
up in the assumption that she will find their statements abhor-
rent. When I was a kid, people – adults and children – would
casually say things like 'Lerr 'em starve', and 'Send 'em all 'ome',
with a sharp snarl-grin, as if to say, *I don't mean it really, well I do
mean it but I haven't thought about it enough to work out whether I mean
it more than I don't.* (I emphasize the word 'casually' to make a
point about the banality and tedium of everyday bigotry: the
way it's expressed without thought. There's nothing casual about
the emotions it expresses.) Also, for some, Charnelle and Kelly's
statements will only provide confirmation of what they already
believe: that working-class people are ignorant racists. The two
young women's definition of belonging is entirely defensive,
pre-emptive even; they don't allow themselves to allow others.
The authors of this study note that you don't have to be white to
be accepted on the estates in question, as long as you 'know and
follow the unwritten rules of living there': that you sound, present yourself and behave exactly like everyone else. This, perhaps,
is the very essence of respectability: a dread of non-conformity.
If someone in your community refuses to conform, why do you
need to bother conforming yourself? It also reveals how subject-
ive, and therefore how slippery, the notion of 'being respectable'
is. In order to stay respectable, you have to stay within the
boundaries of a community – social or geographical – in which
your version of respectability counts. Staying respectable might

mean speaking in a way that sounds 'proper' in the context of local speech patterns, but which would sound common outside of them. Similarly, having 'self-respect' could mean being a bit tasty with your fists in one area, but being reserved and solicitous in another. If you leave that community, such a carefully constructed way of being might not work, and then where would that leave you?[17]

There is a way in which people who are already isolated persistently and repeatedly refuse opportunities to become less so. This compounding response to isolation is a symptom of shame and underconfidence, which may or may not be symptoms of the rejection and humiliation brought about by social stratification. If you feel out of sorts in a group which itself has learned that it is cast out, then where do you go? One way of coping – possibly the worst way of coping, both in individual and social terms – is to retreat inside yourself, to turn away from others. The Labour Party has in its clumsy way tacitly endorsed this strategy in its periodic attempts to address the 'social and cultural reasons' for Labour's unpopularity among some working-class voters. A review of its policies conducted by Jon Cruddas, MP for Dagenham on the eastern outskirts of London, between the 2010 and 2015 general elections periodically returned to a theme of working-class conservatism and what middle-class, instinctively liberal Labour politicians and activists are meant to think and do about it. Maurice Glasman, a Labour peer and reader in political theory at London Metropolitan University, waded in and out of arguments for limiting – and in one interview stopping – immigration to Britain on the grounds that British citizens deserved to feel as though their rights as workers were more important than those of workers from elsewhere. (Example quote: 'Britain is not an outpost of the UN. We have to put the people in this country first.'[18])

In 2011 Glasman announced that Labour would not be able

truly to connect with lost or disgruntled working-class voters
unless it were to be seen 'reaching out' to the racist, xenophobic
English Defence League. At around the same time, Glasman and
Cruddas developed a working formula for their party's future
appeal to working-class voters based on 'family, faith and flag'.
Cruddas, from a working-class Catholic family, framed his ideas
around Catholic social teaching and liberation theology, which
taken together emphasize mutuality, commitment and social
continuity. Glasman, for his part, had worked with immigrants
from South America, West Africa and Eastern Europe at the
East London Communities Organisation (TELCO), through
which he developed and led the London Citizens campaign to
improve wages and conditions for workers in the East End of
London. Crucially, given the irony of his later pronouncements,
London Citizens also campaigned to formalize the status of
illegal immigrants.

   To me, it seems as though the only way Glasman could have
followed his progressive work with London Citizens with such
a grimly conservative line on immigration is by mentally separat-
ing the working-class people he worked with at TELCO and
the working-class people 'out there' whom Labour needed to
'win back' from the BNP and Ukip. The former must have
appeared to him as organized, active and representing the future
of cities such as London; the latter, meanwhile, were bewil-
dered, atomized victims in places where progressive thinking
could not reach, so there was no alternative but to treat them as
separate entities. My impression is that Glasman knew plenty of
people in the first group, but did not know any in the second.
In the run-up to the 2015 general election, Labour's then leader,
Ed Miliband, saw the problems inherent in this approach and
attempted to marry the two by employing Arnie Graf, an
American community organizer, as an adviser. Once the election was over, Graf wrote an article relating how Labour's

central staff had found it impossible to find a worker on the minimum wage to speak to Miliband for a press call, because none
of them knew any. Which kind of says it all.

In August 2011 a series of riots erupted in several British towns
and cities, sparked off by a north London demonstration protesting against the death of a local man, Mark Duggan, at the
hands of the police. In their unfocused way they bore greater
resemblance to the spate of riots on peripheral council estates in
1991 and 1992, which seem to have slipped from the collective
memory more quickly than those in Brixton, Toxteth and
Handsworth in the eighties. In Birmingham, another young
man, Haroon Jahan, died during the 2011 disturbances. His
father, Tariq Jahan, made a public appeal for calm on the streets
of Winson Green, the inner suburb in which he and his family
lived. During and after the riots, members of the government
stated that places such as Winson Green and Tottenham, where
the rioting was concentrated, represented evidence of a 'broken
Britain', in which the social fabric had decayed due to the collective moral laxity of their residents. Jahan commented
afterwards: 'I don't see a broken society. I see a minority of
people who took advantage of the country when the country
was in crisis. They didn't think of the country and only thought
about themselves, their own personal greed and satisfaction.'[19]

Two years after the riots, a Channel 4 documentary series was
made about James Turner Street in Winson Green, its participants giving permission on the basis that they were to be
depicted as members of a strong, mutually supportive community. The programmes that resulted, shown under the title
Benefits Street, seemed designed not to highlight such a community, but instead tacitly to encourage its viewers to denounce the
welfare state and to insult the people who'd agreed to be filmed.
A social media hashtag flashed up thirty seconds before each

advertisement break, with the implicit instruction that viewers express the first thoughts that came into their heads. Selective, choppy editing robbed viewers of the chance to see the participants' lives depicted in any full and rounded way: many individual scenes lasted under a minute and often comprised exchanges that, while seemingly not staged, were clearly influenced by the presence of cameras. The point of the series, Channel 4 maintained, was to initiate debate on the subject of poverty and benefits dependency in Britain: handily enough for a government which, as *Benefits Street* was being broadcast in January 2014, was engaged in a systematic propaganda war against people in poverty. In the programme, the political and creative media elite looked united in their efforts to reinforce class divisions based on suspicion and hatred of those who don't 'do' respectability in the way they ought to. Yet few people in the creative media would consider themselves to be doing the dirty work of an aggressively right-wing government: *Benefits Street* was, rather, an example of unwitting collusion based on shared degrees of privilege and ignorance. In these hands the appearance of class mutates but the effects stay the same.

What does all of this mean for the notion of 'respectability' today? The essential problem is that, increasingly, we are born into geographical areas which ever more closely map a sharp social and economic hierarchy. In Britain, far more so than in other European countries, if you are born poor, in a poor area, the chances are that you will remain poor or close to it for the rest of your life.[20] If you're born rich, in a rich area, the likelihood is that you will find a way – or will have ways come to you – to stay rich and socially privileged throughout your life, and that your children will do the same. Advantage is hoarded by privileged people remaining in close proximity to those who are similarly privileged; likewise, its lack. There is a subtle, collusive process that is engaged in by both left and right to maintain the solidity of this structure. (Anyone would think class divisions are needed in order to maintain the sanctity of the political spectrum.)

Most people's lives are sustained and at times improved through the application of large doses of pragmatism, both at an individual and a political level. One clear example of this is home ownership. The majority culture in Britain favours owning your own home, even though it has become less, not more common to do so. Many who favour renting, because of the flexibility it offers, eventually make the decision to buy a home if they can afford it simply because private renting in Britain is expensive, inconvenient and legally biased towards landlords as opposed to tenants. Some council tenants who believe that, in an ideal world, the Right to Buy should not exist have nevertheless bought their homes because they recognize the stability and the possibility of economic advancement it brings.

In my experience, 'getting on' has meant a constant assessment of what is important and what isn't, in order to avoid having to swallow a lot of bullshit related to notions of consumption and distinction. What's regarded as such depends on the individual, though to me it has always meant trying to work out what is necessary to a comfortable lifestyle – now that I can afford one – and what is simply 'the done thing' to own. Bullshit to one may mean material goods; stocks and shares; Range Rovers (or Volvos if you're concerned with really fitting the bill). To another it may mean the overarching need to be pleasant all the time – not direct in speech, but endlessly circular. To yet another it may mean subsuming one's natural interests in favour of studying subjects that help you to get on in life: doing maths and physics, for instance, when you'd rather do art. (The middle-class version of this is studying medicine or law when you'd rather do art, not because it will help you get on, but because you, or perhaps more accurately your family and friends, want you to stay just where you are.) It is when people don't care either way about conforming to the middle-class version of 'respectable', and simply want comfort and security for themselves and their families, that promoters of social-mobility-as-creed start to worry. There's a degree to which this applies to both sides of the political divide, but for different reasons.

In this sense recognition is synonymous with acceptance. Social recognition is available to the socially mobile only if they 'do' social mobility the right way. To those on the right who regard social mobility as a good thing in itself, there is almost no point in undertaking upward mobility if it doesn't involve taking out a wholesale subscription to mainstream values, which often, though not always, means the dominant middle-class set of values. I think here of Richard's grandparents, whose identities were so bound up with feeling pride in dominant institutions such as the police and the royal family that they renounced the Labour Party on this principle. This set of values places overarching emphasis on self-reliance, careful planning and above all a version of self-respect which puts often severe, though voluntary, restraints on public and private conduct.

Coming from the left is the latent fear that social mobility deadens revolutionary impulses, and for that reason should either be discouraged or denied. For others who regard the concept of social mobility more sceptically – arguing that it is a byword for deference, class treachery and individualism – there is still a noticeable desire to corral people into middle-class homogeneity. Those who disdain social mobility on the grounds that 'there aren't enough middle-class jobs to go round' tend to overlook the fact that most middle-class people today had working-class grandparents, if not parents, and that as great a degree of employment creation is now taking place in highly specialized, highly skilled professions as in routine jobs[21]. It's of a piece with the denial of privilege that goes with pretending an experienced teacher is as equally a part of 'the 99 per cent' as an agency worker in a chicken factory. It also has striking parallels with the regular – generally right-wing – complaint that 'too many people' go to university, and that the admission of half a million young people per year into higher education has only diluted 'standards'. They've been saying that since the days of Kingsley Amis, who, as an English lecturer at Swansea in 1960, complained that, given the perceived quality of his current students, 'MORE WILL MEAN WORSE'.[22]

The most famous, and possibly symbolic, representatives of New Labour's extreme pragmatism were Oasis, the most successful British band of the nineties. Shortly after the 1997 general election, their singer Noel Gallagher attended a now-infamous drinks party at Downing Street, having his photo taken, glass of champagne in hand, engaged in conversation with Tony Blair. Oasis were recognizably and thoroughly working class in presentation and outlook; they were who they were. They renounced book-reading – which of course wound up any working-class person who actually enjoyed reading books – and in their earlier songs concerned themselves exclusively with escape, glamour and the prospect of future affluence. Their most potent lyrical statements, written by Gallagher while on the dole in his native Manchester, were about the power of dreams. At their commercial peak in the mid-nineties Oasis were like a formative friend, a mentor from back home, who gives voice to your dreams and cheers you on, but who eventually you reluctantly leave behind because they never quite appreciated that there's all sorts of versions of being a rock'n'roll star. There's more than one dream to live.

Gallagher's lyrics dealt in vast platitudes that make everyone feel united, such as being free to do what you want, needing each other, believing in one another, wanting to fly, feeling 'supersonic'. But they refused to go further than that. It's not that they couldn't explain in greater detail and with greater wit the iniquities of their upbringing and their profound desperation to escape it. They just didn't want to, because they thought it would be too much of a bummer for everyone. They had the ambition, luck and doggedness to get out, only to spend the next fifteen years banging their heads, equally doggedly, against an invisible ceiling. Oasis were, in fact, the definition of doggedness: a Beatles tribute act who could never understand that what made the Beatles extraordinary was the application of their intelligence and curiosity to a form which their elders regarded as worthless. One of their most plaintive expressions of something or other came in the song 'Live Forever', which rhymes 'pain' with 'rain' but never quite gets to the point of what it is that's so painful. Existence or trapped wind, I'm never quite sure.

Compare the cereal-packet wisdom of Noel Gallagher with the compassionate witness borne by one of his heroes, a 23-year-old Paul McCartney, in songs such as 'Eleanor Rigby'. Or Morrissey, in his songs 'Late Night, Maudlin Street' and 'Break Up the Family', for whom Manchester was also a place that had to be got away from (for better or worse), and who can only reflect on what's good about the present by comparing it to the past. I'm not saying Oasis didn't possess or create something of value. They genuinely did bring people together, or at least produced a sense that people could be brought together, across divides, for the middle class and working class to put aside their vested interests and get Labour elected, or at least to try to prevent those southern poshoes Blur from getting to number one. But they remind me of the frustration felt by Jarvis Cocker at the emptiness of drug-induced fraternity in Pulp's 'Sorted for Es and Whizz', and Hoggart's personality-evading pulp fiction writers in the fifties.[23] The writer and historian of teenage culture, Jon Savage, notes that 'Oasis were so big that they could have done anything they wanted to – they could have done incredible things with their position, but they chose to put themselves in a box and be a malign influence.'[24] Oasis said 'no' to everything except the money, the instrument of physical escape. Once they had feathered their nest they saw no reason to leave it.

What Oasis did have going for them was their unselfconscious commitment to the idea of pop music bringing people together to forget about their problems, rather than giving people licence to obsess over them. In spite of – or perhaps because of – his shortcomings as the lyrical representative of the revolutionary vanguard, Noel Gallagher has for over twenty years given interviews that show him to be clever, perceptive and extremely funny, the personification of Hoggart's 'mickey-taking dissident'. For him pop music is a vehicle for momentary escape rather than permanent transcendence: a totally working-class viewpoint which for all its conservatism acknowledges the fact that depression is the greatest enemy of action. Might as well feel uplifted – and uplifted in solidarity, however fluffy and apparently apolitical such solidarity was – for three minutes than be brought down in perpetuity. Oasis updated the pub singalong, where everyone felt warm towards each other: got, in Hoggart's remembered phrase, 'real friendly' for the night.[25]

In *The Uses of Literacy*, Hoggart barely reflects on pop music, largely because he was writing at its birth. He talks in detail about the central role of music in the self-created cultural life of working-class urbanites, but when the book was published in 1957 Cliff Richard had yet to release a single and Elvis was a brand-new star. Yet you sense an in-built distaste for the idea of pop-songwriting factories, a distaste so profound that he would have had his work cut out to analyse them effectively.

He regarded jukeboxes – which played imported American 7-inches – and milk bars, erroneously, as things which had the potential to fundamentally destroy the creative capacities of working-class adolescents. Yet it's clear that from the fifties onwards, pop music both reflected and helped to shape the sense of liberation from anxiety and grind that had characterized working-class life before the war. Hoggart didn't foresee that this meant pop stars could become allies with their fans, as much as idols. Self-actualization is a project unknown to the working-class subjects of his book.

Yet all the colourful persuasiveness of the things that have been offered to you drains away once you encounter life's goods in their unaffected, truthful form. It's tempting to put quotes around 'truthful', as it sounds such a moral word; something Hoggart himself may have hesitated at before thinking to himself, No, there *is* a difference between a cynical mass culture and the kind of culture we can produce if we're encouraged to do it ourselves, and it has to be measured and confronted if we're to get anywhere at all. You can be raised and somehow nourish yourself on a diet of 'sweet-cakes', to use his own term to describe the unfulfilling rush gained from the indiscriminate consumption of popular culture. But you've got to know what it is you're getting out of it.

Hoggart looked at the culture around him and saw that, for instance, club singers, and the songs they sang, revealed an instinctive sympathy with their audience.[26] In his account, the club singer – along with circuit comedians and the blind piano-player whose hand reaches 'out to the spot where he knew they put his pint' – was one of the figures at the centre of working-class social life. He termed it the 'big dipper' style of singing, or 'the verbal equivalent of rock-making, where the sweet and sticky mass is pulled to surprising lengths and pounded; there is a pause in which each emotional phrase is completed, before the great rise to the next and over the top'. The style arose, he wrote, from 'the need to draw every ounce of sentiment from the swing of the rhythm' in order to communicate fully with the audience. 'The result,' he suggested, 'is something like this:

> *You are-er the only one-er for me-er*
> *No one else-er can share a dream-er with me-er*
> (pause with trills from the piano leading to the next great sweep)
> *Some folks-er may say-er . . .*'[27]

Céline Dion, Whitney Houston, Mariah Carey and latterly Beyoncé and Rihanna, are the current patron saints of amateur singers, but they are only the latest in a long line of melismatic entertainers. In 2012, the artist Grayson Perry visited a social club in Sunderland as part of his research for *The Vanity of Small Differences*, his ambitious series of tapestries on taste and class. In the Channel 4 series that documented this groundwork we see Perry watching a tearful woman in late middle age holding on – tenaciously, but tenderly – to the arm of a young club singer while he performs a ballad she has requested. It turned out that the singer's mother had died not so long ago, and the woman holding on to his arm had been one of her best friends. Comparing the scene with a visit to the opera, Perry later wonders, 'Do you cry a more vintage kind of tears at Glyndebourne?'

Hoggart knew from his close studies of social club 'turns' and the postwar proto-celebrity magazines such as *Picture Post* that sometimes the urgency to communicate overtakes the message being conveyed. If you walk around with a thousand thoughts shuttling in your head, there are only going to be so many that make it out into the world. You have to admire the person who conveys the impression that his fleeting notions have formed an orderly queue in his mind, ready to slip out one at a time like a tablet of bubblegum from a dispenser. That's not how things work generally. Such restraint has to be worked at and practised, consciously or not. I'm not saying I wouldn't in all probability have cringed had I been at that club, and tried to align myself with the dignity of the singer, who manages to carry on his performance while being physically hampered by his fan. But Perry is right to question a hierarchy of emotional display which states that it is more dignified to be seen weeping openly – if silently – at the opera than it is simultaneously to sing, cry and seek physical affirmation in a social club.

Hoggart's fellow traveller, the novelist and critic D. J. Taylor, believes that 'mass culture' does have the power to 'steal us from the sense of who we are', but nevertheless is impressed, and not altogether surprised, when innovation springs from the ground upwards and 'scares the taste-formers stiff'.[28] In my early teens a band came along that seemed to represent this apparently contradictory desire both to destroy the weapons of middle-class soft power and to seize them for their own use. The Manic Street Preachers were four boys from South Wales, self-evidently from respectable working-class backgrounds, desperate to display their intelligence, honed and politicized against a background of social abjection. They looked incredibly provincial, wearing white jeans and terrible make-up, and must have known it, but then they would go on Radio 1 and talk about French philosophy. (First-generation university-goers, obviously.) It was something about beating the complacent middle classes at their own game, wiping the bloody floor with them. You'd have to come from that world for such a contradictory position to make any sense. You have to know what it's like to be both bound by respectability and want desperately to reject it; you have to love your parents and the security they gave you – at base, to respect their respectability – to want to flout the rules of respectability altogether. Theirs was a position I understood. It was reflected in something they once said about 'crusties', or alternative types, whatever you want to call them, hating men in suits because wearing a suit meant you were The Man. Ah, said the Manics, but Nye Bevan wore a suit and he created the NHS. In order to be truly radical, to really stick it to The Man, did that mean you had to hate the NHS and the working-class, suit-wearing Welshman who brought it into being?

What I loved – and still love – about the band was that they hated posers: they hated figures who attacked the present order of things from a position of safety and complacency. This included those who tried to get on the side of working-class people by pretending to loathe anything to do with common decency, good presentation or being articulate. I only loved them more when, at one Glastonbury festival, they had a row with the salt-of-the-earth songwriter Billy Bragg about having requested the use of their own, reasonably sanitary, portable toilet backstage. Bragg believed that as socialists they should be happy to use the same toilets as everyone else. The Manics told him, in effect, to stop being so sodding pious; their bass player, Nicky Wire, declared that he 'wouldn't let him piss in my toilet for all the money in the world'. They were perfectly aware that not wanting to share the indignity of fetid festival toilets left them wide open to being called hypocrites, but they had the means to avoid the discomfort and were buggered if they were going to deny themselves. The Manics also quoted Arthur Scargill, the combative mineworkers' leader, on the sleeve of one of their singles: 'My father still reads the dictionary every day. He says that your life depends on your power to master words.' They took this quote as an article of faith, echoing it in the improbable chorus to 'Faster', their 1994 Top 20 hit, which name-checked Norman Mailer, Sylvia Plath and Harold Pinter. If you were from a certain kind of world, to grow up in the eighties and nineties and succeed in learning how to spell represented another victory over dark forces.

Any residual belief that pop music still represents a merito-cratic route for talent to prevail can't, alas, be sustained given the current landscape. The music journalist Simon Price highlighted the fact that, at one point in 2011, seven of the top ten British albums were by performers who had been privately educated. Countless major British artists, including Florence Welch of Florence and the Machine (Alleyn's School), Lily Allen (Bedales), Frank Turner (an old Etonian), Mumford and Sons (King's College School) and Chris Martin of Coldplay (Sherborne), attended elite public schools, apparently showing that the lim-ited meritocracy of the grammar, technical and art schools has been reversed by an expression of cast-iron confidence incul-cated through private education.

Neil Tennant of the Pet Shop Boys has his own theory of how pop music culture has changed to reflect the changing times:

> Think about the albums that changed things in the sixties: *Ser-geant Pepper* is not a 'personal' album . . . the only ideology nowadays is pure individualism expressed through sentimental-ity. That means we've lost the sense of the communal that pop used to express. The shared experiences. Instead, pop music is wrapped up in itself – about Me, not about Us, which is the way it should be.[29]

In this context, when an act comes along that appears to be somewhat less posh – particularly a guitar band, as 'urban' acts such as Professor Green and Dizzee Rascal are assumed (cor-rectly in those cases) to have come from the working class – it tends to get seized upon as proof of an 'authentic' working-class voice reasserting itself in its rightful field.

Britain's current biggest-selling guitar band, the Arctic Mon-keys, are a case in point. Though their singer, Alex Turner, has never denied being the child of two schoolteachers, he has built a durable image of proletarian obstinacy and 'authenticity' based on the fact that he and his band members come from the working-to-lower-middle-class Sheffield suburb of High Green. His lyrics on early albums – recorded while the band were still in their teens – documented rough, marginal lives and were delivered in a grating Sheffield accent. Their first album – titled *Whatever People Say I Am, That's What I'm Not*, a quote taken from Sillitoe's *Saturday Night and Sunday Morning* – showed on its cover a rough-looking bloke with a cigarette flopping narkily from the side of his mouth. (An aside to this: it was revealed in 2014 that between 2005 and 2009 the four band members invested £1.1 million of their collective earnings in Liberty, an offshore tax shelter also used by Sir Michael Caine and the singer-songwriters George Michael and Katie Melua.[30]) If there's ever been a band for whom the phrase 'trying too hard' was invented, it's the Arctic Monkeys. The rank fishiness of their proletarian stance was epitomized by their refusal to perform on *Top of the Pops*, a programme which generations of working-class children, among them the future stars Johnny Marr and Boy George, dreamed of appearing on one day. Numerous artists, from the dancer Michael Clark to singers Ian McCulloch and Neil Tennant, are quoted as saying that watching David Bowie's 1972 *Top of the Pops* appearance, when he flung his arm around guitarist Mick Ronson as they sang the chorus to 'Starman', changed their lives. You could hardly keep Oasis – brought up under Thatcher – off *Top of the Pops*; the Arctic Monkeys, a generation younger, thought they were better than that. Better than us.

Conclusion – Up the Hill Backwards

In 2015 a visit to Aldi is not, for me at least, the same experience as it was in 1993. I no longer struggle back on the bus with tins of peaches in a handle-less cardboard box. Now I come armed with my jute bag, a reliably sturdy vessel for bottles of cold-pressed rapeseed oil and Pinot Noir. Aldi operates a two-tier system, reflecting the disparate degrees of economic and cultural capital of its customers. You can still get your staples cheaper than anywhere else, with an added layer of quotidian luxuries on sale for members of the urban middle class who love a bargain but wouldn't starve if they couldn't go there. Because my class struggle is over, I can go to Aldi for fun, for additional delight in a life already full of it.

Here's another memory. At the end of my first year of secondary school, I idolized – from a safe distance – a girl in the fifth year because she genuinely looked and behaved differently from all the other girls I knew. Her gait, her style of dressing, her way of speaking and of observing the world were not mediated by the belief that without boys' approval she was nothing. She was simply herself: a sixteen-year-old who knew her own mind and – it seemed to me – faced with confidence the adult world and her impending release into it. Actually, she was a Mod: a little less rare in the late eighties than now, but rare enough where we lived, especially for young teenage girls. She wore jeans and boots, had a part-shaved, part-feathered soul-girl hairdo and, even better from my point of view, didn't wear any make-up. I thought that was brilliant: all that time saved for herself and not wasted on boys. What I loved about her – or, more likely, the idea of her – is that she was with us but she had her own world, her own frames of reference, which weren't just taken from everyone else. It was a lot to do with her sense of self-respect, which I can only assume was sufficiently in tune with what I regarded as respectable. Once I reached her age, tee-tering on the steps of the sixth-form college, I convinced myself that I was now fully free, able to pick and choose from the abun-dance of opportunities that had suddenly emerged. Through a combination of education and good luck, the fog had lifted. Or had it? The difference between me and her was that she felt able to be herself while staying in the same physical space of the estate, whereas I felt able to assert myself only by leaving it. Per-haps it was because Mods were working class: it was a self-made movement. She felt safe to be who she was where she was. I didn't. We can argue the toss over which of her cultural habits she'd chosen freely and which were still broadly in the everyday stream of things for people of her class and time, but together they constituted for her the makings of 'a good life'. I still think about her now, even though I barely knew her.

There's obviously some way to get from *there* to *here*, isn't there? I knew all about the place I wanted to get away from – the place I inhabited in mind and body – but very little about where it would require getting to in order to get away. Then it dawns on you that the wall in the head is something you're unlikely to escape fully without erasing your mind altogether. I've tried to draw some sort of picture of how this is built from outside and within, and how utterly strong is its force in society because it is essentially what our society is made from: real walls bolstered by figurative ones, physical dimensions matched by psychic ones. By default I've dwelt here on institutions: the library, the school and the university, and their role in moulding my charac-ter as surely as the places I've lived in.

Libraries were, and are, the haven: the public institutions

whose walls were porous and whose doors were always open. Libraries were where I went to, and where I still go to, in order to learn without prejudice. Schools – well, schools are a double-edged sword. The schools I went to arguably taught me more about injustice than I've experienced before or since. In many ways they were experiments in social justice which, for a lot of the people who went to them, succeeded only in reinforcing unfairness. But there are *schools* – buildings containing all the elements required to replicate the class system in miniature – and there is *school*, an institutional ideal dedicated to encouraging a love of learning and to which I'm eternally grateful.

Universities are the places where I dwell now: the place I always wanted to get to, ever since seeing that girl with the totemic carton of Ribena on the Warwick University campus. I spend a lot of time on university campuses and in university libraries: always with my swipe-card, barred without it. Warwick was known as a 'plate-glass' university, based on the architectural style of the sixties wave of 'new' universities. The term 'plate glass' is apposite: you can squash your nose up against it or run at it, full pelt, not realizing there's anything coming between you and a concussed head. It feels as though I spent my early years squashing my nose against plate-glass walls – cupping my ear to them, too – then made a run for them. In the invisible wall there was an invisible door just wide enough to bolt through, which, on looking back, appeared never to have been there. I am close to forty now and it's only in the very recent past that I've been able to visit the place I came from, the place that was once my home, without believing it to be some sort of vortex that had to be outrun, outwitted. (There's that fear again of falling back, the anxious root of respectability.) In this, remember, I'm a bit behind Richard Hoggart: he put the age at which the socially uprooted person might once again be able to 'smile at his father with his whole face' at around twenty-five.

I don't pay money for my university privileges, paying instead with social and cultural capital. University got me to a place where I could make use of who I knew as well as what I knew. Over the years I've accrued advantages like loyalty points, the bonuses getting bigger every time I've moved a notch up the social ladder. That is how I've found it to work. Filling in 'The Great British Class Survey' on the BBC's website in 2011, I was entirely unsurprised to discover that I was now part of the 'established middle class': gregarious, keen on the arts, immersed in culture at all levels yet part of an emerging cultural elite that is somehow able to make social and economic gains from knowing the 'right' kinds of people and things.

Both Hoggart and Raymond Williams warned that this might happen. Changes in the pitch, tone and content of our popular media, most notably in mass-market magazines and in television, over the last few decades mean that we stand to learn much less from the media that 'naturally' surrounds us – that is, the magazines, papers, music and broadcasting channels to which we gravitate according to our class – than we once might have done. These changes have the potential to cement us culturally within our class, leading to an ever-greater gap between what is out there and what we believe is 'for us'. Reinforcing this is the constant – if often unconscious – process of social sorting which takes place in our education system, broadly funnelling middle-class pupils towards academic subjects, followed by university and the professions, and working-class pupils towards poorly valued vocational courses and ancillary jobs.

Reading tabloids gave me literacy, but they couldn't give me everything I would need to have a different life, not in a society that has different kinds of newspaper for different social classes. The dignity inherent in choosing to take the *Mirror* and not the

Sun had no value outside the parameters of working-class respectability. (There is another form of respect – respect for the dead – which rightly fuels the continued boycott of the *Sun* in Liverpool following its coverage of the Hillsborough football disaster in April 1989.) I found out about broadsheets and went to them for greater depth of information, but also through them gained a degree of cultural leverage that was needed for life outside those parameters. There was a new language that needed to be learned if I was to function in a new world of knowledge. There were new tastes that had to be acquired: for olives, for ground coffee, for continental travel. You learn about all of this in the big papers. You need to know the names of theatre directors as well as football managers, just as you need to learn that Farrow and Ball aren't a comedy double-act.

Equally, there is a world which remains unknown to those schooled only in the broadsheet lexicon of taste and distinction. Heron Foods; Home Bargains; BrightHouse – do you visit these? These days, every couple of weeks I go back to the precinct where I spent the mornings as a child with my mum and grandad picking up the egg custards and the betting-shop pencils. (These mornings stand out in my memory as what the sociologist Les Back has called 'luminous fragments of class feeling'.[1]) We take my son to the soft-play room and café, and when he puts the vinegar on his chips, just as I used to, and my mother blows them cool for him, just as she did for me, the years between us collapse and I'm as happy as it's possible to be. There is no need to be elsewhere in order to feel this way.

I've written here about the ways people are kept apart, and keep themselves apart, by the methods we use to sustain class in society. I have tried to show the impact of class segregation, through housing and schooling, on minds and relationships that are being formed. I've looked at the ways in which, to use the writer Owen Hatherley's words, 'the working class is divided against itself',[2] through the internal application of gradations of snobbery and distinction, assessments of who is 'respectable' and who isn't, who is 'hardworking' and who is 'lazy': all of which aid the quest by those more socially and materially comfortable to ensure that nothing, and nobody, encroaches on that comfort. I hope that by using elements of my own experience I have illustrated some of the shortcomings of a political narrative that places the onus for social mobility – for 'getting out' of the working class and into the middle class – on to individuals, rather than making it possible for everyone, regardless of occupation, to live comfortably. Governments of every stripe encourage individuals to move upwards, to change their class, to trade up, while never acknowledging the emotional costs of doing so.

For his part, Richard Hoggart likened his lifelong preoccupation with educational, social and cultural matters to a delta with four or five main tributaries:

> Their common source is a sense of the importance of the right of each of us to speak out about how we see life, the world; and so the right to have access to the means by which that capacity to speak may be gained. The right, also, to try to reach out to speak to others, not to have that impulse inhibited by social barriers, maintained by those in power politically or able to exercise power in other ways.[3]

What would a classless society look like, anyway? It's almost as though we wouldn't know what we'd do without class. This leads us back to Raymond Williams's passionate argument for a good society, which, he says, 'depends upon the free availability of facts and opinions, and on the growth of vision and consciousness – the articulation of what men have actually seen and known and felt'. The point at which communication becomes genuinely educative, Williams wrote, is when information is shared through open, diverse and informed discussion rather than inculcated from above. 'Any restriction,' he continued, 'of the freedom of individual contribution is actually a restriction of resources of the society.'[4]

The illusory emancipation offered by a free market in goods and services suggests that we can already make an 'individual contribution' through the things we choose to consume, and through the way we display those things to others. It's simply a matter of aspiration: you don't need money to be trendy, but you *do* need taste, and if you haven't got taste – the right taste – then more fool you. A classless society wouldn't necessarily be one in which everyone had the same amount of money, a similar income and identical assets, though it would help in some areas of life. I believe strongly that social division is to a great degree caused by political decisions that have created an economic hierarchy out of basic needs such as shelter, transport, food and fuel. One of the most egregious aspects of the return to *laissez-faire* economics since the late seventies is the deregulation of things that had been subject to regulation since the end of the Second World War, which in turn meant comparatively greater equality in terms of how they were accessed. It's in areas like these that the social and economic aspects of class meet, and where – because of this – government policy can make a significant difference, for better or worse, to people's daily experience.

I can only speak in this way because I have been through this process myself. I have undertaken that risky, lonely journey from one class to another, and every day I feel a mixture of gratitude and elation to have had the chance to do so, because it has given me the life I have now. I am endlessly grateful to my parents for giving me a level of confidence in myself and my abilities that they didn't always have in themselves. I feel elated because I somehow got to the other side, to the place where life is easier, in one piece. But what about those who try, and don't?

Or those who, rightly, don't see why they have to choose sides in the first place? Until we recognize the psychological impact of class, the way it builds those walls in the head, social mobility will always be double-edged. Learning, art and culture can be catalysts for forging connections between the classes. They can be used to unite as well as to divide, to liberate as well as to limit, but only if we are included, and have the confidence to include ourselves, in their creation.

Notes

Introduction

1. Hoggart, R., 'Introduction' to George Orwell, *The Road to Wigan Pier* (Penguin, 1989), p. vii

1. You're Not Supposed To

1. Offer, A., 'British Manual Workers: From Producers to Consumers, *c.* 1950–2000', University of Oxford Discussion Papers in Economic and Social History, no. 74 (December 2008), p. 25
2. Hoggart, R., *The Uses of Literacy* (Penguin, 2009), p. 16
3. Ward, L., 'Where you live can be crucial to your future', *Guardian*, 8 September 2007
4. Willis, P., *Learning to Labour: How Working Class Kids Get Working Class Jobs* (Routledge, 1978)
5. Ibid., p. 3
6. Charlesworth, S. J., *A Phenomenology of Working-class Experience* (Cambridge, 2000), p. 61
7. Lerner, M., *Surplus Powerlessness: The Psychodynamics of Everyday Life – and the Psychology of Individual and Social Transformation* (Humanities Press, 1991)

2. This Is My Truth

1. Hoggart, R., 'Growing Up', in Goldman, R. (ed.), *Breakthrough: Autobiographical Accounts of the Education of Some Socially Disadvantaged Children* (Routledge, 1968), p.103

2. Bernstein, B., 'Elaborated and restricted codes: their social origins and some consequences', *American Anthropologist*, vol. 6, no. 6 (December 1964), pp. 55–69

3. Kerswill, P., 'Socio-economic class', in Llamas, C., Mullany, L., and Stockwell, P. (eds.), *The Routledge Companion to Sociolinguistics* (Routledge, 2006), p. 7

4. Thompson, J. B., 'Introduction', in Bourdieu, P., *Language and Symbolic Power* (Polity, 1992), p. 1

5. Hoggart, R., *The Uses of Literacy* (Penguin, 2009), p. 165

6. Williams, R., *The Long Revolution* (Pelican, 1969), p. 48

7. Foucault, M. (ed. Colin Barton), *Power/Knowledge* (Pantheon, 1980), p. 155

8. Wroe, N., 'The uses of decency', *Guardian*, 6 February 2004

9. Hoggart, *Uses*, p. 58

10. Skeggs, B., *Formations of Class and Gender: Becoming Respectable* (SAGE, 1997)

11. Jackson, B., and Marsden, D., *Education and the Working Class* (Pelican, 1973)

12. Steedman, C., *The Tidy House: Little Girls Writing* (Virago, 1982)

3. Respectable in the Eighties

1. Evans G., *Educational Failure and Working Class White Children in Britain* (Palgrave, 2006)

2. Skeggs, B., 'Haunted by the spectre of judgement: respectability, value and affect in class relations', in Sveinsson, K. P. (ed.),

Who Cares About the White Working Class? (Runnymede Trust, 2009)

3. Benjamin, W., 'The newspaper', *Selected Writings Vol. 2: 1927–1934* (Harvard, 1999), p. 741

4. Hoggart, R., 'Growing Up', in Goldman, R. (ed.), *Breakthrough: Autobiographical Accounts of the Education of Some Socially Disadvantaged Children* (Routledge, 1968), p. 105

5. Office for National Statistics, *Social Trends 41* (February 2011)

6. Massey, D., *Space, Place and Gender* (Polity, 1994), p. 163

7. 'The measure', *Guardian Weekend*, 28 August 2010

8. Hanson, M., 'Bananas in north London – whatever next?', *Guardian*, 5 August 2010

9. Moorhouse, G., *Britain in the Sixties: The Other England* (Penguin, 1964), p. 23

10. Williams, R., 'Culture is Ordinary', in Jim McGuigan (ed.), *Raymond Williams on Culture & Society: Essential Writings* (Sage, 2013), p. 1

11. Hoggart, R., 'The *Daily Mirror* and its Readers', *New Society*, 27 October 1966, collected in *Speaking to Each Other: Vol. One – About Society* (Penguin, 1973)

12. *Daily Mirror*, 23 January 1984, p. 1

13. Hoggart, R., *The Uses of Literacy* (Penguin, 2009), p. 36

14. Reported in Jack, I., *Before the Oil Ran Out: Britain in the Brutal Years* (Vintage, 1997), and Davies, N., *Dark Heart: The Shocking Truth about Hidden Britain* (Chatto & Windus, 1998)

4. Respectable in the Nineties

1. The Bill Douglas Trilogy comprises *My Childhood* (1972), *My Ain Folk* (1973), and *My Way Home* (1978)

2. Gillies, V., 'Raising the "Meritocracy": Parenting and the Individualization of Social Class', *Sociology*, vol. 35, no. 5 (December 2005), p. 839

3. Evans, G., *Educational Failure and Working Class White Children in Britain* (Palgrave, 2006), p. 11
4. FOI release, 17 March 2011: https://www.gov.uk/government/publications/gcse-results/gcse-results
5. Gillies, 'Raising the "Meritocracy"', p. 845
6. McRobbie, A., 'The culture of working-class girls', from 'Working-class Girls and the Culture of Femininity', MA thesis presented to Centre for Contemporary Cultural Studies, University of Birmingham, 1977
7. *Pet Shop Boys Annual 1989* (World Publications, 1988)
8. Bernstein, B., 'Elaborated and restricted codes: their social origins and some consequences', *American Anthropologist*, vol. 6, no. 6 (December 1964)
9. Smith, Z., *White Teeth* (Penguin, 2000)

5. Snakes and Ladders

1. Hoggart, R., *The Uses of Literacy* (Penguin, 2009), p. 265
2. Mitchell, J., 'Essay VIII', in Goldman, R. (ed.), *Breakthrough: Autobiographical Accounts of the Education of Some Socially Disadvantaged Children* (Routledge, 1968), p. 139
3. Marsden, D., in Goldman, *Breakthrough*
4. House of Commons Education Committee, *Participation by 16–19 Year Olds in Education and Training*, fourth session 2010–11, vol. 1, published 19 July 2011
5. Timmins, N., *Five Giants: A Biography of the Welfare State* (HarperCollins, 1996), p. 66
6. Kynaston, D., *Modernity Britain: Opening the Box, 1957–59* (Bloomsbury, 2013) p. 207
7. McKibbin, R., *Classes and Cultures: England 1918–51* (OUP, 1998), p. 270
8. Kynaston, *Modernity Britain*, p. 219

9. Ibid., p. 218

10. *Billy Liar*, directed John Schlesinger (1963)

11. Barnett, D., 'Ken Barlow's warning to would-be authors', *Guardian*, 12 August 2008

12. Allsop, K., 'Pop Goes Young Woodley', in Mabey, R. (ed.), *The Great Society: Class* (Anthony Blond Ltd, 1967), p. 127

13. Halsey, A. H., 'Educational Priority', quoted in *Unpopular Education: Schooling and Social Democracy in England since 1944*, Centre for Contemporary Cultural Studies (Hutchinson, 1981), p. 11

14. Todd, S., *The People: The Rise and Fall of the Working Class 1910–2010* (Hodder, 2014), p. 221

15. Ibid., p. 223

16. Ibid., p. 228

17. Hoggart, *Uses*, p. 264

18. Kynaston, D., *Modernity Britain: A Shake of the Dice, 1957–62* (Bloomsbury, 2014), p. 193

19. Cook, C., 'Grammar school myths', FT.com, 28 January 2013

20. McRobie, H., 'No easy way to tackle the Oxbridge class divide', *Guardian*, 25 August 2008

21. The journalist Nick Davies reports on the phenomenon of middle-class and working-class comprehensives and their respective school cultures in *The School Report* (Vintage, 2000)

22. Cook, C., 'London's GCSE lessons for the rest of England', 10 September 2014, accessed at http://www.bbc.co.uk/news/uk-29128559

23. Reay, D., 'What would a socially just education system look like?', Think Piece, Centre for Labour and Social Studies, July 2012, p. 6

24. Ibid., pp. 6–7

25. Department for Education statistics published 17 July 2012, accessed at https://www.gov.uk/government/statistics/destinations-of-key-stage-4-and-key-stage-5-pupils-academic-year-2009-to-2010

26. *BBC News* report, 30 March 2009: news.bbc.co.uk/1/hi/education/7971834.stm, page accessed 18 August 2011

27. Reay, D., Crozier, G., and Clayton, J., ' "Fitting in" or "standing out": working-class students in UK higher education', *British Education Research Journal*, 2009, pp. 1–18

6. Drive a Knife in the Wedge and Twist It

1. Willmott, P. and Young, M., *Family and Kinship in East London* (Pelican, 1958)
2. Winnett, R., 'Meet the "Neets": Britain's new underclass', *Sunday Times*, 27 March 2005
3. Roberts, B., 'MPs' plan to house yobs in containers', *Daily Mirror*, 21 June 2005
4. Butler, P., 'Policymakers seduced by neuroscience to justify early intervention agenda', *Guardian*, 6 May 2014
5. Smith, L., 'John Bruer: "Growing up in poverty doesn't damage your brain irretrievably" ', *Guardian*, 6 May 2014
6. Patterson, C., 'Thanks, Nick, but more choice is not what some parents need', *Independent*, 19 June 2010
7. O'Hagan, A., 'Diary', *London Review of Books*, 25 March 2010
8. Quotation by Terence, the Roman playwright and former slave
9. 'Shannon Matthews found hiding under bed with her stepfather's uncle', *The Times*, 15 March 2008
10. Bauman, Z., 'Happiness in a Society of Individuals', *Soundings*, issue 38 (Spring 2008)
11. Mantel, H., 'Every writer has a "how I became a writer" story', *Guardian*, 6 September 2008
12. Mantel, H., 'Diary', *London Review of Books*, 11 June 2009
13. Department for Business, Innovation & Skills, BIS Research Paper no. 57, '2011 Skills for Life Survey: Headline Findings' (December 2011), p. 5
14. Charlesworth, S., Gilfillan, P., and Wilkinson, R., 'Living Inferiority', *British Medical Bulletin* (2004), vol. 69, issue 1, pp. 49–60

15. Merritt, S., 'Dad, I could've killed you', *Guardian*, 26 February 2006

16. Charlesworth, Gilfillan and Wilkinson, 'Living Inferiority', p. 56

17. Shepherd, J., 'Universities don't like common people, do they?', *Guardian*, 3 February 2009

18. Shepherd, J., and Curtis, P., 'Middle-class pupils have better genes, says Chris Woodhead', *Guardian*, 11 May 2009

19. Whitley, J., 'If Billy Elliot had been a painter . . .', *Daily Telegraph*, 10 September 2007

20. Bennett, T. et al, 'Cultural Capital and the Cultural Field in Contemporary Britain', CRESC Working Paper no. 3, published by Centre for Research on Socio-Cultural Change, University of Manchester, June 2005

21. Brooks, D., *BOBOs in Paradise: The New Upper Class and How They Got There* (Simon & Schuster, 2000)

22. Savage, M., Devine, F. et al, 'The Great British Class Survey – Results', *BBC Science*, 3 April 2013; http://www.bbc.co.uk/science/0/21970879, accessed 8 August 2014

23. http://www.tuc.org.uk/economic-issues/touchstone-pamphlets/everyone-thinks-they-live-middle-britain, accessed 20 May 2014

24. Atkinson, W., *Class, Individualization and Late Modernity: In Search of the Reflexive Worker* (Palgrave, 2010)

25. Ibid., p. 90

26. McKnight, A., 'Downward mobility, opportunity hoarding and the "glass floor"', LSE CASE research report for the Social Mobility and Child Poverty Commission (June 2015)

27. Cook, C., 'The fall of Kids Company', *BBC News*, 12 November 2015

7. Who's Respectable Now?

1. Ratliff, E., 'Geoff Dyer on "Otherwise Known as the Human Condition"', *Paris Review*, 19 April 2011
2. Offer, A., 'British Manual Workers: From Producers to Consumers, *c.* 1950–2000', University of Oxford Discussion Papers in Economic and Social History, no. 74 (December 2008), p. 25
3. Social Exclusion Task Force, 'Aspiration and Attainment amongst Young People in Deprived Communities', Cabinet Office: short studies, published December 2008
4. Meek, J., 'Where will we live?', *London Review of Books*, vol. 6, no. 1, 9 January 2014, pp. 7–16
5. Dorling, D., *All That Is Solid: The Great Housing Crisis* (Penguin, 2014)
6. Baggini, J., *Welcome to Everytown: A Journey into the English Mind* (Granta Books, 2007), p. 50
7. Ware, V., 'Towards a sociology of resentment: a debate on class and whiteness', *Sociological Research Online*, 2008
8. Jones, O., *Chavs: The Demonization of the Working Class* (Verso, 2011), p. 223
9. Pearce, J., and Milne, E-J., 'Research findings: community and participation on Bradford's traditionally white estates', Joseph Rowntree Foundation, 2010, p. 38
10. Goodwin, M., 'Forever a False Dawn? Explaining the Electoral Collapse of the British National Party (BNP)', *Parliamentary Affairs* (2013), p. 2, downloaded from http://pa.oxfordjournals.org/ on 5 March 2013
11. Garner, S., Cowles, J., Lung, B., and Stott, M., 'Sources of resentment, and perceptions of ethnic minorities among poor white people in England', DCLG (Department for Communities and Local Government) for the National Community Forum (2009), pp. 8, 31

12. Todd, S., *The People: The Rise and Fall of the Working Class 1910–2010* (Hodder, 2014), p. 354

13. Goodwin, M., and Milazzo, C., 'How Labour is failing to grasp Ukip's appeal to angry white voters', *Guardian*, 24 June 2014

14. Beider, H., *White Working-class Voices: Multiculturalism, Community-building and Change* (Policy, 2015). p. 1

15. Seabrook, J., *City Close-up: Blackburn* (Penguin, 1973)

16. Rogaly, B., and Taylor, B., *Moving Histories of Class and Community: Identity, Place and Belonging in Contemporary England* (Palgrave, 2011), pp. 192–3

17. Ibid., p. 199

18. Riddell, M., 'Labour's anti-immigration guru', *Daily Telegraph*, 18 July 2011

19. Hasan, M., 'I don't see a broken society', *New Statesman*, 17 August 2011

20. Dorling, D., 'Class segregation', in Lloyd, C., et al, *Social-spatial Segregation: Concepts, Processes and Outcomes* (Policy, 2015), p. 363

21. 'Britain's workforce in 2022: From a nation of pen-pushers to an army of carers', *Independent*, 4 June 2014

22. Kynaston, D., *Modernity Britain: A Shake of the Dice, 1959–62* (Bloomsbury, 2014), p. 86

23. Hoggart, R., *The Uses of Literacy* (Penguin, 2009), p. 244

24. Bolton, M., 'Class war on the dancefloor', *Guardian*, 3 September 2008

25. Hoggart, *Uses*, p. 65

26. McGrath, J., review of *The Uses of Literacy*, in *Popular Music*, vol. 29, no. 2 (Cambridge, 2010), p. 317

27. Hoggart, *Uses*, p. 132

28. Taylor, D. J., 'Whatever happened to popular culture?', *New Statesman*, 15 July 2002

29. Rogers, J., 'Word to the Wise', *The Word*, January 2011

30. Price, S., 'Arctic Monkeys: from men of the people to tax-dodgers', *Guardian*, 11 July 2014

Conclusion – Up the Hill Backwards

1. Quote from Les Back's talk on '*The Uses of Literacy* Today' at 'Celebrating the Life and Work of Richard Hoggart' event, Goldsmiths, University of London, 31 October 2014
2. Hatherley, O., 'Who will stop them?', *London Review of Books*, 23 October 2014, pp. 13–26
3. Wroe, N., 'The uses of decency', *Guardian*, 6 February 2004
4. Williams, R., *Communications* (Penguin, 1965), p. 111

Acknowledgements

This book took a very long time to write, during which I relied on frequent interventions from friends, family and colleagues to keep me going. To borrow Richard Hoggart's words yet again, this time from his autobiography, it was 'a huge cuckoo in an already full emotional nest and at times I hated its voracity and its assumption that it had to be served first'.

I have a lot of people to thank: first, my mother and my husband, without whose help looking after our son and daughter I literally could not have written the first draft. David Kynaston and Joe Moran gave unwavering support and advice after reading early versions of it, as did Owen Hatherley, Aditya Chakrabortty and Gerry Mooney. My agent, Caroline Dawnay, and her assistants Olivia Hunt and Sophie Scard were endlessly patient as I cranked out each chapter. Matt Weiland, Craig Taylor, Ian Jack, John Urry, Andrew Sayer, Diane Reay and Danny Dorling all helped me to clarify what I wanted to write about. Helen Conford and Tom Penn have been brilliant editors; I'd also like to thank Emma Bal and Bela Cunha for their work in publicity and copy-editing respectively. Thanks to colleagues at Liverpool John Moores University and Lancaster University, and to the staff of the following public libraries: Chelmsley Wood Library, the Library of Birmingham, the Picton Reading Room at Liverpool Central Library, Swiss Cottage Library and Lancaster Central Library. I am grateful to Paul Hoggart for inviting me to a celebration of his father Richard Hoggart's life and work at Goldsmiths, University of London, in October

2014, and to everyone who has given me a chance to consider and explore the ideas presented here through talks or in print during this book's long gestation. In particular, this includes Hugh Levinson and Adele Armstrong, who in 2010 commissioned from me an essay series for BBC Radio 4, *Wall in the Mind*, out of which the first draft of this book grew.

Thank you, David Bowie. Thank you to Richard, for being both 'there' and 'here'. And to Jamie, Peter and Erin: I love you.